PROJECT MANAGERS
AT WORK

Bruce Harpham

Apress®

Project Managers at Work

Bruce Harpham
Toronto, Ontario, Canada

ISBN-13 (pbk): 978-1-4842-2667-4　　　　　ISBN-13 (electronic): 978-1-4842-2668-1
DOI 10.1007/978-1-4842-2668-1

Library of Congress Control Number: 2017952194

Managing Director: Welmoed Spahr
Editorial Director: Todd Green
Acquisitions Editor: Susan McDermott
Development Editor: Laura Berendson
Coordinating Editor: Rita Fernando
Copy Editor: Kim Burton-Weisman

Distributed to the book trade worldwide by Springer Science+Business Media New York, 233 Spring Street, 6th Floor, New York, NY 10013. Phone 1-800-SPRINGER, fax (201) 348-4505, e-mail orders-ny@springer-sbm.com, or visit www.springeronline.com. Apress Media, LLC is a California LLC and the sole member (owner) is Springer Science + Business Media Finance Inc (SSBM Finance Inc). SSBM Finance Inc is a **Delaware** corporation.

For information on translations, please e-mail rights@apress.com, or visit http://www.apress.com/rights-permissions.

Apress titles may be purchased in bulk for academic, corporate, or promotional use. eBook versions and licenses are also available for most titles. For more information, reference our Print and eBook Bulk Sales web page at http://www.apress.com/bulk-sales.

Any source code or other supplementary material referenced by the author in this book is available to readers on GitHub via the book's product page, located at www.apress.com/9781484226674. For more detailed information, please visit http://www.apress.com/source-code.

Apress Business: The Unbiased Source of Business Information

Apress business books provide essential information and practical advice, each written for practitioners by recognized experts. Busy managers and professionals in all areas of the business world—and at all levels of technical sophistication—look to our books for the actionable ideas and tools they need to solve problems, update and enhance their professional skills, make their work lives easier, and capitalize on opportunity.

Whatever the topic on the business spectrum—entrepreneurship, finance, sales, marketing, management, regulation, information technology, among others—Apress has been praised for providing the objective information and unbiased advice you need to excel in your daily work life. Our authors have no axes to grind; they understand they have one job only—to deliver up-to-date, accurate information simply, concisely, and with deep insight that addresses the real needs of our readers.

It is increasingly hard to find information—whether in the news media, on the Internet, and now all too often in books—that is even-handed and has your best interests at heart. We therefore hope that you enjoy this book, which has been carefully crafted to meet our standards of quality and unbiased coverage.

We are always interested in your feedback or ideas for new titles. Perhaps you'd even like to write a book yourself. Whatever the case, reach out to us at editorial@apress.com and an editor will respond swiftly. Incidentally, at the back of this book, you will find a list of useful related titles. Please visit us at www.apress.com to sign up for newsletters and discounts on future purchases.

—*The Apress Business Team*

*This book is dedicated to the love of my life,
my wife, Dr. Carolyn Harris*

Contents

About the Author

Bruce Harpham, PMP, is the founder of Project Management Hacks career website. He is also an award-winning blogger for *IT World Canada*. In 2016, TimeCamp named him as one of the top 123 Top Influencers in the Project Management Industry. His articles on project management, engineering careers, IT strategy, cybersecurity, leadership, and innovation have appeared on ProjectManagement.com, Success.com, Monster.com, CIO.com, CSOonline.com, and in *InfoWorld*, *College Recruiter*, *Profit Guide*, and other publications.

Harpham has been interviewed by the *Globe & Mail*. He has appeared on several industry podcasts, including *The Project Management Podcast*, *The People and Projects Podcast*, and *The Engineering Career Coach Podcast*.

Harpham holds the Project Management Professional (PMP) certification and certifications from the Canadian Securities Institute. His professional experience and projects focus on the financial services industry.

Harpham pursues his passion for education as an alumni volunteer at the University of Toronto. He is also fundraiser for various causes, including the Toronto Public Library and the United Way.

He has a bachelor's degree (history and political science) and a master's degree in information studies from the University of Toronto. He also has a master's degree in history from the Western University (London, Ontario). He lives in Toronto.

To learn more, please visit ProjectManagementHacks.com.

Acknowledgments

Most great projects require a team of people. This book was no exception.

Thank you to each and every interviewee profiled in this book. Your generosity in sharing your time, insights, and career experiences made this book possible.

My thanks to several authors and interview experts who have inspired and informed my approach. Jessica Livingston (author of *Founders at Work* (Apress, 2008) and Josh Steimle (author of *Chief Marketing Officers at Work* Apress, 2016) paved the way for me to understanding the opportunity at Apress. Robin Speziale, (author of *Market Masters: Interviews with Canada's Top Investors* (ECW Press, 2016) provided helpful advice and suggestions. I have been inspired and informed by Andrew Warner's interviews on the *Mixergy* podcast. Timothy Ferriss, author of *Tools of Titans* (Houghton Mifflin Harcourt, 2016), directly inspired several of the questions I asked in this book. Reading his book *The 4 Hour Workweek* (Harmony, 2009) in 2014 inspired me to create my website, ProjectManagementHacks.com.

Thank you to Gary Vaynerchuk and his team for their many inspirational videos. In particular, the YouTube videos "Overnight Success" and "Hard Work & Patience" inspired me to overcome the obstacles and surprises I faced in this project.

At Apress, I would like to thank the excellent team of editors, designers, and professionals who developed this book. Robert Hutchinson worked with me in 2016 to design the book. Rita Fernando and Susan McDermott have been excellent editors in guiding me through the publishing process.

Thank you to my editors at IDG and ProjectManagement.com. Cameron McGaughy, my editor at ProjectManagement.com, has encouraged me to cover a wide range of topics in project management. Edward Murray, Amy Bennett and Jason Snyder at IDG have worked with me to publish a variety of articles on business technology, the Internet of Things, and other exciting developments for CIO.com, CSO, and other IDG publications. Thank you for your support.

Thank you to my managers and colleagues at the Bank of Montreal. Richard Livesley, Kathy Irvin, Yousif Jaurji, and Ali Soheil have been highly supportive in my efforts to learn more about project management and grow my career. Your support was important in learning about the field. I appreciate the professionalism and organization that you bring to your work.

Thank you to my parents, Joan and Fred Harpham. As I grew up, I had a constant hunger for books and learning. They were wonderfully supportive in my education through books, taking me to the library, international travel, and beyond. Your love and support has been highly important over the years.

This book is dedicated to my wife, Dr. Carolyn Harris. Her success as an author, historian, and lecturer continue to inspire me. Her constant love, encouragement and support during this project made a tremendous difference.

Introduction

"You've been living in Project World for so long you've probably forgotten that for a long time, projects didn't matter so much... Think about Apple, Google, director James Cameron's team, Ideo, Pixar, and Electronic Arts. These are project-centric organizations. Each one of these organizations consists of groups of committed people who ship projects. No projects, no organization."

—*Poke the Box* by Seth Godin

Project management matters more than ever before. Once the province of large companies and governments, project work has spread across the economy and our lives. Consider this: in 2013, the Project Management Institute estimated more than 15 million project jobs would be created by 2020. Even better, the Institute has found that project managers are consistently highly paid. According to Project Management Salary Survey (ninth edition, published in 2015), the median salary for project managers in the United States is over $100,000. That just leaves one problem: How will organizations meet the demand for the next generation of project managers?

Some organizations have developed career paths and training programs. Other organizations have a less structured approach. You may simply need to develop a few project skills so that you can finally achieve some of your personal goals. Or you may be seeking to acquire the skills needed to build skyscrapers, networks and submarines! Whatever your situation, you may find the existing project management literature too technical to suit your needs.

Even though project management is a relatively young profession, there are plenty of resources available. You can find project templates. You can find standards. These are all helpful. Yet, you may be left wondering how to translate those ideas and methods into your career. You may be considering questions like this:

- How do I get ahead in the field?
- How do I get promoted?
- How do project managers stay organized and productive?
- What books should I read to become more effective?
- How do I become a better leader?

These are some of the questions that I explored by interviewing some of the world's most successful project managers. I wanted to know how people found their way into the profession. Even further, I was curious to understand how projects unfold across a variety of industries and experience levels. In presenting this book to you, I hope you will be both inspired by the interviewee's examples, and find ideas, techniques, and recommendations to grow your career.

Throughout the interviews in *Project Managers at Work*, you will find several recurring themes. Project stories, leadership, lifelong learning, career development, and productivity are the key themes that you will discover in this book. A combination of hard won experience, professional discipline and the passion to never stop learning drives these project managers to the top.

1. From Stories to Lessons Learned: Reflecting to Improve Performance

The "lessons learned" concept is important to project management success. By reviewing how the project unfolded, you can find ways to improve your performance on future projects. In the interviews, I asked professionals about what they have learned from their challenges and triumphs at work. You will also find out about how these leaders have put these lessons to work by changing their organizations.

To make the most of your lessons learned, integrate those insights in your ongoing processes. For example, change a checklist, document template, or other process to include your insights.

2. The Many Paths to Leadership: Choose the Right Path for You

The traditional project manager faces a unique leadership challenge. She has to deliver the project through the project team. However, many or all people on the project team report to other managers. Leading successfully in this context requires paying close attention to relationship development, networking, and influence. It's also important to note that there is no single road to leadership success. Leadership is more about skills, attitude, and vision than personality. If you're interested in moving to senior levels of responsibility, demonstrating your leadership ability is absolutely essential.

To develop yourself as a leader, look for opportunities around you. Consider pursuing a leadership role through a professional association or a charitable organization. You will build your skills and make the world a better place in the process.

3. Lifelong Learning: Grow Your Knowledge with Books, Experiences, Mentors, and Beyond

Graduation day is no longer the end of the learning journey. Like accountants and lawyers, project managers are committed to ongoing professional development. In fact, some project management certifications, such as the Project Management Professional (PMP), have a formal requirement for ongoing professional development. If you have an employer who understands the value of learning and development, make the most of that support to learn and grow. Remember that learning can come in multiple formats and styles. You can learn from books, mentors, reflecting on your experiences (especially mistakes), and other areas.

For an excellent introduction to business and rapid skill development, I recommend the following books by Josh Kaufman: *The Personal MBA: Master the Art of Business* (Portfolio, 2010) and *The First 20 Hours: How to Learn Anything . . . Fast!* (Portfolio, 2013).

4. Career Development: Practical Ways to Get Ahead

In most organizations, you do not start as a project manager as your first job. Generally, you first develop your skills in a specific discipline, such as software development, engineering, finance, sales, or consulting. If you're determined to transition into project management, pay attention to the strategies used by the professionals profiled in this book. Networking, asking your manager for opportunities, and developing yourself as a leader are all time-tested strategies to grow your career.

If you are unfamiliar with networking, study this skill and put it into action. First, read *Never Eat Alone, Expanded and Updated: And Other Secrets to Success, One Relationship at a Time* by Keith Ferrazzi and Tahl Raz. Second, reconnect with current and former coworkers, managers, and classmates. Third, start to reach out to new people who are in the careers and jobs that interest you to find out about their experiences.

5. Improve Your Productivity

With the right productivity system, you can achieve your priorities and head home at a reasonable hour. Your productivity approach needs to include both the tactical matters such as managing your calendar and strategic matters such as setting meaningful goals. Several of the professionals profiled in this book also highlight specific techniques, like time blocking and restricting yourself to a 40-hour workweek. Experiment with their techniques to improve your productivity and get more valuable activities done.

Once you finish reading this book, I would ask you to take two actions:

- Choose at least one idea from the book to apply to your life and career.

- If you find the book valuable, please write a short review sharing your thoughts on Amazon.com. It's one of the best ways to spread the message.

Warm regards,
Bruce Harpham
Toronto, Ontario, Canada

CHAPTER 1

Michael Lubrano

Senior Program Manager, Google

Michael Lubrano *started at Google in 2011 as a program manager in NetOps. He eventually moved to Search Features/Experience, working on user-facing features that impact billions of people around the globe. Lubrano graduated from Excelsior College with a degree in liberal arts, with philosophy and ethics concentrations. Prior to joining Google, he worked with the US government (NASA, the Department of Defense, and the Department of State) and in the private sector, including overseas postings, primarily in the Middle East.*

Lubrano *started the program management fireside chats and annual summit at Google. He manages projects in search and teaches leadership and related topics at Google for program managers.*

Bruce Harpham: How did you first get involved in project management?

Michael Lubrano: I started off as a software engineer at a company that was a contractor for NASA. About a month into my role, the division manager decided to leave and start his own company. When that news came up, the question came up: "Who is going to take over this organization?" While my project was going well, I saw the impact of a lack of leadership. Since S&K Technologies was a small company, it was easy for me to call up the president. I proposed to him that I take over running the office and all the projects.

© Bruce Harpham 2018
B. Harpham, *Project Managers at Work*, DOI 10.1007/978-1-4842-2668-1_1

In my view, I considered myself a mediocre software developer compared to my colleagues. I was surrounded by people who were ten times better than me at software development. For me to get ahead in my career, I realized that I would have to do something different—an activity that I was exceptional at. I was excellent at building relationships, moving projects along, and providing technical judgment. In contrast, I was only "OK" at writing the code itself. That was a transition point for my career development.

Harpham: What were you working on in terms of projects and products at this organization?

Lubrano: I was working with NASA's manned spaceflight program. For example, we worked on Project Green Book. This tracked all the data and measurements relating to the space shuttle landing process. This included everything from tire pressure as the shuttle hits the runway to how many heat-absorbing tiles were lost in flight. All this data goes into the Green Book system. We created a digital version of the resource so that users could add, retrieve, and use data easily every time the shuttle landed.

We also worked on a MER [mission evaluation room] project. I contributed to the system that tracked two different types of issues. First, it tracked anomalies and "funnies." Anomalies would be something like a nut and bolt that just flew by one of the astronauts in space. Now we have to track those items. The MER system had to figure out where that bolt came from, how it happened, and related data. In contrast, a "funny" is something like: "We ran out of paper." A relatively minor problem that needs to be tracked. NASA tracks absolutely everything. As a result, there are a huge number of databases at the organization to manage all of this data.

Harpham: How did you come to be working with NASA?

Lubrano: Here's how I got the job at the contractor supporting NASA. Previous to that role, I was a programmer at a small privately owned company in Springfield, Missouri that manufactured alarm panels.

I always felt that I was a good teacher and communicator. At this time, there were ColdFusion discussion forums where programmers discussed technical issues, asked questions, and got answers from other people. I often went on the forum to answer questions and help people solve programming challenges. It turns out the director of the company that ended up hiring me was posting questions on this discussion forum! I was consistently the person who was answering his questions. Then, one day, he reached out to me via the forum with a message: "Hi, I work with NASA. You seem to know technology. We'd like to talk to you!" That's how that job came about.

Harpham: Giving back to the software development community translated into a major career opportunity for you.

Lubrano: Yes, it did.

Harpham: From your work with NASA, what's a project that you're particularly proud of working on?

Lubrano: I was proud of the work we did after the Space Shuttle Columbia explosion in 2003. The Green Book project was important to that investigation because it meant there was better information to understand how the shuttle operated.

There was a major effort to investigate and understand what happened. The challenge with government projects is that they're slow and tend to be complicated. Government requirements also tend to change frequently, so you never really have a sense of what you are meant to deliver at the start of the project. As a result, it's difficult to make either the waterfall or agile models work. There is constant change that you simply have to deal with all the time.

I remember having to work with our teams and tell them, "We don't have a product manager in this context. Therefore, we have to function in different roles." It's another example of the classic cartoon about building a swing on a tree. There's one panel called "What the Engineer Delivered," another on "What the Manager Wanted," and yet another on "What the Customer Wanted." The punchline is that each panel of the cartoon shows a very different result. Getting clarity on what we were asked to deliver was a constant struggle.

Harpham: What is a project management principle that you learned the hard way?

Lubrano: Thinking back on projects I worked on with NASA and the Department of Defense, a principle comes to mind: not making a decision is a decision.

There have been times where I did not have a bias to action. I suffered as a result. That created problems within the project and it hurt team morale. I've always said that it's better to make a bad decision than no decision.

I remember working on a project at the Shaw Group, a construction company that builds chemical plants and other facilities. We were not getting approval to install Internet connections in China. I could not get a decision from the Chinese government or our company, despite escalating the matter to higher levels. The project floundered as a result. I kept trying to "do the right thing" by getting our company approvals and going back and forth with the Chinese government. Instead, I wish I would have made a decision on my own.

Even today, I see technical program managers have a similar problem. They often lack a sense of ownership for the problem. They think they need to ask permission. I have a personal motto: proceed until apprehended. This is a principle that I tell every single person on my team. It's a principle that I preach to everyone in the field. You are here to make decisions or facilitate the process to get a decision made. If you are not getting decisions made, you're not doing your job on projects and programs.

When I worked at the Shaw Group, I wasn't owning the problem. It was another epiphany moment. I said to myself, "I'm never going to let this happen again."

Harpham: I think part of the problem is that project management methodology puts a strong emphasis on planning, monitoring, and controlling. It may encourage the view: "Oh, I should just monitor this problem. Once it turns red, I will act on it."

Lubrano: Yes, that's exactly right. I have a lot of maxims that I've developed over time to guide my approach. Proceed until apprehended and taking ownership of the problem early is a much better approach.

I also advocate the "T" model for approaching your career development. Program managers need two competencies. First, the breadth across the domain they're working in, such as software engineering and construction. By breadth, I have to know what a bulldozer is and have a high-level understanding for how software development works. I don't necessarily need to know how to write software code, however. Breadth is the top part of the T.

The vertical part of the T is depth. I often tell my team members about the importance of depth in their product area, such as search engineering or Google Suggest. You don't need to know how to write the search engine code. That said, you should know how the search and ranking model works. You should know the architecture. You should know exactly how the data flows through the system—step by step. Program managers generally decide to operate at a high level of detail. They miss the depth.

When you don't have the T model, you run into several problems. You lose credibility on the team because they realize that you don't know what you're talking about. And they don't leverage you. Second, you cannot proactively identify issues if you lack depth.

Harpham: Can the vertical depth be applied to other domains, such as procurement or vendor management?

Lubrano: Let's take the vendor management case. The horizontal aspect of your expertise is that broad area, "vendor management." However, the depth area could be something like handling call center vendors. In that case, the person would understand how to transition, implement, and manage call-center vendors. Generally, program managers sit at the high level of "vendor management" and avoid developing depth.

Harpham: When you see it done well, how do people develop this depth? Does it come from direct work experience as a technical person? Or some other method?

Lubrano: Knowing how to learn and learning quickly is vital. One of the best aspects of working for Google is that I work with the smartest people in the world.

That's also the greatest challenge in working at Google. By any measure, Google staff members are the best learners that I have ever seen. People here pick up information, synthesize it, and put it into action quickly.

One of my program managers joined the team and immediately studied Google Suggest in depth. Google Suggest is a feature on the Google search engine where you type a few letters in and you see a list of suggested searches. Shortly after joining the team, she had to learn the entire Google Suggest system in order to solve a number of highly complex problems. Beyond learning the technology, she also had to meet all the people—the team leads, engineers, and others—who work on this product. She had to learn all of this and start coming up with solutions within a month. She started out as a relatively junior program manager and had to cover all of that.

Harpham: How did you transition from organizations where you're launching satellites into space [and serving institutional customers] to Google, which has a different emphasis? How did you teach yourself and get up to speed when you joined Google?

Lubrano: Google provides a "ramp" period. There's a running joke that it takes six months to a year before you are able to do anything here. There are so many systems to learn! A brand-new person coming into Google will just take a while to learn the "Google way." If you switch to another part of Google later, the "ramp up" period is easier to manage.

I started in network operations at Google and had networking experience to build on. However, I didn't understand the Google approach to projects and programs. It took me about a year to learn and get my feet wet working on smaller projects. Google's management facilitates this process. There's an understanding that it takes time to get up to speed.

Harpham: Let's turn to your perspective as a manager. How do you support new people to grow and develop?

Lubrano: It depends on the situation. Every human is different, after all. I have regular one-on-one meetings with everyone on my team. Some of my past managers had this idea that coaching, mentoring, and one-on-ones would be done the way the manager wanted it to be done. That view is based on the premise that you have limited capacity as a manager. The way you "scale up" yourself as a manager when you have a large team is you impose a standard process: "This is the way that I coach people, period."

That same-size-fits-all approach to people may scale, but it is not effective. I take an individual approach to coaching based on personality, their role, and level of authority. It's one of the few practices I've seen here that doesn't scale. I tend to avoid giving directive orders when somebody comes to me with a problem. I typically avoid diving into the details of the problem. Instead, I ask them some questions, like: "You're struggling to get the product manager to agree to the change. Why?" And then I follow up with: "Well, the proposed change pushes out the product manager's schedule by a month." I coach them individually. In some cases, the person may struggle putting themselves in another person's shoes, so I role-play to help with that point. Another person may struggle with saying no.

Harpham: Efficiency is important but it doesn't apply to everything, especially when it comes to working with people.

Lubrano: People do not scale well. Processes and technology scale well. Imagine if you're depressed or have psychological difficulties, you may consult a counselor for advice. The counselor has training and a process, but they customize their approach to that individual.

Harpham: What is your view on relationship development and associated skills?

Lubrano: If you're not an expert at relationship development, you should not be a program manager. That's what we do. We are network brokers. We're master communicators—the glue who connects everyone together. If you cannot build relationships and credibility quickly, you're going to have a problem and have no business being a program manager.

Harpham: What do you mean by "developing credibility quickly"?

Lubrano: There are two books that radically changed my thinking on how to interact with people. First, *Crucial Conversations: Tools for Talking When Stakes Are High* by Kerry Patterson, Joseph Grenny, Ron McMillan, and Al Switzler [McGraw-Hill Education, 2011]. This book is mandatory reading for everybody on my team. This book changes the way you speak to people, especially in difficult or controversial settings in the workplace. It talks about how we think and how emotions impact our thinking.

The second book is *Getting More: How You Can Negotiate to Succeed in Work and Life* by Stuart Diamond [Crown Business, 2010] on negotiation. By developing empathy and putting yourself in other people's shoes, you build trust. When other people see that you're solving their problem rather than creating new problems, it makes a big impact. Instead of solving tactical problems, you start to solve strategic problems. That's when people start to say, "This person is valuable."

Sadly, many program managers have the reputation of adding complexity in many companies. We have this horrible reputation of adding process and slowing down work. Yes, we need process and reports so that other people understand what we're doing. However, people on the project team are more likely to do that work if I've built trust with them and they trust me. For example, an engineer may ask for some additional developers to make a product launch.

As a program manager, I can go out and negotiate with another team to get that support. When your team sees your contribution, it builds credibility and trust.

Harpham: What are some other ways that you build relationships?

Lubrano: At Google, there's free food for employees. A brilliant consequence of that benefit is that many people eat together each day. When you eat with people, you get to know them. I know every person on my team: when they go on vacation, we're Facebook friends and so forth. The mentality that a manager needs to build walls doesn't work. The more that you open up, the more that people tend to open up to you.

Harpham: How do you connect with people who have a "closed off" style or who don't like to open up?

Lubrano: Crucial Conversations comes into play here. I learned how to engage by saying, "I feel like you're struggling to make this decision. I think that you're upset. Is that true or am I misreading it?" Whether it's over politeness or fear, there's this impression that we cannot talk about emotions or how we're feeling in the workplace. When you open that can of worms and you get it into the open, it changes everything. The other person tends to open up. They may say, "Yes, I'm upset. I feel like you're stepping on my toes."

You may have to confront some harsh truths in the process. Someone you work with on a project may not feel you provide value or that you're trustworthy. If someone is closed off to you, find someone they like and trust to get advice and seek to understand the problem.

Harpham: It's important to know both direct and indirect approaches to building relationships are crucial skills to have.

Lubrano: Overall, it's a question of showing empathy. Take this example: I get the feeling that a person is putting up roadblocks everywhere I go. Then I ask myself, "How does my project impact him?" It turns out that my project measures his team's performance and he doesn't like that. He may feel that I'm a threat to his status or career. This is the thought pattern that you need to think through: What is the other person's motivation? What are that person's feelings?

Program managers just don't do this thinking when it comes to empathy. By putting your idea into the open with the other person, many people will open to you. That said, there will be a small number of people who will not respond. For those people, you may need to take an indirect approach. Ask other people in that department for their input and insight on the person you're struggling with. You may not get a direct answer, but eventually you will see a pattern in what other people tell you.

Harpham: I understand that you've given a presentation on the eight traits of a great technical program manager [TPM]. What are those traits?

Lubrano: Here are the eight traits that I've identified for great technical program managers:

1. They partner with everyone.

   Leaders are masters at building relationships, even with seemingly difficult people. This is not optional. You must be able to do this in order to succeed.

2. They proceed until apprehended.

   Program managers take calculated risks. A common refrain is to ask for forgiveness rather than permission. Leaders know when to make decisions with limited information and when to wait for more details. They're not limited by analysis paralysis. Movement in the wrong direction is always better than staying put. To use a combat analogy: in a firefight, you don't stay in one place—you keep moving.

3. Program managers are visible.

   Technical leads tell me "I have no idea what my program manager does." That's bad. In every project and program, you have to be seen. Leaders have proximity to their team. Unfortunately, I see too many project professionals locked in their office all day working on spreadsheets or other documents instead of engaging with people.

4. Leaders conquer their fears.

   Leaders act "as if" to achieve their goals. You act as if you have confidence. It's like you're hacking your mind to become effective. Building relationships doesn't come naturally to everyone. However, you can develop those skills over time. For example, start by asking a few questions in meetings. I sometimes like to use a self-effacing question to understand something: "I have a dumb TPM question. How does this application really work?" In my experience, there's usually at least one other person in the room who would like to ask the same question, but they're too scared to do it.

   Impostor syndrome is especially strong at Google. I'm not talking about embellishment or overstating your skills. You should not have a fear around engaging people, yet this fear exists.

5. They never give up.

    Think about US Navy SEAL training. Hell Week is part of the training program. It's an extreme test of endurance with minimal sleep. Nobody really understands what separates those people who make and those who don't. On some level, it comes down to never giving up.

    It's the battle of mind. We accept defeat way too soon or don't give our full strength. Refusing to give up means that you keep working. You may have to try a different strategy to solve a problem.

6. They have depth.

    Recall the T model. The top part of the T is decision-making, planning, and the skills that program managers are known for. The vertical part of the T is the depth. Leaders are voracious learners. Consider Elon Musk: he built his first company in the technology industry and now he's in the space industry with SpaceX. If you talk to him about space, he understands it. He may not be a physicist, but he knows the field because he's consumed so much information over time.

    It is possible to change industries and succeed. However, you have to work twice as hard to learn the fundamentals and earn credibility with the team.

7. They understand people.

    Understanding motivation is crucial to being a leader. I can walk into a room and determine who's bored, who's angry, and who's engaged within ten seconds. We should be masters at "meta": the body language and related behaviors that go beyond verbal communication. We have to be amazing observers and put that understanding into action.

    Consider the different motivations of my daughters at one point in time. My older daughter wanted more freedom, so we agreed she could stay out an hour later if she took care of her responsibilities. My other daughter had a different concern. She wanted money and we took that into account.

8. Program management leaders have vision.

    All leaders are dreamers in some way. I remember
    when I started coding in the 1990s. I knew I would
    stay in this industry when I would dream in code.
    Leaders cast a vision in a way that everyone can
    understand. It may come naturally to some people.
    Everyone can learn this. By the usual measures, Elon
    Musk is not charismatic if you listen to him speak.
    But he has a tremendous vision—to put people on
    Mars—and he executes on it, which draws passionate,
    capable people to him.

    I'm also inspired by Major Richard Winters. He was the
    leader in *Band of Brothers.* He has all of those qualities.
    When I read *Band of Brothers,* I was struck by the fact
    he was an amazing leader. I encourage people to read
    Band of Brothers by Stephen E. Ambrose [Simon &
    Schuster, 2001], as well.

Harpham: Any other rules that you swear by?

Lubrano: There's one other rule I use on my team. I call it the "twenty-percent rule." Only twenty percent of our time should be paying "the program management tax." That means meeting notes, schedule management, building a report for distribution, and so forth. That should only be twenty percent of your workweek. The remaining eighty percent of the time, you will unblock people, solve strategic problems, accelerate velocity, and similar activities. Our role is not to be report writers, not to create schedules or act as a coordinator. I hate that word "coordination," because that's not what we do. We manage projects and programs.

Every problem will be solved differently depending on your level. Let's say there are a large number of bug reports coming in. The junior engineer may say, "I will act as the triage point, personally." That's a tactical solution. In contrast, a senior program manager may suggest setting up a rotation with different people handling the bug reports on different days. An even more senior person will take this approach: "I'm going to pull myself out of the rotation and I'm going to build metrics and dashboards so that anybody can use this model." That approach means anyone can take over the model and tools, and the solution can scale up. All three approaches solve the problem, but they use different methods. By limiting traditional program management activities to twenty percent of your time, you have the capacity to address systematic problems.

Harpham: What are the differences between those approaches to problem solving?

Lubrano: The solutions vary in terms of scalability, the impact of the solution, and the solution's elegance.

Harpham: Would you recommend delegating out tasks if you see the "program management tax" activities exceeding the twenty percent of your time?

Lubrano: Yes, because those problem-solving activities are more valuable. When people come to me and ask for a program manager, I ask them why. Sometimes I get this response: "Well, we need all the 'program management tax' activities." With that response, I will assign a program manager to the requesting group for a few weeks as a test.

At that point, I ask a few questions to the technical lead: How many reports have you read? How many meeting minutes have you read? The usual answer to both points is zero. In that scenario, I realize that they really want an administrator, not a program manager. It's a mistake to view program managers as senior-level admins—people to take notes, track a schedule, and so forth.

Harpham: What does your productivity toolbox look like in terms of tools and practices?

Lubrano: Every program manager has to send out reports or send status updates. To be productive, I think about everything as a problem that I need to understand. Consider a report that I have to produce on one project: that report is probably not going to work on another project. I started with the question: "Who is my audience for these reports?" In my case, the audiences are executives, technical leads, the project team, and other project stakeholders. All of those groups have different communication needs.

I developed a model that solves all of those needs. The model showed the project broken up into major "tracks." Each track had specific goals [not milestones]. Next to each goal, we had milestones, which were expected to be completed that quarter. Last was a status. The only thing TPMs had to fill in was the status for the week. And we had a simple red-yellow-green model for the track. We developed agreed-on definitions of what red-yellow-green meant across the project. It was a very simple report that many different groups could follow.

Finally, I wrote a story and included an executive TL;DR [too long; did not read—a very brief summary], which was no more than three sentences at the top of the document. Every audience was served with one document and each audience knew which parts addressed their needs.

The result? People read the report! When it didn't come out on time, which sometimes happened, people asked me where it was. When has anybody ever asked you about a status report? It usually never happens. I look for solutions that completely solve a problem. Building something special for each request does not scale.

I also use a time boxing strategy to organize my time. I will not exceed my time box. If I say that I'm only on a project ten percent of my week, I will not go over that. Being religious about time boxing is the only way you can survive.

Focus on a single area is another way to enhance productivity. If you are working on five unrelated projects, you will likely be ineffective because you cannot develop meaningful depth. I give everyone on my team one domain to focus on: one person has core search, one person has Google search on Android, and so forth. It's also important to make the project size appropriate. You don't give a large number of tiny projects to a program manager. For small projects, it is better to assign those projects to people who are interested in project work and would like to explore it [e.g., folks who are interested in becoming program managers]. That's a good way to build a pipeline of talent for the future.

Harpham: Looking ahead of the next few years, which opportunities and trends are you most excited about in your work? Whether that is technology or something else.

Lubrano: I think about robots and artificial intelligence. In some circles, there is a fear that robots will take over the world. There will be industries that will suffer disruption and change through this trend. Program management is likely here to stay for the foreseeable future. As long as people are doing challenging work, there will be a cadre of people at organizing and accelerating that work. In the future, there will be greater levels of complexity to manage as software and technology continue to take on simple tasks. The automation of the human workforce will have far-reaching consequences—and that extends to program management.

Chapter Summary

- Recommended books include *Crucial Conversations: Tools for Talking When the Stakes Are High* by Kerry Patterson, Joseph Grenny, Ron McMillan, and Al Switzler and *Getting More: How You Can Negotiate to Succeed in Work and Life* by Stuart Diamond.

- Networking: Lubrano attracted career opportunities by contributing his expertise to online forums. Answering questions and helping others is an excellent way to grow your career.

- Adopt the "T" model for your career. Develop a broad knowledge of your domain (e.g., software development) and then go deep on a specific area (e.g., Google Suggest) to understand how that product works. This approach enhances your credibility and productivity at work.

- Proceed until apprehended. Keep yourself and your team moving to maintain momentum on your projects and programs.

- The program management tax: Lubrano recommends that program managers limit their time spent on program management activities (e.g., reports, plans, and, schedules) to 20% of their time. Use the majority of your time to develop relationships, solve problems, and keep the project moving.

David Woerner

Chief Engineer, NASA

David Woerner *has more than 30 years of experience as a systems engineer and manager at NASA's Jet Propulsion Laboratory. This includes being an office manager for the Mars Science Laboratory (MSL) mission that successfully landed on Mars on August 6, 2012. He is currently applying his technical expertise, engineering skills, management tools, and leadership to some of NASA's challenging developments as a member of NASA's Radioisotope Power System Program. He is the Radioisotope Thermoelectric Generator (RTG) integration manager for the program and is the Chief Engineer of the Nuclear Space Power Office at JPL. He is presently leading the engineering of an enhanced Multi-Mission Radioisotope Thermoelectric Generator (MMRTG). He is also leading a cross-agency team to engineer the next generation RTGs.*

Woerner has worked on such missions as Galileo (to Jupiter), Cassini (to Saturn), Magellan (to Venus), Mars Pathfinder, and MSL. He was the chief engineer of the avionics for the Mars Pathfinder mission that successfully landed on Mars on July 4, 1996. Shortly after that, in the late 1990s, he managed the X2000 Project that developed the RAD750 space processor that is still regularly flown.

Woerner earned his BS degree in aerospace engineering from the University of Colorado and went on to earn his MBA from the University of Southern California. He is the chair of the board of directors for the IEEE Aerospace Conferences. He has won numerous NASA awards, including NASA's Exceptional Service and Exceptional Achievement medals.

© Bruce Harpham 2018
B. Harpham, *Project Managers at Work*, DOI 10.1007/978-1-4842-2668-1_2

Bruce Harpham: How did you get started in project management?

David Woerner: During my studies at the University of Colorado, I worked with NASA as a student. After I graduated, I joined NASA JPL, and I have worked through a variety of roles ever since then.

I had good mentors and excellent opportunities at the organization. In the late 1980s to early 1990s, flight projects at JPL exploded in number. As a result, there was increased demand for project management skills to get those projects completed. Overall, it's been a combination of deliberate strategy on my part to find interesting projects and a bit of luck in opportunities coming through.

Harpham: What was the NASA project you worked on while at the University of Colorado?

Woerner: While I was an undergraduate, the University of Colorado built and flew a spacecraft called the Solar Mesophere Explorer [SME] in the 1980s. The university hired fifteen undergraduates from the engineering college to work on this project, and I was one of them. That project opened the door for me because I met people from JPL and NASA.

It was a great opportunity because we were introduced to computer systems much more advanced than what was available at the university. I was in computer science class with people who had to use an old mainframe computer while I had the opportunity to work on a modern "cut and paste" computer. At that time, "cut and paste" capabilities were unheard of on campus. In fact, one of my classes involved using punch cards! This was a major contrast in the technology we had available.

We would call ground stations around the world for the project, such as Ascension Island in the Atlantic or one in Australia. We set up the communications between NASA, the satellite, and the various ground stations. It was a part time project for us, about twenty hours per week. The University paid us a decent salary and managed to keep the project and our studies going.

Once we all graduated, JPL hired all but one of the fifteen students. We effectively had a two year head start on everyone fresh out of school who was applying for work at JPL. It was a very exciting moment for me to join JPL. When I came to JPL for the job interview, I had a camera around my neck. I was so thrilled to be there, interviewing for a job I would die to have. It turns out that I was a natural fit for this organization.

Harpham: How long was that first satellite in operation for?

Woerner: It was in operation long after I graduated from the University of Colorado [CU]. It was virtually free for NASA to fly because students and professors did most of the work on it. They kept it running for a long time.

The Laboratory of Atmospheric and Space Physics [LASP] was the first university lab in the United States to build and fly their own spacecraft.

SME was a simple spacecraft relative to many of the spacecraft that the US was flying at the time. We could measure nitrogen and nitrous oxide in the atmosphere with it. We could see the factories running up and down the country because of their nitrous emissions. We could actually pin point specific factories based on their pollution. It was a novel experience. It was a successful project.

Harpham: What was your role in the Mars Pathfinder mission, which landed on Mars in 1997?

Woerner: I started working on this project right after my work on the Magellan mission, which was launched to study Venus in 1989.

At that time, Dan Goldin became the administrator of NASA. His motto was "faster, better, cheaper." It was a revolution for NASA. We had a reputation for building big missions, such as the Apollo missions to the Moon, the space shuttle, and so forth. He wanted us to focus on small satellites to see what we could do.

JPL set up a concurrent engineering laboratory where they put fifty to one hundred junior engineers like me in a room. We were supported by a few "gray beards" [highly experienced engineers] to make sure that we didn't screw up too much. We had the mission to create the Mars Pathfinder. My assignment was chief engineer on the avionics system for the lander. That included designing the electronics for the cruise phase, the entry and descent phase, and the ground operations phase. It was an exciting two and a half years!

I had never had that much responsibility in my life. It was a lot of fun, and I enjoyed working with some really bright people.

Harpham: How did you get involved in the project?

Woerner: At the time, I had a mentor who I was close with. When the opportunity came up, he put my name forward, and I was picked. I was happy to accept the assignment. When you have a mentor like Joe Savino, it makes a big difference. He was listening to people in various parts of the organization to find opportunities for people that he knew. He actually pushed me out of the division he led because he felt that I had broader interests that could be explored in other divisions. That experience forced me to grow and that was for the better. I had greater responsibilities such as leading teams, for risk management, and for more.

Harpham: Pathfinder was a step up in responsibility for you. From a project perspective, what did you find most challenging?

Woerner: Risk management was a major challenge. I like to compare Mars Pathfinder [launched in 1996] and the Mars Science Laboratory [MSL] [launched in 2011]. On Mars Pathfinder, NASA gave us $125 million to build and fly that spacecraft, which is a ridiculously small amount of money in that context. The leadership put a bunch of energetic young people in the room to work on this and we went at it. We managed to pull it off.

Working on the Mars Pathfinder mission meant working ten to twelve hours per day, six days a week. At the same time, it was fun. We had white boards on the walls that displayed our progress on hardware, software, and other aspects of the mission. It looked like a crazy factory as we worked on the mission.

From an engineering perspective, we had to do "seat of the pants" engineering. That means operating without two or three engineers to back you up in case you made a calculation error or something of that nature. You had to get it right all on your own. That alone raised the risk dramatically.

Turning to MSL, it was a nuclear mission. The MSL included a nuclear power source, which was a challenge to manage. We had the resources to double check our calculations.

Harpham: Were you also working with a fixed launch date in addition to a fixed budget?

Woerner: Yes, we had a fixed launch date to meet. I'm working in an organization that prides itself on getting everything right when it comes to these missions. We do occasionally fail but the culture at JPL emphasizes getting everything right. The tools and processes developed to prevent failure can get in your way when you're trying to do something fast and cheap.

This was the conceptual problem with the "faster, better, cheaper" model. That concept was in tension with the anti-failure processes and tools that had developed at NASA. It caused some friction for us. Management put a wall around us so that those historical tools and processes would not get in our way.

Harpham: Once you had finished your work and you saw the mission launch into space, what surprised you at that point about the rest of the mission?

Woerner: Tony Spear, the project manager for the mission, fired me after the launch. [Laughs] I knew when it launched that the mission wasn't going to succeed. I couldn't believe that we actually pulled the launch off on time. Until about a week before the mission hit the Martian atmosphere, I was convinced it wasn't going to work.

I had seen the telemetry come in during the cruise from Earth to Mars. I had seen the reports and data on all the subsystems operate correctly. It was great to see it actually work as expected for the most part.

When it hit Mars, the lander bounced multiple times against the surface with airbags. While it went through this bouncing and landing process, we lost communications because the antenna was oriented poorly and our receiver could not lock on. At one point, it was out of lock for about a minute—we were stunned. Fortunately, it came back. After that point, it worked flawlessly.

Harpham: It was a surprise that the mission went as well as it did?

Woerner: It's a mental stress test in a way. You've just created this mission. You know it was done on the cheap. You know it was done on a short schedule. Further, you know it was the first time you've had this level of responsibility on a mission.

Harpham: How does the Pathfinder mission compare to the MSL mission?

Woerner: Mars Pathfinder was completed in about two and a half years. MSL was conceived in 2003 and got a green light for a 2009 launch. Ultimately, it turned into a seven-year development process because we discovered problems when we hit the five-year mark. We discovered two of the subsystems were having serious design problems. We had to cancel the launch and postpone it two years.

My role in the MSL mission was managing and engineering the nuclear power system and the launch vehicle. It was about $400 million for those items—about $200 million for the nuclear power system and about the same for the launch vehicle. For my work, the stakeholders included NASA Headquarters, the Kennedy Space Center and their contractors, and the US Department of Energy and their contractors. US regulations require the US Department of Energy to oversee the manufacture of nuclear power systems. Fortunately, we could tell them how we wanted it made for our purposes. I was instrumental in the design and integrating the nuclear generator into the spacecraft.

On the launch vehicle side, I had a similar challenge. You have to get the nuclear power system through the side wall of the rocket. We required a pair of special doors in the rocket fairing: one to insert the nuclear generator and bolt it to the spacecraft, the other to charge the cooling system on the spacecraft. This whole installation process was done about a week before the launch. To get ready to do that operation required more than eighteen months of preparation.

The preparation involved many stakeholders. We had reviews with community leaders in Florida, and others. Florida's leaders were important because they had to be prepared in the event of a launch accident involving nuclear materials. We also had to work with the US Air Force, the FBI, and others concerned with national security issues. We had to upgrade the launch complex because there had never been a nuclear launch at the site. That meant new security systems, increased redundancy for electrical systems, and much more.

For example, the nuclear power system generates 2,000 watts of heat. When put inside the MSL spacecraft, the generator would act like a heater in a Thermos bottle. If we lost power to the air conditioning system cooling the spacecraft, everything would start to heat up. That's a major problem because the spacecraft's pressure tank and fuel tank are close by—they could overheat, burst, and start a fire. The air conditioning system required three separate power systems to minimize the risk of power failure.

Harpham: Let's turn to the stakeholder management issues. Had you worked with these stakeholders before, such as the Florida authorities, the US Air Force, and others?

Woerner: It was new for me and new for many of them as well. It turns out that NASA flies one of these nuclear-powered missions about once a decade. Therefore, people come and go through their careers at these organizations. You might have some experience with a few of the stakeholders but many of the people were new to the process.

Over time, you learn where everybody's sensitivities are and what their needs are. Once you learn those points, you address them to the best of your ability.

Since we were working on a nuclear system, there were hard safety requirements to learn to live with. We could not just walk into a building that has the nuclear generator. We could not allow people near it. We had to adopt a hyper-safety attitude. While I had experience with space flight before this time, I had not worked on nuclear matters or with the Department of Energy. After seven to eight years working with the Department of Energy, I loved them. Once I saw them in operation, I was impressed by how detail oriented they were. I still sometimes wonder about other countries with nuclear capabilities and whether they are as diligent in handling nuclear materials.

Harpham: How did you handle schedule challenges on these projects?

Woerner: The schedule options for launches are forced by the physics of the problem. To maximize launch vehicle performance, there are only a few times each decade when you would choose to launch to Mars—those occur about every twenty-three months. The orbits of Mars and Earth dictate when it is best to launch. If you were to launch at a different time, it would take more energy. JPL had a mission scheduled for a 2016 launch to Mars but it had to be rescheduled due to problems. It's a problem we face all the time. An actual launch period is typically about three to four weeks long for an interplanetary mission, so there is not much flexibility when you run into problems close to the launch period.

For the MSL mission, everybody was taking orders and trying to get their work done. The project was burning through its reserves attempting to solve problems. We relied on the engineers to come forward and confess their difficulties. We had to assess the value of fixing each specific problem. Everyone kept going and we kept trying to put your best foot forward. Eventually, we could mathematically prove that we were not going to make the launch date.

NASA had always known we were not playing an easy game. For instance, changing requirements made it difficult to get work done. Dollars, schedule, and people all get tight as you approach the launch date. The conversation got kind of ugly at that point even though we had put in "pressure relief valves" earlier in the process.

When we were setting up our budget, people wrote two sets of requirements. One set of requirements was for the case when everything went well. The backup requirements were there to give us schedule relief or budget relief when the original plan did not work out. Backup requirements might eliminate a scientific instrument from the mission or slip the launch as examples. It would not be pretty to make a change. Making changes like those has the potential to harm the institution's reputation and its likelihood to do future missions. However, sometimes you get forced into those situations.

The engineers couldn't manage to solve problems on two of the subsystems on MSL. This came to a head about eight months before liftoff.

Harpham: I understand that you've continued to be involved in nuclear space power systems following that mission. What's your current focus in that area?

Woerner: Right now, I'm the chief engineer for the Nuclear Space Power Office at JPL. I'm also the RTG [Radioisotope Thermoelectric Generator] integration manager for NASA. NASA has a program for radioisotope power systems—they serve as my sponsor. One task I have is to enhance the design of the type of power system flown on the MSL rover. That generator design was started in 2003 and it was ready to go by 2008. As a result, we have a few of those generators in storage on Earth. One of them is promised to a 2020 mission to Mars. The others are unassigned right now. The development cycle for these systems is about ten years from start to finish. That means it takes ten years to develop a nuclear power system for a five-year mission, you have to start the nuclear power system before any specific space mission is approved.

We have been working on ways to improve the design and productivity of the nuclear power system, which was first designed with MSL in mind. We're currently transferring those designs to industry for further development. The enhanced design will produce about twenty-five percent more power at the beginning of its service life. At the end of its service life, power production will be fifty percent higher than the current model. It's a significant power boost for long lived missions of ten years or more. These generators are typically designed to run for about seventeen years.

In addition, I'm running a study to develop concepts for the next generation of generators. These will replace or supplement the current system that we're building enhancements for. These will be long lead projects and require extensive coordination across multiple government agencies and laboratories.

Harpham: This long lead time has an impact on requirements. You might know what some of the missions will require but other missions haven't been developed. Yet, you have to imagine what is required and act accordingly.

Woerner: You have to guess what the scientists and others will require because they haven't conceived of the possibilities yet. You take your best shot at it based on past experience and what they can tell you today. It's an interesting challenge.

Harpham: How does it work with the industry partners to get the equipment built?

Woerner: The enhancements we're building for the RTG were developed at JPL over the last twenty years by a few of our scientists. When the MSL landed on Mars, we had high confidence that we could start to transfer this technology to industry. We are going to do the upgrade for about $30 million compared to the cost of producing a novel generator for about $200 million. By starting the development process early, we lower the risk of later problems.

Harpham: How does the interaction between NASA and industry unfold?

Woerner: The generator is a structure made up of subcomponents. My purview is to make sure all of the components hang together successfully. The technologists and the industrial partners have weekly meetings, and I participate in those to provide my input. We also have gate reviews because this is a technology transfer—we are aware of the potential to delude ourselves on the project. These gates reduce the likelihood that we're fooling ourselves on our progress. On this project, we have three gate reviews spread over several years.

Harpham: How do these gate reviews work?

Woerner: Before the gate reviews, we write down criteria that we have to pass successfully at the next review. For example, the system has to generate X amount of power. The system has to be able to survive the launch environment. We get agreement with our customer on the success criteria for a gate review. The engineers have to stand up and prove that they have met those criteria. We also bring in outside consultants and the Department of Energy for advice on designing these gate reviews.

Harpham: You mentioned that self-delusion is a major challenge on these projects. How do you approach that challenge?

Woerner: Third parties, such as consultants and the Department of Energy, are helpful in addressing self-delusion. We go looking for people who are good at seeing our blind spots and exposing them to us. On the other hand, it's a small community and we know most of the players already.

Recall the earlier example of the slipped schedule with the MSL launch? Everyone was working hard and trying to look good for NASA. At some point, we realized we were in trouble and realized we had to add two years to the mission before launch. Tests and gate reviews can reduce the chance of getting hit by delusions.

Harpham: If you compare the project management processes you're using today versus the 1990s, where do you see the greatest improvement?

Woerner: Risk comes to mind first. When we did Mars Pathfinder, risk was not really an area of focus. We did have one person on Pathfinder who worked on risk, and we did have a short list of risks that were transformed into requests for funds.

In contrast, we had a meticulous approach to risk on MSL. Every subsystem and every engineer had baskets of risk. They understood where all the problems could arise. Further, they understood the probability of a risk occurring and the cost if they did arise. At the project level, that information would be put together, and we could see how project risk evolved over time.

In this business, risk is hugely important. It's not practiced uniformly across NASA though. JPL has its own rules on how to approach risk. The risk approach used on MSL was transformative for me: how to manage money and the burndown of money to address risk. We were given some reserves, but how would we know if we had enough reserves? Risk analysis helped on that point.

Harpham: How do you segment risks and treat them differently? In the financial industry, some risks are well understood and can be managed with insurance or other methods. In contrast, other risk types are harder to forecast and mitigate. How do you approach these risks?

Woerner: Almost all risks are not the sole property of the person who thought them up. They start out that way, but then they get expert review and the relevant parties are identified. The question becomes: can you budget some amount of money to mitigate a risk and if it becomes a problem and what is the likelihood of that happening? The less you know about the risk and its probability, I think you have to budget more money against it.

Risks are then graded into categories. At JPL, we use five categories for risk that consider the likelihood and consequences of the risk event occurring. A project might say, "Category 5 risks would consume one-fourth of the project budget." So if I had found something that risky on the project, I would probably change the spacecraft or mission design significantly to mitigate the risk. In contrast, a risk category 1 event might cost a work month of effort to address.

MSL cost over $2 billion, so a twenty-five percent budget impact is very significant. That scale made it painful for managers to ignore risk.

Harpham: What is your approach to mentoring others in the organization?

Woerner: My experience has changed from when I first started at JPL. I now view a new hire as someone who has no experience. In contrast, someone who might be acceptable for a technical job might have seven to eight years of experience. A good person for a challenging job will often have over ten years of experience.

The brand-new person—two years or less of experience—is somebody you give mathematical and technical problems to and review their work with them. You encourage them to keep a notebook, learn the JPL basics relating to performance expectations, and doing engineering. There are also some classes for new hires to help them get up to speed. That's my approach to mentoring someone at that level.

If we're talking about someone with seven to ten years of work experience at JPL, that's the kind of person I love to get onto a complex project like a nuclear power system. I start throwing graduate level work at them—they get juicy problems to chew on, challenges that will keep them up at night. With the right kinds of problems, they will work long hours and have a good time doing the work.

I've seen two kinds of problems people can work on. There are problems that suck—these cause people to walk away from their job and look elsewhere for a new opportunity. On the other hand, there are juicy problems, and people will love you for assigning those.

Last year, I worked with an exceptionally bright person who had graduated from Cal State Fullerton. He was just head and shoulders above everyone else around him. He knew how to put together and deliver presentations about his engineering work, and he did great engineering.

Other people are harder to bring out of their shell. In that way, you have to use unique approaches. I have one person working for me who is quiet and doesn't ask many questions. In this case, I am taking a proactive approach to engage him. I gave him a journal article and asked him to discuss it with me within a week. That process encouraged him to open up, dive into the technical approach in the article, tell me what he learned, and then I could find out what he should learn next.

Harpham: What defines a juicy problem where you're happy to be up late working on it?

Woerner: A juicy problem looks like this: "Don't tell me what this electrical circuit does. Tell me how it will fail, and why it fails. Even better, tell me the math and physics behind how this component will fail. What are the other functions that could be done with this component that nobody else has come up with yet?" That's an example of a juicy problem. Send them on a voyage of discovery. Find the wonderment in a challenge.

The idea is to encourage people to think broadly about a problem. If I gave somebody an equation to solve, they could probably do it in a flash. However, that doesn't advance our understanding. Instead, I want to know where the inflection points are in the equation, what happens if I invert two of the parameters, or what does this equation mean for the hardware we're using?

In a way, solving a particular problem is only part of the goal. The real goal is to change how a person thinks about the world around them. If you hire an engineer, and you only have them build flight computers, that person will be good at those computers. Instead, I would have them build a flight computer in the context of all the scientific instruments on a mission and the environmental forces on the computer, and identify design changes to make the computer more resilient against failure, and other factors. Explore and envision a rich multi-dimensional world, not a one-dimensional world.

Harpham: For the reader who is interested in changing their career path from engineering into project management, how would you suggest they pursue that move?

Woerner: Let's start with the assumption that you have opportunities to do projects. That may not always be the case, however.

A person's home organization has to promote them relentlessly. A new person coming into projects tends to start at a disadvantage compared to more experienced project managers. If you want to get into project management, you've got to have the skills or the capability to be successful. Nobody wants to give a multi-million-dollar mission to an engineer without project experience. You've got to build up to that level slowly. That's the JPL approach: give people smaller projects to grow on.

To reach the project management level, you need more than skills with schedules, finances, risk management, and all those management bins labeled with buzzwords. People skills are essential for success. A person needs to have managed four or five people in a semi-stressful context. Projects are stressful, so a person needs to be ready for that. From there, career growth will be about adding responsibilities to your job. The more complex the job, the more a person will be seen as a leader.

Harpham: If a person has managed a team but has not struggled with stressful conditions, then perhaps they are not ready to lead a project.

Woerner: I agree with that.

Harpham: In terms of managing your daily work, what productivity methods and strategies do you use?

Woerner: There are parts of project management that I find boring—day to day financial management is boring to me—though planning the budget for the year is interesting. Some boring work goes along with any job. The question

I face is—what are the interesting problems and questions I can develop to explore?

I keep myself excited by focusing on strategic activities that have broad impact. I look for difficult questions to work on from an engineering or scientific perspective. I also keep my fingers on technical work to a degree. That prompts me to come up with good questions and assignments for my teams to work on.

Harpham: Thoughtful delegation is a key part of the strategy. For example, problem A would be great for Jane but not problem C.

Woerner: Exactly right.

Harpham: Which books and other resources have been valuable in your outlook and changing how you think about your work?

Woerner: I earned an MBA degree about five years after starting at JPL. A few aspects of those studies were very helpful. I studied with Warren Bennis, a noted author on leadership. I read his books chronologically, so I could see how his thinking on leadership evolved over time. When he first started writing, the books looked at what was a leader and how they did their job. Eventually, his later books, such as *On Becoming a Leader* [Basic Books, 2009] gave me insight into working with people.

I find it helpful to attend conferences and lead those events to learn about the latest research. I've organized an IEEE Aerospace Conference, where I invited leading researchers from around their world to make presentations—similar to a TED talk, but focused on a technical audience with interests in science, aerospace, and engineering topics.

I found *Thinking, Fast and Slow* by Daniel Kahneman [Farrar, Straus and Giroux, 2011] to be helpful in thinking about consciousness and our thinking processes. On the same topic, I've read *NeuroLogic: The Brain's Hidden Rationale Behind Our Irrational Behavior* by Eliezer Sternberg [Vintage, reprint edition, 2016]. I'm interested in brain science and what that tells us about behavior. I'm also interested in the field of behavioral economics—Dan Ariely has some great books in that field. I look for people who are on the cutting edge doing solid work that will teach us new insights.

Harpham: Over the next three to five years, what are some of the science and technology opportunities that interest you?

Woerner: I've worked on seven or eight deep-space missions that have been highly successful. I have also worked on three technology projects, one of which was a major failure. Making my current technology into a success is my focus—we'll know one way or another in a few years. I'd like to see this technology put into production and fly on a spacecraft. There are other pressures in my organization. However, I would like to get this project shipped out the door.

Chapter Summary

- Recommended books include *On Becoming a Leader* by Warren Bennis, *Thinking Fast and Slow* by Daniel Kahneman, *Neurologic* by Eliezer Sternberg, and Dan Ariely's books.

- Grow your career with mentors. Navigating a large organization and identifying good career opportunities is easier with a mentor. Seek a mentor who can support your growth.

- Risk management: Recognize that you may struggle to identify risks when you are deeply involved in a project's work. To address this situation, consider NASA's approach of bringing in outside experts to provide risk advice.

- Create multiple sets of requirements: With a backup set of requirements, you can respond more quickly to major changes such as missing a launch window.

- Use gate reviews. Define certain performance or success criteria that the project has to meet at predefined stages before the project can advance further.

- Develop people by giving them challenging problems. Adapt Woerner's approach to grow staff by handing them substantial problems that occur at work in order to learn how they can be solved.

Tamsen Mitchell

Agile Coach, Salesforce

Tamsen Mitchell *is an agile coach at Salesforce, with over 17 years of experience in the software industry. She facilitated agile transformations in three companies and coached multiple teams on agile software development. Mitchell's background in architecture laid a foundation in traditional project management. After deciding that designing buildings that actually obeyed the laws of gravity was not for her, she thought that virtual buildings would be much more fun. This led to a producer role in the video games industry, first at The 3DO Company, and then at Shaba Games (later Activision Blizzard).*

Mitchell has always been around strong and creative storytelling environments, where thinking outside the box was nurtured. Her next industry jump landed her as a project manager at Pixar Animation Studios, working with the research and development team and the stereographic (3D) department. Mitchell later moved to LinkedIn to become a technical program manager. This was where her interest in coaching grew. She currently specializes in crafting learning and development programs that maximize the retention and engagement of the participants at Salesforce.

Bruce Harpham: How did you get started in the world of project management?

Tamsen Mitchell: I have had a winding career path. I studied architecture at the Mackintosh School of Architecture, University of Glasgow. I originally thought I would move into the architecture profession. I found that I enjoyed the creative and theoretical challenges of architecture work. During my studies, I had a one year placement at a firm to learn more about how architecture is practiced.

© Bruce Harpham 2018
B. Harpham, *Project Managers at Work*, DOI 10.1007/978-1-4842-2668-1_3

I decided to come to San Francisco for that experience. It was an opportunity to combine travel and professional experience.

In San Francisco, I was essentially working as an architecture intern at several architectural studios. The harsh reality of work as a professional architect was quite a shock to me! After that experience, I decided that I wanted to move into a different field. While in San Francisco, I met fellow British expats who happened to be involved in the video game industry—many of them were engineers and other technical professionals. Learning about the video game industry was exciting. It occurred to me that I could use my architectural knowledge in games—to design buildings and other structures—without having to worry about building codes. That idea would later lead to work in a variety of roles in the video game industry.

Following graduation, the contacts I had made in San Francisco helped me find my first job in the video game industry. I found that the planning and project management skills I developed through my architecture studies came in very helpful. Within a year of working in the video game industry, I moved into my first project management role. That first role involved project management at the portfolio level—managing release dates and activities across multiple projects.

Harpham: What was one of the most complex video game projects you worked on?

Mitchell: I got started in that industry in the 1990s when it was dominated by console systems like PlayStation and Nintendo.

From a project perspective, this meant multi-year projects to produce a game and then shipping the game on a CD or cartridge. In contrast, today's games are delivered as a download or as a "software as a service" model. In those earlier projects, there was no easy way to publish a patch or update to the product.

There are two sides of the video game industry. There's the publisher side—and the developer side. The publisher has a focus on sales, marketing, and distribution. The developer side has a focus on creating the code and content of the game itself. I was working as a producer on these games on the publisher side at The 3DO Company. At one point, I was managing about fifteen or so different product lines, such as High Heat Baseball, the Army Men series, and Jonny Moseley Mad Trix, from a portfolio management perspective.

Harpham: What other project roles did you encounter in the video game industry?

Mitchell: A few years later, I moved into a different type of project management in the video game industry. I moved to the developer side of the industry. I was hired as the company's sole project manager at Shaba Games, a small developer, which was later purchased by Activision Blizzard, a large publisher.

When I started at that developer, there were around forty people working there. In addition to engineers, there were artists, animators, designers, and other professions. Eventually, the company grew up to 150 people at its peak in the late 2000s.

I managed the development of Tony Hawk's Thug 2 Remix for the launch of the Sony PlayStation Portable. This was a "port" project—i.e., the game had already been made by a different company, and we were converting it to run on a different piece of hardware. The team was small—maybe twenty people. It launched in 2005. It was a technically challenging project: the game was to run on an unknown piece of hardware with limited information of the technical specs and a brand-new format [i.e. the UMD mini disks]. We could never run the code to test it on actual hardware from the actual media until after it was released. On top of that, the original game had to be highly optimized to run on the reduced hardware spec.

During this time, I also got involved in video game projects with new types of challenges. For example, I worked on a Spider-Man video game. It's a major intellectual property and you have to work effectively with Marvel [owner of Spider-Man] on it. There are also actors involved and intellectual property law considerations to think through.

Harpham: On these projects working with Marvel and other franchises, what did your role look like?

Mitchell: I was managing the engineers and artists to execute the project. I would also work with other people at Activision, our parent company, as they focused on marketing, and working with third parties and related activities. It was my role to move the project forward and ensure that constraints [e.g., Marvel's restrictions on their intellectual property] are followed.

Harpham: I'd like to make sure that I'm clear on structure of the industry. Can you define the difference between a developer organization and a publisher?

Mitchell: The developer organization makes the game. They write the code, create the art, the story, the game play, and so forth. The publisher, in this case, is similar to a book publisher in some ways. The publisher will manage copyright considerations and other similar activities outside the project. For example, the developer may say, "We'd love to use a certain song in our game." The publisher would then manage the request and explore whether or not it was feasible to purchase rights to use that music in the game, given our budget and the license considerations.

Harpham: Would the developer and publisher be different divisions of the same company or totally distinct entities?

Mitchell: It depends—they may be units of the same company or separate. The people who are passionate about making games generally go to work at a developer. In contrast, the publisher side is more about the business of making and selling games.

Harpham: You have worked in several different industries: architecture, video games, and software services. How did you approach changing industries in your career?

Mitchell: Aside from my studies, I wasn't in architecture that long, so it was relatively easy to make a switch. In the mid 2000s, I started to get interested in the agile methodology for managing projects. The principles and the mindset is the same when it comes to using agile in different industries. I treated my changes to different industries with this view: I understand planning, prioritization, and related skills. Then I would ask, "How do these skills apply in this other industry?"

Once I moved to a new industry, I started to ask a few questions. For example, what is the technology stack [e.g., is it LAMP—Linux, Apache, MySQL, PHP] in use here? Who is the customer and what do they want? I had to become very good at learning the different technologies and customer needs in each place. From the 2000s onward, I had one stable skill set—agile and project management—that I could use in each new role. Around that stable core, I would then learn new technologies and related industry knowledge to succeed in each industry.

After working in the movie industry, I joined LinkedIn. There were interesting challenges in that move because of the scale of users and technology involved in running LinkedIn. It was also a new experience to work on a web-based product, which is quite different from games distributed on CDs or consoles.

Harpham: What other questions did you consider when you moved to a new industry?

Mitchell: It was helpful to consider the organization's history and understand what mistakes and problems they suffered in the past. That history tends to inform risk management—certain risks tend to be better understood due to an organization's history.

I also found that the teams and units I joined often did not have a formal project management process or role in place. At this point, I've also learned whether or not a given company is going to be a good fit for me: Are they interested in improving and using better project management practices?

Harpham: What have you learned about company culture through your experiences?

Mitchell: When it comes to technology companies, I've noticed certain patterns. Some companies are technology led, design led, or product led. For example, Google is known for strongly emphasizing technology: engineers and technologists have significant influence and authority. In contrast, design and designers have a much greater role at Apple. You can also have customers that are focused on the product or a problem.

LinkedIn was heavily technology focused, with a major emphasis on the product. This culture is probably influenced by the fact that many senior LinkedIn technology people came from Google. I've found that some companies that have a technology or engineering focus don't always appreciate the value of project management. To illustrate with an extreme example, an engineer at such a company might say, "I'm an engineer. I call the shots here." That attitude may diminish the role and contribution of the project or program manager.

Harpham: What was your response to this environment where the value of project management is not recognized?

Mitchell: In short, you have to prove the value of project management. I believe that seventy percent of this job is relationship building and treating people like people [rather than treating them like robots]. When you're working with software engineers all day, relationship and people skills may not be at the top of their list. You start by showing the engineers that your contribution makes their life easier and more effective.

At LinkedIn, my approach was to build strategic relationships with the engineering leadership and the product leadership. My goal was to understand their concerns: What do they want to fix? I take a baby steps approach: let's fix the problem you're facing right now. For example, you have trouble with release planning. Let's figure it out and improve that process. By improving release planning, it helped that group to become more reliable and predictable in their work.

Harpham: What was valuable about helping the department to become more predictable?

Mitchell: By predictable, I mean that they could make an estimate for work and then achieve that estimate. If the group said a given project would take a month to complete, we would generally complete it in a month. That predictability increased the group's standing in the eyes of senior management. The strong relationship that I developed with this group made it possible to give them support and direction to improve.

In other cases, I've seen project managers treated almost like "bean counters." For example, engineers might say, "Oh that project manager is constantly referring to their Gantt chart. They're annoying me by asking for progress updates." It's better to start the relationship with a focus on the person's needs [e.g., to improve estimation accuracy and delivery] rather than starting the conversation with technical project management questions and comments.

Harpham: If you were starting a new relationship with someone important in your work, how exactly would you develop that relationship?

Mitchell: It may sound a little corny at first. Start with this simple principle: being able to listen closely to a person when they answer questions. I like to ask questions, like "What has gone wrong in the past?" or "What have you tried before to solve this problem?" In a way, this approach is almost Coaching 101. Asking non-judgmental, open-ended questions makes a big difference. In terms of attitude, it's important to show true curiosity to that person's position and problems.

When I started at Pixar and LinkedIn, here was my approach: I would say, "Hey, let's grab lunch and chat." I wanted to understand what was happening in the business. My first step would focus on the team or the organization's leaders and managers. I would seek to find out what they care about, what they value, and what their goals and vision are for the group or teams. I want to find out where I can help. More specifically, I wanted to understand the stakeholder's situation. What do they see as problems or challenges? I'm seeking to develop a "relationship map" of the department to see how people relate to each other and understand the history of those relationships.

Harpham: Were the people you met generally open to your relationship development approach?

Mitchell: It depends on the person I'm reaching out to. Some people are interested in engaging with you, and some are not. You have to take their predisposition into account as you work at getting to know people. If you approach someone and they don't want to engage, I back off and direct my efforts to other people who are open to connecting. I find that when people have pain points in their work, there is often a willingness to discuss those points, so that can be a good opening.

In fact, I find that few people are asked about the problems and pains they're experiencing. It tends to go unnoticed and that leads to a resentment building up.

Harpham: How does coaching fit into the picture?

Mitchell: When I was working at LinkedIn, I was responsible for the delivery of various products, including the identity team, which oversees your LinkedIn profile. In that work, I coached people on ways to work better together and make their lives easier. Over time, I became interested in coaching people, compared to the traditional nuts and bolts of project management. I realized that coaching was interesting to me, and so I decided to make that my focus.

I wanted to embody the servant leadership model. I view my role as "I'm here to help you" rather than "I'm judging whether we messed up as a team."

Consider this analogy: agile coaches are like vampires in that you have to be invited in. Unless you're invited in, you're not going to have much of an impact. Your advice is not going to be wanted. If you are invited in, there's a desire for help, because the team is in trouble or perhaps they're curious about learning how to do better.

This analogy also helps me to prioritize my time. If I'm not getting a good reception in one area, I can step back and look at other places where I can make a contribution. You have to remember that you can't fix everything!

Harpham: Can you share an example of a department "hitting rock bottom" and inviting you in to assist them?

Mitchell: The technology organization at Salesforce is massive and there are less than twenty agile coaches here. Therefore, we had to choose carefully where it makes sense to use our time.

In some cases, the department may reach out to me directly to ask for support. In other cases, the relationships I've built with leaders and other people in the organization bring situations to light. I might hear something like "There's pain in this team. They're in trouble. Could you help them?"

I sometimes also see problems come up on our internal bulletin board. If people post messages like "How on Earth do we do X?" or "We can't do Y!"—those are triggers that I may be able to help that group as an agile coach.

Harpham: Let's say that you're brought in to help a new department tomorrow. How do you start your agile coaching process with them?

Mitchell: I start by defining coaching. I define coaching as a balance of teaching, facilitating, mentoring, and actual coaching based on agile and lean principles. Next, we create a coaching agreement to define our work together. That agreement will cover questions like "What do you expect from me?" and "What do I expect from you?" It's like setting up a set of working agreements. That agreement also covers feedback and the form that feedback takes. The agreement also covers "How do we know if we're succeeding in our work together?" The group and I both define the agreement.

Harpham: Is there an educational or training component to the engagement, where you're teaching agile methods and techniques?

Mitchell: Yes, in some cases. Overall, the agreement is about coming up with the rules of agreement for the coaching process.

Harpham: What happens next in an agile coaching engagement?

Mitchell: I like to start with an agile retrospective. That exercise helps people to open up about their pain points: what's going wrong and what the "bright spots" [activities and processes that are functioning well] are in their work. Partly, I'm looking for extremes: What are the greatest pains the group is suffering? Likewise, what are the group's greatest strengths that can be built upon?

There's an element of mentorship in this work. In some cases, I draw on specific examples of successful practices that I've used in my own experience. However, I generally limit how many suggestions I provide because I want the group to engage in the process and develop their own solutions.

The coaching agreement usually has principles like "I promise to give you honest feedback in a constructive manner." If that is stated up front and agreed to, that principle sets the tone for the work. With that in place, I may identify certain dysfunctional habits. For example, I may observe a discussion in a retrospective and point out, "Is that type of comment in line with providing honest feedback in a constructive manner?" That's when you can have a breakthrough in the group recognizing their habits.

Harpham: What kinds of systematic dysfunctional patterns have you seen occur repeatedly in your work?

Mitchell: Teams or individuals will rush to fix a problem before they have properly analyzed the problem. Put another way: they're jumping to solutions as opposed to figuring out the problem. That's a key dysfunction that I often see.

I also see people not honoring commitments in their work. I also see people not understanding the meaning of an estimation versus a guarantee. I also see misalignments between a product person and the team members doing the work. There's also a whole category of interpersonal problems: single points of failure, back stabbing, and hero worship, for example.

In terms of solutions, I see many groups attempt to solve a human dynamics problem by using a process solution. People don't like talking about soft skills and human dynamics problems at work, even though that may be the most effective path to a solution. As an agile coach, I sometimes serve as a mirror and show them: "This is what is going on in your department. Do you recognize this?"

Harpham: Can you walk me through an example where you helped a group solve dysfunctional practices?

Mitchell: Recently, I had an informal coaching conversation with someone I met earlier during a Scrum Master Foundation workshop I delivered. He mentioned that he had been given the assignment of "making his team more predictable and better at estimating." At first glance, that's a fairly common assignment. I started to explore the issue by asking questions like "What has the team tried?" "What's going wrong?" and "What actions might you have done differently?"

It turns out that the team never broke down work into smaller pieces. Therefore, there was a lot of guessing in terms of coming up with estimates for how long work would take to finish. As a result, it's no surprise that these poorly developed estimates tended to have accuracy problems.

I explained a few ideas to get the person moving in the right direction. However, I made it clear that I would not be providing a comprehensive solution: he had to engage in the process as well. I also asked him to complete a few steps on his own and then come back to me to discuss it in a few days.

Harpham: You're pointing out the critical value in taking the time to properly identify and define the problem before moving on to a solution. What is your overall approach to problems and the problem-solving process?

Mitchell: I generally start with the premise that the "obvious" solution to the problem may not be correct. I may have some instinct for the problem and the solution, but I keep that in check for a period of time. I allow myself the time and space to look around and explore other aspects of the environment. For example, is there a cultural problem? What about conflict within the organizational hierarchy?

I recently heard from a department where they claimed to have communication problems. Their solution? Hold more meetings. It turned out that the team was spread out over a variety of time zones around the world. Therefore, any given meeting time would frustrate at least one team member who had to come in early or stay late to attend the call. The group never directly spoke about how this difficulty affected them. In this case, it was an organizational problem instead of a being a communication problem.

Harpham: You encourage people to slow down in their problem-solving process. Let's put solution A to the side for the next hour and explore the problem more deeply.

Mitchell: At a basic level, there are objective ways to identify and fix a problem. There are also subjective ways to approach the problem.

Harpham: What's the difference between an objective and subjective approach?

Mitchell: Process-driven approaches would be an example of the objective approach. That is the approach often favored by engineers. The objective approach may be encouraged by a manager who phrases their need for improvement by saying, "This department needs to increase its agile velocity,"—i.e., focus on improving a metric.

The subjective approach may define the problem by saying, "We need to focus on how we resolve problems on our team." Or, "What are our shared values for working together?" I often find that engineers and most businesses are less interested in that kind of conversation. However, those "touchy feely" conversations are often the best way to solve a problem.

Harpham: Based on your observation of seeing other agile coaches in action, what mistakes do you see novices make?

Mitchell: It's easy to feel like you have to fix everything. It's not your job as an agile coach to create the solution and implement it for someone else. That's not teaching them to fish. You're not there to provide the answers. You're there to facilitate the learning process.

There's also a tension to manage in this role. On the one hand, you're generally recognized as the agile expert in the room. On the other hand, you don't want to lapse into arrogance and order people around. As a coach, it's important to have the mindset that there's always more to learn and discover. That perspective keeps you improving personally and keeps you from falling into the arrogance trap.

Harpham: Speaking of learning, what are some of the books and resources that have been most valuable to you professionally?

Mitchell: I took a great course called Training From the BACK of the Room! by Sharon L. Bowman. It covers how to construct and present information as a trainer or teacher. The approach is based on cognitive science ideas related to how people learn and use information. Fundamentally, it teaches how to create and deliver content so that people will remember it.

Turn the Ship Around!: A True Story of Turning Followers into Leaders, by L. David Marquet [Portfolio, 2013] is a great book. It's a great exploration on leadership and how to empower your team. I've read that book a few times. One of the insights I've taken from the book: start by establishing trust. The problem is not with the people.

I've also taken several excellent courses with the Agile Coaching Institute. Lyssa Adkins, author of Coaching Agile Teams [Addison-Wesley Professional, 2010], is one of the people behind the course. I found their Integral Agile Wizardry course quite helpful. A number of my questions and techniques have come directly from my studies with the Institute. They opened my eyes on how to properly coach.

I also quite liked Scaling Up Excellence: Getting to More Without Settling for Less by Hayagreeva Rao and Robert I. Sutton [Crown Business, 2014]. They're experts from Stanford. I learned from their insight that "the bad" is stronger than "the good" in many organizations. Therefore, bad problems have significant impact and need to be nipped in the bud.

Harpham: What habits and systems go into your personal productivity strategy?

Mitchell: Multi-tasking hurts my productivity, so I make a point to avoid that behavior. I like to have time to think deeply and process what's happening. I sometimes wonder if I have that process correct: how I know if I've done enough reflecting and that it's time to move to execution.

When I become particularly overwhelmed with distractions, I like to use the Pomodoro Technique [i.e., set a timer for twenty-five minutes to work without interruption on a task, and then take a short break and continue the process]. When I use the technique, I tell people that I am using it and not to interrupt me during that time. It's a great technique to help me focus. In fact, we've made it into a bit of a game at the office. Some of my co-workers have bought me some silly hats to wear. It's a good way to signal "do not talk to me while I have the hat on." This approach helps me to get into a flow state where I'm exceptionally productive.

My productivity approach also covers how I manage technology. I have two smartphones: one is my work phone and one is my personal phone. When I get home at night, I plug in my work phone for charging and turn it off. I do not touch that phone until I leave for work the next day. If I didn't do that, I would constantly be checking my email.

From a self-management standpoint, I'm ruthless with how much work in progress I have at any given time. I hate not being involved in an activity, especially if it might impact me. However, I've gradually realized that I have to set limits on my work and let other people do their work. I tell myself, "There are other people who are perfectly capable of doing this work. I don't have to be involved in each and every project." This practice helps me to keep my perfectionist streak under control.

Harpham: Do you find project management practices helpful in other areas of life?

Mitchell: I just planned my wedding using the Trello application! It worked out well. It was helpful to have everything documented so that we could both work on the project and balance the load. After all, a wedding is a project that involves a lot of people.

Chapter Summary

- Recommended books include *Training from the BACK of the Room!* by Sharon L. Bowman, *Turn The Ship Around!: A True Story of Turning Followers into Leaders* by L. David Marquet, *Coaching Agile Teams* by Lyssa Adkins, and *Scaling up Excellence: Getting to More Without Settling for Less* by Hayagreeva Rao and Robert I. Sutton.

- Education is not destiny. Mitchell earned a degree in architecture and went on to work in video games and social media, and at Salesforce. You can make the move to a new field.

- How to change industries: To aid your move to a new industry, use Mitchell's orienting questions. Who is the customer and what do they want? What is the technical "stack" used here to create products and services? Who are the important leaders and managers?

- How to build credibility for yourself (and project management): First, identify the top problems as defined by management. Then, start to take baby steps to solve those problems with your skills and project management methods. That wins you the credibility to propose other changes and improvements in the long term.

- The most common dysfunction: Rushing to fix a problem immediately rather than taking the time to define the problem first.

Isabelle Tremblay

Director, Astronauts, Life Sciences and Space Medicine, Canadian Space Agency

Isabelle Tremblay *began working at the Canadian Space Agency (CSA) in 1998 as a research and development engineer in robotics. She received a bachelor's degree in mechanical engineering and a master's degree in aerospace engineering from the École Polytechnique de Montréal. She is also a graduate of the International Space University (ISU), where she completed the Space Studies Program. In 2001, Tremblay joined the CSA's systems engineering group, where she worked as senior engineer and technical manager in the context of international and complex space exploration projects, namely, the Canadian contributions to the NASA's Phoenix Mars lander mission, which operated on Mars in 2008, and the James Webb Space Telescope, which will be launched in 2018. More recently, she was manager of the projects/ program portfolio and headed the CSA's Corporate Investment Management Office, where she led the development and implementation of the new Canadian Space Agency project governance and monitoring framework and other initiatives, with the objective of improving the CSA's organizational project management capacity. She was recently appointed as the Director, Astronauts, Life Sciences and Space Medicine.*

© Bruce Harpham 2018
B. Harpham, *Project Managers at Work*, DOI 10.1007/978-1-4842-2668-1_4

Tremblay is currently on the board of directors for the PMI-Montreal, a chapter of the Project Management Institute. Over the years, she has been involved in numerous initiatives for popularizing and promoting science and technology among young people and the general public.

Bruce Harpham: How did you first become interested in the space field?

Isabelle Tremblay: It was a lifelong dream for me. As a child, I was fascinated by space exploration. I read books about it all the time. At the time of the Voyager 1 launch in 1977 [the first human spacecraft to leave the solar system], I was five years old. That mission certainly inspired me about the possibilities of space. I knew from an early age that I had to be involved in the space field.

Harpham: The Voyager mission in particular stands out as an inspiration?

Tremblay: In addition to Voyager, there were a few other sources of inspiration. Before I learned how to read, I received a book on space [a French translation of Moon, Sun, and Stars (New True Book) by John Bryan Lewellen]. I still keep the book in my office. One section explains the phases of the Moon. It looked fascinating and I wanted to understand what it was. I was highly motivated to learn to read so that I could read that book!

If I had to think of a single moment that made the difference, it was meeting an astronaut as a child. My father is an electrical engineer and he took me to his office one day, in the 1980s, because they had a special guest visiting. It was an astronaut, if I remember correctly. He talked about his training and experiences with the space program. It was an exciting experience yet also intimidating. I was the only child in the room. I was so impressed with him that I could barely say anything beyond hello.

My father was also a major source of inspiration. I was fascinated by science and technology, in general, and he took the time to answer my questions and encourage me.

Harpham: What are some of your personal "rules of thumb" that you've developed to manage projects?

Tremblay: It's important to have the courage to make hard decisions on projects as soon as possible. When there is a persistent issue or some other problem, it's tough to make adjustments to a project's scope. When you work on science missions as I do, our clients are scientists who depend on our projects to carry out their research. Personally, one of my career motivations to work in the space field is that I wanted to enable scientists to explore space. Therefore, my team and I are highly motivated to give as much performance as we can on the projects and technologies we create.

Of course, our ability to deliver these capabilities is constrained by cost and schedule. For example, we may have a mass problem with a spacecraft system.

In simple terms, the spacecraft may be too heavy with too many different instruments. On the Phoenix mission, we had to reduce the mass of our instruments. It was very difficult to make the choice to remove [or descope] components and capabilities, because it was still quite early in the project. Usually in the preliminary design stage, given the low level of definition, it's recommended to retain some margin to make sure that your instruments will fit within the mass, volume, and power requirements that have been allocated. Unfortunately, that margin was reduced due to other changes on the project. In this example, "descoping" meant reducing the scientific capabilities of the system to fit within the requirements. That meant disappointing scientists and researchers to a degree.

If you delay difficult decisions on your project, including where you have to compromise on requirements from a stakeholder, that will likely make the project more difficult for you, since usually the more you wait, the more constrained the decision space or alternatives become. Unfortunately, you don't have full and complete information when you make these difficult decisions. For example, you have no idea if your allocation on the spacecraft will be increased again in the future. You cannot count on the unknown or be overly optimistic about future conditions to avoid the discipline of making hard decisions. You have to accept some uncertainty and risk.

Harpham: That's a great principle to guide your approach to project decisions. Do you have guiding principles in relating to other people on the project?

Tremblay: It's important to compose diverse teams, as well as seek out and listen to people who have different opinions and views than yours. They spot problems and opportunities that you may not be aware of. You may not be able to achieve a perfect consensus on the project. In those cases, you and the team have to accept that the solution is not perfect, accept the residual risk, and move on.

Harpham: Let's look at project decision making given uncertainty. How do you approach those situations, especially when you know you have to make a decision to move ahead?

Tremblay: The key is to be transparent in communication: share all the information you have—and respect all opinions—to cultivate trust within the team. It's human nature to be uncomfortable with uncertainty. It's much easier to make decisions when you have all of the facts, but that's not always possible. When you share information, and have a reputation for transparency, it's much easier to accept uncertainty.

On the James Webb Space Telescope project, we faced a situation where an instrument had to be completely redesigned. As we were struggling through these issues, new technology became available that helped us to achieve our scientific objectives in a different way. These changes required completely thinking through the project and revising the specifications for the instrument. We also maintained flexibility in the definition and design process so that further refinements could be made efficiently to meet a very constrained schedule.

Harpham: Let's look at the James Webb Space Telescope in more depth. Overall, what was the objective of the telescope project and what was your role on it?

Tremblay: The James Webb Space Telescope is the successor to the Hubble Space Telescope. It will observe the universe in a different spectrum than Hubble and will be seven times more powerful. Hubble can see the near infrared, visible, and ultraviolet light. James Webb will see near-infrared and mid-infrared light. That capability is interesting because it will be able to see through dust clouds surrounding objects to better observe their structure and understand how they form. The telescope will able to see much further into space, see the very first stars and galaxies, and provide greater detail. With this telescope, we'll also be able to "travel back in time," and see the universe as it was after the first 100 million years following the Big Bang.

The scientific objective of the telescope is to help us to better understand the origins of the universe: how the first stars formed, how the first galaxies formed, and so forth. We also want to look at exoplanets—planets beyond our solar system. One of the Canadian instruments on the telescope, called NIRISS—the Near Infra-Red Imager and Slitless Spectrograph, will provide capability to directly observe exoplanets and study their composition. We can also look at the question of whether life could exist on those planets.

Harpham: This telescope sounds like it will be a major leap forward.

Tremblay: Definitely! It's interesting if we compare it to Hubble. Originally, Hubble was designed to last for about five years. It ended up lasting much longer. [Hubble was launched in 1990 and it has been in service for over 20 years.] With the James Webb telescope, we will be able to gather much more information about the universe and explore new questions. The planned launch date for the telescope is 2018.

Harpham: What was your role on the James Webb Space Telescope?

Tremblay: I worked on the Canadian contribution to the telescope as the lead systems engineer [i.e., technical manager] for the Canadian Space Agency. The CSA invested $37 million in the Canadian contribution to the Phoenix mission (the Meteorological station). The number of people directly involved in the project varied though project phases, from about 10 to 40.

We worked on two instruments: the FGS [Fine Guidance Sensor] and the NIRISS [Near-InfraRed Imager and Slitless Spectrograph]. The Fine Guidance Sensor looks at a given area of the sky, compares that data to a catalog, identifies star patterns or constellations, choses a guiding star, and provides telescope positioning information with an accuracy of a millionth of a degree. If the observatory is kept stable and focused, then we are able to obtain excellent images for research. Without stability, you will get blurred images.

Harpham: Looking back on your work on this project, what was surprising about the telescope?

Tremblay: Prior to working on the telescope, I worked on the Phoenix mission, which was also an international mission bringing together scientists from all over the world. When I joined the James Webb Space Telescope project, the project had reached the detailed engineering phase. This was different from Phoenix, where I was involved from the beginning to the end [i.e., from feasibility studies to operations].

The James Webb Space Telescope project was distinctive due to the size of the team working on it. It was an order of magnitude larger than previous projects I had worked on. For example, we had large workshops during which we held science, technical, and project management meetings with a large number of stakeholders. At one of the workshops, there were well over two hundred participants. When I inquired about the size of the project team, I was told that the workshop attendance represented about ten percent of the team members. This means that a few thousands of people—from space agencies, universities, and industry—were working on the project. In addition, this project required working remotely with people based in different locations around the world, mainly in the United States, Europe, and Canada.

Harpham: Let's look at the stakeholder management aspect of the project. How do you approach engaging and leading such a large number of stakeholders?

Tremblay: It's a challenge. However, we have a few advantages that make the whole process easier. We work with a group of people who are passionate and highly engaged in the project—scientists, engineers, and others who are enjoying their dream jobs. I also found that holding regular face-to-face meetings makes a major difference to build trusting and lasting relationships.

Conducting meetings and conference calls is a challenging area in some cases. I find that tightly focused and specialized meetings tend to be the most productive. When you have a broader subject to cover in a meeting, and it is necessary to involve a more diverse group of participants, that breadth means the meeting tends to be somewhat less efficient for the participants, timewise.

Harpham: Do you face challenges in terms of holding conference calls with people from different time zones around the world?

Tremblay: For the most part, the projects I contributed to involved working mainly with American team members. Therefore, the time zones were only a few hours apart at the most.

Harpham: Let's turn to the Phoenix mission. What was your contribution to this Mars project?

Tremblay: The Phoenix mission was proposed in the context of the NASA Scout Mission Program, an initiative where a competitive process was conducted to select relatively low-cost science missions, with a budget of around 400 million US dollars, complementing major billion-dollar Mars missions. These smaller missions were led by a principal investigator. That scientist would assemble a team to design and perform the mission. A Canadian company—MacDonald, Dettwiler and Associates Ltd.—was part of the team led by Peter Smith, the principal investigator who submitted a proposal to NASA. This proposal for the Phoenix Mars lander won the competition! Once the competition was awarded, the Canadian Space Agency became involved and sponsored the Canadian contribution. Although I followed the competition very closely, I really became involved when the CSA entered the project.

Harpham: What was the scientific objective of the Phoenix mission?

Tremblay: In brief, the mission was to look at the habitability of Mars. Scientists wanted to know whether Mars could have once supported life. To answer that question, we look for signs or traces of life as we know it. We know what life looks like on Earth and use that knowledge to guide our search for life elsewhere. For example, we look for sources of energy that life could use and byproducts of life, like methane.

NASA's motto at the time was "follow the water." They were looking for water in the solar system as a clue to finding life. The mission went to the northern part of Mars, in an area called Vastitas Borealis, at about seventy degrees of latitude, which is very close to the North Pole. We were looking for water ice in that area that had been detected before by the Mars Odyssey orbiter.

The Canadian contribution to Phoenix was a meteorological station. It looked at the atmosphere to measure clouds' dust content, diurnal and seasonal cycles, and related phenomena. Phoenix landed on Mars in May 2008 and it ended up lasting several months, until November 2008. Originally, Phoenix was planned to run for three months. Since the mission was very successful, it was extended over five months. Eventually, with the Martian fall coming, and the sun lower on the horizon, the Phoenix's solar panels could not collect enough energy to continue operations, and one day we lost communication with the lander.

Harpham: What happened after you lost communication with Phoenix?

Tremblay: Most probes to Mars had landed near the equator. Phoenix landed in the far northern part of the planet. In that area, part of the north polar ice cap, the temperatures go very low during the winter [below −100°C] and a thick layer of dry [carbon dioxide] ice accumulates on the ground.

The Phoenix lander wasn't designed to survive the Martian winter. Scientists expected that the lander would become completely covered with ice in the winter season. Later on, images taken from Mars orbit showed that Phoenix was badly damaged by the winter.

Overall, Phoenix was a highly successful mission. It landed safely on Mars, operated longer than planned, and all mission objectives were met.

Harpham: What was your approach to risk management on this project?

Tremblay: Risk management is an important aspect of any space mission. We used several methods to assess risk on the project and set aside sufficient reserves to manage the risk. We think a lot about what could go wrong, and compromise a mission to develop our risk management plan. Throughout the project, we reassess risk continuously based on changes to requirements, issues that occur, and other factors.

Harpham: How do you approach managing unknown risks? Risk management often uses historical events and loss events for analysis, but that approach does not address new and unprecedented risks.

Tremblay: We have to keep reserves for the unknown. Fortunately, we have great information from previous space missions that guide our planning and risk management. No single team will have a comprehensive knowledge of possible risks. Multi-agency missions have the benefit of a wider understanding. The Canadian Space Agency's risk management approach is also well informed by our partnership with NASA.

We have comprehensive project reviews at each phase of the project that include a risk discussion. Those reviews are supported by experts from outside the project who challenge every aspect of the project. We're never completely successful in predicting the unknown, but we're getting better each time. It's critical to have the right people in the room on the project review meetings. In addition to experts, we have lessons learned databases to inform our approach.

In addition, we have some technical methods to explore and reduce risk and the unknown. We use simulations to verify if the systems we design will meet the required performance. For example, we develop structural and thermal software models and simulations to verify if a proposed design can survive the launch vibrations and extreme temperatures to which it will be exposed in space. Over the course of the project, we also build a series of prototypes of increasing fidelity, and subject them to various tests. We test these models in a simulated space environment. A good principle is to "test as you fly": make your testing conditions as close to the actual mission as possible. In space projects, there is no margin for error. Once a spacecraft is launched, we cannot generally fix it, aside from implementing some relatively minor software workarounds remotely.

Harpham: This gives me a sense of some of the risk management strategies and techniques you use. For example, bring in outside experts to provide new perspectives on risk at project reviews. Invite the internal team to challenge each other on risk. Finally, continuously identify new risk areas as the project unfolds rather than limiting that activity to the start of the project.

Tremblay: We always have to monitor risks, update our risk database, reassess likelihood and impact, and reconsider mitigation measures.

When issues arise, we link them back to risks that were anticipated. Or we take note of it where it was an "unknown unknown." We continuously evaluate if we have enough resources to deliver the project given known and potential issues or risks.

Harpham: One of your past assignments at the Canadian Space Agency was leading the Corporate Investment Management Office. What was the purpose of the project, and what was achieved?

Tremblay: My role was to improve the organization's project management capacity. When I started in that role in April 2014, we were in the process of developing a new project management framework—the investment governance and monitoring framework. It's based on leading best practices and the Canadian government's requirements for projects to achieve value for money, demonstrate sound stewardship of funds, and ensure accountability and delivery of project outcomes within time and cost constraints. The fact that the US government recently adopted new legislation on project management is of particular interest, since it is a natural and important partner for Canada. In Canada, policies and requirements for the management of projects are established by the Treasury Board Secretariat. They are similar to US legislation and requirements.

In addition, standards from the Treasury Board Secretariat, a part of the Canadian government, require assessing the risk and complexity of projects and an organization's capability to carry them out. Here's how it works: you start by assessing the project management capacity of an organization. Then, you evaluate the risk and complexity of a project. If the result of this evaluation exceeds the assessed capacity of the organization, then you need to seek Treasury Board approval to undertake the project.

When I arrived, the CSA was developing a framework to implement the Government of Canada's project management policy requirements. We developed a stage-gate model for projects. In addition, I was involved with developing new monitoring and reporting tools for the agency's projects.

Harpham: Would you need to call the Minister for approval at a certain level?

Tremblay: We don't directly call the Minister. For anything major that goes to the Treasury Board, the Minister is informed and involved in the decision that the CSA will undertake those projects. Every project has to be strategically aligned and have a business case to justify it. During my assignment at the Corporate Investment Management Office, I also had the opportunity to observe the executive committee in action as they reviewed investment proposals and made decisions about which projects to approve.

Harpham: What aspect of this project management governance change has been most beneficial to the organization?

Tremblay: The new governance committee has a challenge function. It challenges all requests for new investments and monitors the progress of approved projects. Essentially, project teams benefit from the broad experience and diverse expertise of senior executives composing our governance committee. They provide valuable inputs and raise important questions about the projects we're considering. The stage-gate process has also been beneficial. Before undertaking each stage or phase of a project, you must pass a gate and obtain a decision from the organization's leadership to move forward with the next phase. The governance committee challenges the proposed project plan [I.e. scope, cost, schedule, and risks] to ensure that the project team can deliver as expected, per the plan, with confidence.

At the same time, the governance or challenge function is perceived as a constraint. It introduces more steps to undertake and review projects. There is also a challenge to present the right level of detail to the leadership, which is required to enable informed decision-making by our senior executives. However, this healthy challenge function is essential, in particular in the government context, where we are spending public funds.

Harpham: What is the approach to communicating with the executives on this governing body? Engineers and scientists may be interested in all of the technical details, while executives may prefer a high-level summary highlighting key decision factors.

Tremblay: Absolutely. We have a series of dashboard reports that summarize our projects and projects' performance for the leadership. These reports have standardized metrics or indicators designed to inform senior executives about project scope, cost, schedule, risks, and issues. If there's a desire to add more information to reports, we question whether adding more detail is helpful. The key questions become: Why are we reporting this information? How is it helpful to our executives to make a decision? Is it helpful for an executive to know that "project X passed a test readiness review"? What does that mean? Is it an important achievement, and why? What is the significance of that point?

There are also reporting requirements that go beyond our agency. For example, we have to inform other government departments, and their senior executives, up to the Deputy Minister's level, on our activities. How do we report the right information to those audiences with the right level of detail? That's all part of this new project management framework.

Harpham: What does your personal productivity system look like in terms of habits, goal setting, and organization?

Tremblay: In a leadership role, my priority is the team and the organization. It is to create and maintain the conditions that will contribute to our success. The other important aspect is to clearly and concisely articulate and communicate our purpose—the vision, mandate, and measurable objectives for the team. This facilitates cohesion, communication, and efficiency. Keeping the momentum is also key—by creating short term-wins and incrementally delivering on commitments.

Harpham: What books have you found most valuable for your professional growth?

Tremblay: Books on leadership mainly. Leadership can be expressed at all levels of an organization. Two books stand out: Simon Sinek, *Start with Why: How Great Leaders Inspire Everyone to Take Action* [Portfolio, 2009] and *Leaders Eat Last* [Portfolio, 2014]. I also like reading on how to foster a growth mindset in individuals and organizations.

Harpham: Let's turn to the future. What's on the horizon for space science and exploration for the next several years?

Tremblay: We live in exciting times for space exploration. Efforts to commercialize activities in low Earth orbit will intensify over the next few years. The commercial sector is getting more active in space, and that brings faster progress. In the next ten years, I think we'll see space tourism develop and more humans than ever before will go into space. As low Earth orbit becomes commercialized, humans will travel further in the solar system. We will be able to explore the solar system, including the Moon, Mars, and beyond. Human space exploration is more than an adventure—it's the expression of our propensity to explore the unknown. It is deeply rooted in and intrinsically stems from our survival instinct. It may seem far-fetched, but going into space, and extending human presence beyond Earth, is the future of humanity.

The Canadian Space Agency will be involved in these projects and missions in the future as well. In 2017, there's an astronaut recruitment campaign currently underway in Canada. That's a good sign! One of our astronauts, David Saint-Jacques, will also be the third Canadian to participate in a long-duration mission on the International Space Station. We're also preparing for the next big step in exploration, and the future of human spaceflight in deep space, pushing the limits of our capabilities and inspiring the next generation of Canadians to pursue science and technology.

Chapter Summary

- Recommended books include *Start with Why: How Great Leaders Inspire Everyone to Take Action* and *Leaders Eat Last* by Simon Sinek.

- Early career inspiration: Learning about the *Voyager 1* launch in 1977 and meeting an astronaut.

- The importance of courage: Having the courage to share bad news on projects (e.g., an unavoidable reduction in scope) is important.

- Stakeholder management on a large space project (i.e., the James Webb Space Telescope): When managing hundreds or thousands of stakeholders, use workshops dedicated to specific themes to engage each group.

- Risk management lessons from space projects: Start with the premise that no single team will have all the information to anticipate risks, so collaboration is critical. Use simulations and the "test as you fly" principle to reduce risk.

- Implementing project governance at the Canadian Space Agency: To align CSA projects with Government of Canada policy, Tremblay led the effort to implement the Corporate Investment Management Office. The key practical challenge was to help engineers and other technical professionals recalibrate their communication for this new audience.

Andy Kaufman

President, Institute for Leadership Excellence & Development Inc.

Andy Kaufman, PMP, is an international speaker, author, and executive coach, and president of the Institute for Leadership Excellence & Development Inc. He works with organizations around the world, helping them improve their ability to deliver projects and lead teams. He also teaches project management at Loyola University's Quinlan School of Business in Chicago. Kaufman is the author of three books: Navigating the Winds of Change (Zurich Press, 2003), How to Organize Your Inbox & Get Rid of E-Mail Clutter (Zurich Press, 2007), and Shining the Light on The Secret (Zurich Press, 2007).

Prior to starting the Institute for Leadership Excellence & Development Inc., Kaufman was vice president of US Systems at ACNielsen. He started his career as a software developer at Brokerage Systems Inc. He earned a bachelor's of science degree in business data processing from Northern Michigan University.

Bruce Harpham: How did you get started in project management?

Andy Kaufman: As with a lot of project managers I work with, I didn't set out to become a project manager. After graduating from college, I started as a software developer. Inevitably, software development projects came up but we didn't think of them as formal projects. We thought of it as "we have a release date and we've got to find a way to do it." My bosses at the time were not called "project managers."

© Bruce Harpham 2018
B. Harpham, Project Managers at Work, DOI 10.1007/978-1-4842-2668-1_5

When I was promoted to my first management role, I was managing people who used to be my peers. There were a lot of challenges with that. I made all kinds of mistakes. Over time, I realized there can be joy in organizing a group of people to accomplish something. At the time, I wasn't reading the PMBOK Guide or following stage gate methodologies. I was clueless about best practices. However, taking a group of people and working with them is really rewarding! In fact, I found that more rewarding than delivering a piece of work by myself!

What I love about project management is that we don't just talk about stuff. We have the opportunity to deliver. That is fun! It doesn't generally take us years to deliver either. We get to deliver on a regular basis. I'm the kind of guy that gets a rush from checking off a to-do. There is a set of to-dos when I complete a project, so it brings a great sense of accomplishment.

Harpham: People who are achievement oriented and like to ship work out the door tend to like projects. I also find there's a strong tension between task-oriented project managers and people-oriented project managers.

Kaufman: I think there's room for both task- and people-oriented approaches in projects given the sheer variety of industries and organizations.

Harpham: Can you share an example of an early project you worked on when you were "green" as a project manager?

Kaufman: In my first job, I was hired as a programmer. I soon moved into another role—manager of product development at Baxter. The cool thing about that job: we were writing software that IBM put their name on. We could go to a store and see our product on the shelf. There's something cool about being in the business of creating things and seeing how it helps other people.

In this role, IBM had big expectations for the product, which was automation software for physician offices. There were deadlines, performance reviews, and political issues in dealing with Baxter and IBM. It was eye-opening. It made me realize how stupid I was when I got out of college.

Harpham: What do you mean by "stupid"?

Kaufman: In college, I learned how to develop flow charts, and about programming languages and theory. I don't feel like college prepared me for the people side of work, organizational politics, influencing skills, and other workplace realities. Of course, we have to be good technically—write good code and understand requirements, for example. Unfortunately, I did a horrible job with the first performance reviews I did as a manager. I gave constructive feedback on issues where I also struggled, so there was some challenge around my credibility to give feedback.

I faced the question: what does it mean to lead? Fundamentally, I learned that leading doesn't mean "bossing people around." Early on, I had a mental model about what it meant to be a boss or a leader. My job is to inspire and motivate, not to point out mistakes, act bossy, or pretend that I know everything. That job helped me understand that I'm there to serve and help the team. I learned the value of tapping into mentors as well. There were a few people who were fifteen or twenty years ahead of me and I learned a lot from them.

Harpham: What did you learn from these mentors?

Kaufman: I learned that if you *really* listen to more experienced people— whether they are five or twenty years more experienced—there are valuable lessons to learn. There are technical lessons, people management lessons, and more.

From Rick, I learned about his approach to structuring programming code in a certain way so that it would be easy to maintain and adjust in the future.

From Bob, one of my bosses, I learned about different approaches to documentation. There was a request for documentation for some of the modules in the product. I was young and ambitious, so I volunteered to do it. Bob said, "No, I know exactly what they need." He must have printed off three or four boxes worth of documentation. When I pointed out, "They're never going to read that much documentation," he simply replied, "That's exactly right!"

He understood the difference between what was being asked for and what was really needed. I had a lot of fun during that time and made a lot of mistakes in learning how to lead the team. Even today, I'm thankful for those early days where I first moved into a management role and developed to the skills to manage people successfully.

Harpham: What did you learn about office politics at this stage? Some people dismiss this concept with the thinking that "I should just be able to execute my tasks and that should be it." On the other side, nobody wants to become a master manipulator like Frank Underwood from House of Cards where you're pushing people into the subway tunnel.

Kaufman: Here's a lesson I learned about office politics early on. There's a natural tension between those who promise things and those who had to deliver on the promises. In almost every industry, there's that tension between the project people who have to deliver and the sales or business development group who sell the work.

The dirty little secret of business is relationships. If a project manager has strong rapport with people across the organization, it makes a huge difference. At Baxter, I knew a marketing person who was definitely a "climber." I always felt like I couldn't quite trust her. I'll call her "Julie." It became apparent that if I got to know Julie better outside of work discussions on requirements, due dates, and the like—that Julie became nicer in meetings!

Julie was not warm and fuzzy at all. Yet, you could get her talking about her interests and then we could connect. I realized that building relationships and bridges across organizational boundaries makes a big difference.

Over the years, I've come to realize that "office politics" really comes down to relationships. I've realized that people are driven by different things and we can use that information to work better with them. When you can help other people achieve their goals, then you can work with them on their level.

Let's think of politics as "the way things get done in organizations." Get out of your office or cubicle and build relationships! I learned a lot from interviewing Herminia Ibarra about her book *Act Like a Leader, Think Like a Leader* [Harvard Business Review Press, 2015]. When it comes to networking and building relationships, people tend to build connections with people similar to them. If you're a business analyst, you probably hang out with the other business analysts. Building relationships more broadly is part of the job even though it requires more effort to go beyond your immediate department.

Harpham: If you're highly task oriented, you could add a task to your to-do list, like: Go for morning coffee and invite someone I haven't talked to this week.

Kaufman: At one of my workshops, I suggest putting together a list of people and start connecting with them. Make it simple: once a month, invite someone from that list to lunch or coffee. Otherwise, you will tend to hang around people who are just like you, day in and day out.

Harpham: You've built on your early experiences with mentorship by expanding into teaching workshops in the corporate world and courses at Loyola University Chicago's Quinlan School of Business. What have you learned from that teaching experience?

Kaufman: Teaching has helped me to understand project management more deeply. I coach other people to become better project managers. That means I have to stay sharp on project methods and ideas. As a result, I've developed the habit to keep learning and constantly think of ways to communicate these ideas so that the other person really gets it. I owe a huge debt to all of my teachers because I didn't appreciate all the effort that goes into teaching well.

At Loyola's business school, I teach a project management course as part of a healthcare MBA program. It's a room filled with doctors, administrators and other smart people. They generally don't think of themselves as project managers. I love the experience of seeing students understand the practicality of project management principles to their profession. My favorite compliment is hearing from students after the course that they're using the ideas and concepts in their work.

Recently, I was teaching a course at a financial services organization and ran into someone over the lunch break. She had taken one of my courses a few years prior and she told me, "I took your course a few years ago and got promoted!" I made the point to her: you got promoted because you put the learning into action. When someone embraces the learning, and achieves great results—well, it doesn't get any better than that.

I've taught project management to the United Nations, large companies, and small companies. The problems are all very similar in those organizations. Learning to apply best practices does yield results and better value. Project managers also have a unique opportunity to build credibility because we make promises to deliver and then we either live up to that or we don't. Delivering projects successfully means bigger challenges, opportunities, and projects. I love that about our profession.

Harpham: What was it like to teach project management at the United Nations?

Kaufman: My favorite part of working with the UN is the cultural challenge. Though I have taught workshops on every continent except Antarctica, I've spent most of my corporate career delivering projects in North America. I appreciate that there are differences within different parts of the United States—the East Coast, the Midwest, and the West Coast. At the UN, however, there are far greater cultural differences and capabilities. The people I work with at the UN bring excellent skills to the table including fluency in multiple languages.

In North America, we might talk about software projects or a process change. In contrast, UN project managers are organizing a new government after a national crisis. Or providing services to refugees in the aftermath of a natural disaster. The stakes are huge. Regardless of the situation, understanding what you're trying to deliver and putting a reasonable plan to deliver given your constraints are the name of the game. It's the same blocking and tackling in projects whether you're doing an intervention to help refugees or build software. In the UN, the projects aim to have an impact that will last for generations rather than boosting quarterly earnings at a corporation. That's inspiring for me—to know that I'm helping people to deliver success.

Harpham: Today you run your own project management consulting and training company. How did you get started? Where did the first few clients come from?

Kaufman: Even to this day, I'm still a software developer at heart. I like to break problems down and have an organized approach to thinking problems through. That thinking carried me through several promotions up to the vice president level. With each of those steps, you look at the next step in the path and then you ask yourself: "Do I really want to do that?" As a vice president of systems, I truthfully don't think I was awesome at the role and I didn't enjoy it as much as other roles. Careerwise, I asked myself: "What am I good at? What do I enjoy? And what can I make money at?" You need all three of those points to build a successful career in my view.

I started speaking at conferences and was surprised when one actually paid!
It wasn't enough to build a viable business but it allowed me to interact with
people who did speaking and training full time, such as Karl Weigers, a pro-
lific author and speaker in the software development arena some years back.
When I learned that you could actually build a career in speaking and training,
I asked them how they did it and how they found customers. This was preparation and research I did long before I left my full-time job.

I'm reminded of an insight from Adam Grant's book, *Originals* [Viking, 2016].
There's a perception that people who start a business take massive risks. He
provides compelling evidence that many entrepreneurs start their business
"on the side." I started my business on the side by speaking at conferences
while I still had my job. I found my voice, figured out what I like to speak on,
and determined what people value.

In 2001, I participated in a two-day coaching session with Joe Miraglia,
former senior vice president of HR at Motorola—that covered life purpose
and planning. At the end of it, he told me, "I think you can run your own
business. Based on what you've done in the past and your temperament, you
can do it. However, you need twelve months of living expenses in cash in the
bank before you go into it full time." At that time, I had about six months of
liquid cash, so I was feeling down because it would take a lot longer to further
build up my savings.

At the same time, I was having the "what do you want to do when you grow
up" conversation with my boss at ACNielsen. I told him about my vision. It
turns out that I was able to receive a six-month severance package because
they were going through a downsizing process. I thought I had shot myself in
the foot by suggesting that I leave the company. It turned out to be great timing: the company had to downsize but they had not had a voluntary separation
program. It turned out to be a win-win: they didn't have an ugly process of
letting people go and I received what I wanted for my purposes.

I drive by the offices of ACNielsen from time to time. I say "thank you" to
myself because that process helped me to launch my company as I pass by.

I launched the company on a full time basis in August 2001, shortly before the
9/11 attacks. I did what I knew to win business: I went to my network and
made sales. I did a lot of subcontracting for training companies at that time
who provided project management.

During that first year of business, there were good months and some months
where I made nothing. It took about thirteen months to really get the business
going, so I'm grateful for the advice to have twelve months' worth of savings in
the bank. It's the same advice I'd give to anyone starting a business or searching for a job after a lay off. Hopefully, it wouldn't actually take that long but that
planning assumption gives you peace of mind.

It took a while to get used to variable income each month. But I love what I get to do on a daily basis. I don't think I could do what I'm doing in a traditional job.

Harpham: How long did you run the business "on the side"?

Kaufman: I started the business on the side in 1994 and went full time on the business in 2001.

It all started at ACNielsen when I was running a project using some innovative technology from Microsoft. In February 1994, I got a call from someone at Microsoft who said, "We have a TechEd conference coming up. Would you come and present a short case study during one of the keynotes?" At that time, if I had to present in front of ten people, I was a wreck and couldn't sleep the night before. This would be in front of 7,500 people!

However, I said yes to the invitation even though I was nervous about it. I had two weeks to prepare the presentation and worked with a coach to help me develop my skills. It was the scariest five minutes of my professional life up to that time. The presentation went well enough that they invited me to give an hour long version of the presentation at another conference. I had a very supportive boss who reasoned, "Your conference presentations earn good press for our company and help us with hiring new people." The conference organizers often paid for travel expenses so there wasn't a burden for the company. I also had a supportive spouse in making the transition to a full-time business.

Harpham: So this wasn't a case of tinkering for a few weeks and then quitting your job?

Kaufman: It was years in the making in my case. You don't have to take massive risks to start a business. It's just like risk management on a project. You identify the risks and come up with mitigation plans. In retrospect, I wish that I had made the leap two or three years earlier.

The bottom line for me: I didn't want to be eighty years old someday and regret not starting my own business. Another point was that I had just turned forty. John G. Miller, author of *QBQ!* [TarcherPerigee, 2004], was a mentor for me at the time. His view at the time was that you're not ready to start a company until you're forty. There are plenty of examples to the contrary—however, his comment resonated with me. The fundamental idea is that you want to understand yourself, have learned enough, and have developed enough supportive relationships in order to start a business.

In my podcasting work, Cornelius Fichtner has been incredibly generous to me with his insights and suggestions. I've been surrounded by people who have been generous with ideas and support, if I was willing to ask. That's a good lesson for all of us.

Harpham: In your podcast, The People and Projects Podcast, you bring great positive energy and enthusiasm to each episode. It really shines through your work. Does that energy and drive come naturally?

Kaufman: Some people think that I'm an extrovert because of the podcast. That's not true at all. Depending on the assessment, I usually come out as an introvert or borderline extrovert. That said, I really love this work and I'm guessing it's this passion for the profession that comes through as energy. You don't have to be a raving extrovert to run a successful kick off meeting. It really helps if you like the project! If you can find meaning in your project work, your enthusiasm will become infectious.

Harpham: How have you gone about developing your leadership skills as an introvert?

Kaufman: There's a spectrum or scale between highly extroverted and highly introverted. In the middle of that range, you have people called "ambiverts" that have both qualities.

When I teach this concept, I ask my students where they think the best sales professionals rank on that scale of highly introverted to highly extroverted. They usually assume sales professionals are highly extroverted and the best actuaries are highly introverted. Interestingly, there's some compelling research suggesting ambiverts rule the world! They have a mixture of both tendencies. The challenge with highly extroverted people is that they struggle to shut up while highly introverted people don't speak up enough. So there is a downside to both tendencies.

This research gave me comfort to be myself and "ramp it up" when I need to deliver. In an interview or delivering a training program, I know I need to bring energy to deliver a quality educational experience.

However, I learned that introverts need to have time and space to recharge. That's one of the great insights I picked up from Susan Cain's book *Quiet* [Crown, 2012]. Over the next few days, I'm going to deliver day long training sessions to a group of people. Over the lunch break, I go off by myself to recharge—I don't talk to a single person. I tell the people in the class up front, "I would love to have lunch with you but I need to go off by myself to recharge." When you position it like that, people understand it. Giving myself space and time to recharge makes all the difference.

When I used to be quiet in meetings, I learned a "hack": early in the meeting, speak up. The longer I stay quiet in the meeting, the more likely I will stay quiet all the way to the end. Even if it's just asking a question, it's a way to engage. That's a way to manage my natural inclination to sit back and be quiet.

At the other end of the spectrum, extroverts need to learn ways to improve their listening skills. There are times when listening more and speaking less makes a critical difference in effectively connecting with other people. If they do that, they will be more effective.

Harpham: It's like training for a marathon. Your training run doesn't go all day. You go hard at it for an hour and then you do other things for the rest of the day.

Kaufman: You don't have to pretend to be an Olympic runner. You're ramping it up to do what is necessary to achieve the goal.

Harpham: What advice would you give to the reader who has been on a project team and they're interested in moving to the project manager role? How can they make that transition from their current role to a project manager role?

Kaufman: I see the "accidental project manager" situation happen a lot where people are pulled into a project role. When people make a strategic career move into projects, they start spending time with people doing the work. They ask questions like, "What do you like about your job? How did you get to this job? What do you not like about the work?" Learning about the work and networking goes a long way. A lot of people have heard that suggestion before. The real point is "Are you strategically setting out to learn from other people? Are you putting these ideas into practice?"

I believe in the maxim "You don't get it if you don't ask." Many people don't ask for help or for opportunities. If you spend enough time with project managers, you will learn whether you're interested in the work or if it is right for you. After all, the work isn't easy, there's pressure and significant challenges. Through these conversations, you will find out if the career is right for you. You may also get invited to join one of their projects.

The standard advice is to volunteer for opportunities but it's a tough idea to implement. You probably already have a full set of responsibilities and taking on more responsibilities feel unreasonable. Yet, it is a path that some people use successful to grow their career. Asking to take on a set of tasks and delivering that work builds your career credibility.

I honestly think that project management is a life skill. It's far from a title. Just like time management, conflict management influencing skills are basic skill sets that need to be exercised to be a professional. Project management is like that. We all have work to deliver so it makes sense to use project management skills to be successful, no matter your job title.

As you network more, realize that there will be a time in the future where you see a job posting and go for it. I would encourage readers to think, "Wow, this is a great rewarding way to make a living."

Harpham: What are some of your personal productivity habits and methods that underpin your success?

Kaufman: As mentioned before, the single biggest lesson I've learned is that everything in business comes down to relationships. I'm just amazed that one stakeholder has the ability to create a lot of pain if there is a poor relationship.

I make an effort to learn more about people I work with because then I can customize my approach.

Generally, I like to be the one asking the questions and become curious about people. I even do this when I'm on a cruise or vacation. I like to ask people where they're from, what they love about their job, and so forth. That skill set—having genuine curiosity about stakeholders—is critical to managing our projects. Some stakeholders may be obstacles at first glance but if we're curious about them, we can discover what concerns they have. Likewise, if you have a teammate who is always making negative comments, it could be that they are the canary in the coal mine—they're detecting problems that we need to be aware of.

In the last five years, I've learned the importance of testing your assumptions.

Harpham: What do you mean by testing assumptions?

Kaufman: People sometimes tell you, "Don't assume!". But in projects, that's terrible advice. We always have assumptions. The question isn't whether we have assumptions—rather, the question is to ask what those assumptions are based on. Do we have historical data? Have we checked those assumptions with other people? Do we update those assumptions as we get new information?

In my business, the traditional assumption is that you need to bring a person to your location to deliver training or consulting. Well, remote presentation technology keeps getting better and better, so I'm experimenting with those methods. That's how I question my business model. Project management teaches you to question your assumptions and seek to come up with answers based on that. It's a life skill to question, revise, and act because we have to act in conditions of uncertainty.

Recently, I've developed the habit of asking myself a few questions at the start of each day to guide my thinking. I learned this from interviewing Jim Kouzes about his book *Learning Leadership* [Wiley, 2016]. Jim suggests you start your day like this: "Who I am, what I do, and how I do it matters. What difference do I want to make today?" I think about who I'm going to meet with and how I can help them.

I also use productivity tools like to-do lists, mind mapping tools, and *Getting Things Done author* David Allen's recommendation to put ideas on paper. Why try to remember it all when we have great tools to capture and manage information?

Harpham: Are there specific productivity tools that make a difference?

Kaufman: Evernote stands out. When I read a book, I put my notes in Evernote. When I'm with a client and have an idea to share, I can easily look up the idea from Evernote with a quick search. I also have a paper journal for those cases where digital note taking isn't practical. I also use Todoist for keeping track of tasks. I'm amazed at how fast I forget stuff, so it's important to write it down in a format that I can search.

Harpham: What's your perspective on lessons learned? Sometimes, I see these written in a vague way, such as "Mistakes were made." That may be true, but it's not very helpful. What important lesson have you learned in your career?

Kaufman: There are a number of them that come to mind. I remember reading the comment "if you have an unrealistic schedule, it's your fault as the project manager" in Rita Mulcahy's *PMP Exam Prep* book's section on time management. The PMBOK Guide may not put it that way but it is aligned with the PMI worldview. As project managers, we are responsible for this project.

If we're given an unrealistic schedule, it's our responsibility to point that out and negotiate so that we can be successful. Taking responsibility is near and dear to my heart right now because it seems like we have a whiny culture. If you listen to talk radio, news, or conversations at the workplace, we just complain and point the finger. That often translates into doing nothing. If you take responsibility for a situation, even if it was not entirely of your own making, then you can make progress.

If you don't like where you're at in your career, do something about it. Don't whine about it. You can get better! Life is short, so make the most of the time you have. Ask yourself: "What can I do given the current circumstances?" I'm far from perfect yet this principle has served me well in business and with my projects. It's too easy to blame the stakeholder.

Harpham: I see the responsibility principle at play in meetings when someone says, "I will take on solving X." People give you credit for moving the ball down the field. It will sometimes trigger people to get involved and support you.

Kaufman: Right. Take the view: I'm responsible to come up with a plan to move forward.

Harpham: Looking out over the next five years or so, what trends do you see impacting the practice of project management?

Kaufman: The biggest one is virtualization of teams. Concerns about work/life balance and environmental concerns will mean greater support for remote work and work-from-home arrangements. Availability of talent is another reason for remote work as more people retire from the workforce. Companies will increasingly need to tap into talent beyond their local area. Improving Internet bandwidth and other technologies also encourage this trend.

In my business, I want to get even better at presenting through collaboration tools like WebEx, Microsoft Lync, or other tools. Project managers at companies should ask, "How can I learn to run meetings through these technologies so it is just as good as managing people down the hall?" Leading virtual teams just as effectively as local teams will become a superpower for project managers.

Harpham: Any closing thoughts on project management that we haven't covered?

Kaufman: I'm intrigued by the challenge of using Scrum and similar approaches in new ways. For example, my son is in college right now and he has a heavy course load. I've taught him to use Scrum to manage his homework. He told me, "Dad, I'm two weeks ahead on the homework!" Thinking about ways to use project management methods and skills beyond the traditional project context is an interesting frontier to explore.

Ask yourself what trends are happening that you can take advantage of. There's a wealth of learning resources such as books, e-learning tools and so on while you're at your company. Podcasts are a great example—they are a great way to learn while you drive or do other activities. Years ago, Zig Ziglar used the phrase "automobile university" to encourage people to listen to audio programs while they drive. That approach is still effective today.

Chapter Summary

- Recommended books include *Quiet* by Susan Cain and *QBQ!* by John G Miller

- Relationships and networking: Networking is an excellent way to build a business and a career. Start small by setting a weekly reminder to have coffee with someone in your organization.

- Interested in starting a business? Consider Kaufman's approach to start it as a part-time project and grow it gradually over time.

- Check out Andy Kaufman's podcast, *The People and Projects Podcast,* for great interviews with authors, project managers, and other business experts.

Owen C. Gadeken

Professor, Defense Acquisition University

Dr. Owen C. Gadeken *is a retired professor at the Defense Acquisition University (DAU) located at Fort Belvoir, Virginia. His primary focus is to help project managers become more effective leaders.*

Before joining the DAU faculty, Gadeken was a project manager at the US Department of Energy (DOE) Operations Office in Oak Ridge, Tennessee. Prior to that, he served as an Air Force officer and a civilian engineer working on missile development programs at the US Air Force Air Armament Center at Eglin Air Force Base, Florida.

After leaving active duty, Gadeken continued to serve in the Air Force Reserve. Achieving the rank of colonel, he was the senior reservist at the Air Force Office of Scientific Research in Arlington, Virginia, where he helped manage the basic research program for the Air Force.

Gadeken has a bachelor's and a master's degree in chemistry from the University of Nebraska, an MBA from the University of West Florida, and a doctorate in engineering management from the George Washington University. He is a graduate of the Federal Executive Institute and has served as a Visiting Fellow at the Royal Military College of Science in Shrivenham, England.

© Bruce Harpham 2018
B. Harpham, *Project Managers at Work*, DOI 10.1007/978-1-4842-2668-1_6

Bruce Harpham: How did you get started in project management?

Owen Gadeken: It was through the US military that I became involved in projects. It wasn't my plan at all though. In college, I was studying to be a scientist. Unfortunately, I took out student loans during my studies. At the same time, the draft for the Vietnam War was in place and I had a low a draft number! So, I was looking around for options in the early 1970s.

I realized that if I joined the Reserve Officers' Training Corps [ROTC] that I would have a choice where I served and that I would be an officer. I received an ROTC scholarship for the rest of my undergraduate education. The discipline of the military aligned with the discipline and organization I knew from science and mathematics. After graduating, I was assigned to an Air Force research lab in Florida.

With my chemistry background, I worked on warheads and related materials. The lab was located at the far end of the airfield just in case anything happened. As it turns out, a few years after I left that base, there was an explosion in the lab! Thankfully that didn't happen while I was there.

The military then changed its priorities away from the basic sciences area that was my focus. Instead, the government decided to send this "hands on" research and development work to industry. After working in the research lab for a year, I became an R&D project manager.

Later, there was a switch in emphasis to precision-guided weapons that used smaller warheads. This meant cancelling the entire project area I was working. As a result, I was transferred to the future planning section—we looked at all the equipment and weapons we had in the Air Force inventory and what was on the drawing board. I found that work fascinating. I ended up on one of the larger projects through that work.

Through these assignments, my career moved from science to project management. It was partly a result of my interests but also the priorities of the Air Force.

Harpham: What was that transition like from a professional identity as a scientist to this new role?

Gadeken: I thought it was going to be very difficult. It turned out differently. Back in the 1970s, there were few courses available in project management. After I was in the field for about eight years, I got to attend the project management course at the Defense Systems Management College [DSMC]. The organization was set up by David Packard, the co-founder of Hewlett-Packard, when he became the Deputy Secretary of Defense in the 1970s.

He observed that the military was pulling people from active military service and putting them into project management without much training. It didn't make a lot of sense to pull people in that way.

As I started my study of project management at DSMC, I gained a much broader perspective. I learned how projects were funded, how they were managed and the typical issues and complexities that occur. I thought to myself, "This is really fascinating!" I realized that I would enjoy teaching project managers even more.

At the ten-year point in my career, I made the switch from practicing project management to developing project managers.

Harpham: How did that switch come about?

Gadeken: From ROTC, I had a service commitment to serve four years in the military. After the Vietnam War ended, there was big reduction in all the military services. The colonel I was working for at the time said to me, "Look, you have a good background but promotion opportunities are going to shrink because there are cutbacks. I advise you to get out and pursue a civilian career." I took his advice.

One of things I learned is that if you're working with people you trust, ask them for advice, and listen to what they have to say. It was excellent advice for me. I watched some of my friends get stuck in dead-end positions in the military where they couldn't get promoted due to the cutbacks.

At this point, I transitioned to a civilian career working for the Air Force. Later, I moved to a teaching role at DSMC, which eventually grew to become the Defense Acquisition University.

Harpham: For a civilian reader who is unfamiliar with the military context, what are some of the unique challenges involved in military projects?

Gadeken: It's a very large system. The U.S. Department of Defense spends a significant amount of taxpayers' dollars on projects and related activities. That includes maintaining bases, training, developing equipment, and managing highly complex projects. At the same time, we're in a dynamic environment where there are threats to U.S. national security from major powers and terrorists. To respond to that environment, we develop plans to respond and regularly revise those plans in light of new information.

Finally, our whole budget process is governed by the U.S. Congress. The Congress is made up of representatives from across the country. That body has a lot of competing demands on it for how federal dollars are spent. In many cases, demands in Congress are dynamic and change based on the political situation. For example, which party is in power and which people are on certain committees has a tremendous impact on the military budget. If a certain district has a military base or defense supplier in that area, that factor impacts Congressional actions and projects relating to defense spending.

The funding for our projects is on a roller coaster. It goes up and down. That makes it much more difficult for project managers to lay out and execute a project plan.

Harpham: When it comes to mega projects like a stealth bomber or an aircraft carrier, these projects take a long time to build and put into the field. At the same, there is a roller coaster effect. Do you have to hit the pause button on these projects?

Gadeken: Sometimes the pause button is hit by other stakeholders. One pause button is a decision from Congress to cut the funding for your project. There have been a number of instances where the project is going along successfully. Then Congress makes a decision to change the funding, so you're stuck on hold.

In other situations, you're trying to do something very ambitious. It could be you're developing new technology or pushing the limits of the system. You begin to test the system and you have a few failures. In that case, you have a problem because you will not meet your schedule or plan when you hit unexpected developments. When you push the frontier of technology, systems, and processes to do something innovative, it is challenging to meet a schedule.

When you're in a large organization like the Department of Defense, we have a lot of organizations that affect project management as stakeholders. They are outside of the formal control of the project managers. So, project managers have to constantly cultivate a consensus to keep their projects moving forward. We have separate organizations that do budgets and contract support. Today, we're not in the business of building anything directly—we're in the business of contracting for systems.

There's a real challenge to build a consensus and influence people because there are so many different groups.

Harpham: Is there conflict or tension between the traditional military versus civilian project managers?

Gadeken: When I first started in project management, the traditional approach to selecting project managers was to pick an experienced operational person, such as an ace pilot or a ship captain. Then the leadership would say, "Hey, you're a great pilot. You're now a project manager for the next airplane." Unfortunately, the project manager job is completely different from the pilot job. As a result, many people struggled with these new assignments.

We have a lot of people that have great technical background and experience. The fact that you are a super engineer doesn't necessarily mean you will be a super project manager. Project management is more than engineering. Project management is working with a cross-functional team and outside stakeholders. That super engineer may have a penchant for wanting to have everything be cut and dried while project managers live in a much more chaotic environment. Not everyone makes that transition well.

Harpham: They are used to saying, "Here are the specs, let's start building."

Gadeken: Right. Or if you're a military commander, "Here's pork chop hill. Follow me! We're going to take that hill!" Unfortunately, that approach doesn't work when the stakeholders don't work for you. Instead of ordering people to do work, you have to influence them. That requires a different set of people skills.

In the project management field, there isn't a straightforward hierarchical structure. There are people from across the country on the project—contractors, units in the Pentagon, and so forth. They're all stakeholders and you do not have direct power over them. First of all, you have to know who those stakeholders are. Second, you have to make contact, get to know them, figure out what their interests are, and then build consensus.

Harpham: I imagine that even if you are based in Washington, DC, you will still have to collaborate with people in bases and organizations across the country.

Gadeken: Certainly. In fact, there are a large number of stakeholders across the world. We may award a contract to a company in the United States. However, that company may have vendors and suppliers from across the world. Pulling all of that together is a challenge. There's also a security issue. How reliable is that electronic component we got from some country in the Pacific Rim? How are we going to verify that the component is not a counterfeit and that it has high reliability?

Harpham: As an educator, how do you approach teaching and developing these relationship development skills in your students?

Gadeken: When I started at DAU, we literally taught project management. We taught every discipline and we put different subject matter experts in front of the class for lectures. We figured that the more knowledge we could pump into someone, the better project manager they would be.

Over time, we realized that is a flawed concept for two reasons. First, there are far more efficient ways of transmitting technical knowledge that don't require people to be sitting in a classroom. That led us to a blended learning approach—basic knowledge is covered through online learning programs, which must be completed before you attend the advanced program in residence.

Second, project management knowledge doesn't guarantee success. They have to be able to perform in this environment where you're dealing with people. As you move up through our training program, there is a growing emphasis on people skills: building a team, leading a team, being able to negotiate, and deal with conflict. Those skills are just as important as all the knowledge you have. If you can't apply your knowledge in a changing environment with different stakeholders, you will not be successful.

Harpham: What is your approach to teaching conflict management skills?

Gadeken: We like to use assessments. We use the Myers-Briggs personality type indicator along with an instrument to assess emotional intelligence. We do 360-degree feedback where new students are rated by their boss, peers, and direct reports. They will get a composite picture of how they look as a manager and leader to the people they work with. With that information, they will understand their strengths and weaknesses and decide where to improve.

In my early days on the faculty, I convinced my organization to do a study on the characteristics of top performing project managers in our business. We needed to find out what successful project managers are doing and then use that information as a basis for our future training. While the military changes in some ways—new departments, new names, and so forth—I would argue that the fundamental military project management culture has not changed and therefore the study still has merit.

We had a group of project managers from each service—Army, Navy, Air Force. They were hand-picked for the study and we interviewed them in depth. We asked them to go through some of the difficult situations they faced. We then dissected what they were doing as the project manager. We divided the sample into highly capable project managers and top performers. Almost all the difference between the two groups came down to the soft skills.

Soft skills such as relationship development and political awareness [i.e., understanding peoples' interests] came up as key points. Everyone thought we would get different findings, such as engineering or financial knowledge, but that did not come up in this research. It was fascinating to see that soft skills made a tremendous difference.

Harpham: What does political awareness mean for project managers? What would I notice about someone who has high political awareness?

Gadeken: I think you would notice that they pay attention to how decisions are made in organizations. They pay attention to who seems to be the thought leader in each functional area—the people that carry the most sway when a decision needs to be made or those who are sought out for advice. All organizations have a formal power structure that you can look at—the classic organization chart. It shows job titles—who is at the director level and so forth. That's only part of the picture.

However, organizations all have an informal structure. That includes who speaks to who? Who has known each other for years? Who knows how to get an activity approved quickly when you are racing against a deadline and have to cut corners? When you have political awareness, you have the ability to get work done with the least amount of effort and the least amount of resistance.

This is a learned skill. People can learn this skill if they realize it's important and see that you can get results. For example, if you notice that the commander's executive assistant influences whether or not you can get an appointment to speak with that person. With that knowledge, you can work on connecting with the executive assistant. The assistant may also give informal advice to the commander. Therefore, if you can convince the assistant, there's a higher likelihood they will share that view with the decision maker.

However, I have seen a challenge. If you bring in people with a military engineering background, that type of person tends not to have political awareness. People select that career path because they like the technical challenge or they like the fact that there is always a right answer. Those people tend to be the most difficult to train to be politically sensitive.

At the start of our programs, we have to convince students that soft skills are important. If we do that, we can start the process. If we went directly to case studies, some students will say, "Hmm, I don't see why these soft skills are important."

Harpham: If we take the classical engineer who says "Give me the spec sheet and we'll get it done. Why can't I just get going? The general already signed off on this." How do you broaden their perspective?

Gadeken: When I first came here, we mainly offered traditional lecture style teaching. Thankfully, we have moved to a different model that has some lecture instruction mixed in with other approaches. Today, our methods emphasize case studies and team exercises with hands-on work.

With a case study, we are reading about a real project from the Department of Defense. It's not a case of simply doing a calculation and coming up with the right answer. The political issues are mixed in with the technical design issues. Funding and pressures from Capitol Hill are part of the picture as well. In the real world, all of those issues are in force.

We then ask students, "How would you handle that?" We use a dilemma approach—we take the project up to a specific problem on the project. We then say, "OK, project managers, what would you do here?"

Harpham: What would be examples of these dilemma points that threaten project success in these case studies?

Gadeken: You're working on a big system project that will take several years like a ship or a tracked vehicle. During the course of development, you discover that the threat has changed. Our adversaries now have different systems or weapons—they now have more advanced systems. That means what we're building will no longer work. So, what do you do? Can you modify the system you are building? Do you start all over and build something completely new?

Another example: you're moving along on a project and you're doing a good job. Then, suddenly Congress decides to set your budget to zero for a year or two.

In other words, you're not going to get any more money. Now, we have some overhead funds that allow us to keep the government project team going. But if we have people out in industry building something for us, they can't keep their project team going without additional funding—they're likely to shut down the project. Then a year or two later, Congress allocates further budget and your industry project team isn't there anymore. And now you have to start over with the project to a degree. So, the dilemma would be how to restart the project effectively? These are all real scenarios that have happened on Defense projects.

Harpham: How does the classroom discussion unfold on these case studies?

Gadeken: We hope for out of the box ideas in the discussion. Even our senior decision makers are looking for people who will be innovative in their approach to solving problems.

Unfortunately, the cultural history of the Defense Department has an impact. The culture tends to look for certainty. It's a challenge to take someone who has marched along in a somewhat predictable career path and teach the old dog new tricks. Some people adapt to it better than others.

Harpham: How did you develop this approach to teaching project management?

Gadeken: We looked around for best practices. For example, we went to the Harvard Business School and the [Ivey] business school at Western University in Canada where they have long-standing experience in using case studies. Our cases, for the most part, are real government projects. Lately, we have started to ask students to create their own case studies at the end of their program based on their experience. Some of those cases are included in future sessions of the course. That means we also have fresh material and examples in the course.

Harpham: How do you think about lessons learned and using them to improve performance?

Gadeken: That's a pet peeve of mine. For the entire time I've been here, we've had a periodic desire to try to catalog lessons learned by looking at failed or problematic projects. We then try to derive what went wrong on a given project.

A few observations on the lessons learned process. For some reason, it seems like the project management community has never been that interested in looking at this material. More significant to me, lessons learned need to be understood in the in the context of that project.

When you think there is a lesson learned on one project—"I always want to use this type of contract or technical approach"—that may be exactly the wrong thing to do on another project because the circumstances are quite different. You have to be careful with what you think of as a lesson learned.

There are so many varieties of projects and circumstances that it is difficult to develop general rules.

Harpham: There's a significant challenge in deriving meaningful general principles from lessons learned.

Gadeken: There are principles but it is fairly difficult to generalize across all projects. We have an amazing diversity of projects here. I have people in my class who are working on a new submarine, a new unmanned ground vehicle, clothing for soldiers, and a new satellite. We have people in the Army medical command who are working on new drugs to combat diseases.

Harpham: Turning to project management methodology. How do you negotiate the fact that the statute book may say "do X" or the regulation says "do Y" but the big contractor wants to do it a different way? How do you reconcile these differences?

Gadeken: That's a dilemma. Due to the large bureaucracy in the Defense Department, if you were to actually follow every one of the guidelines, rules and regulations, we might never put anything in the field for war fighters. In some cases, the war fighters not only need new systems but sometimes they need something put into the field rapidly.

Here's what we tell our project managers. Let's get to the heart of the matter—what is the true need? Then look for people that you can work with in these other organizations who can tell you about the flexibility in the policies and procedures. Then you can put in a request to waive certain requirements to get the project done.

We have two systems for project management in fact. The traditional disciplined process includes the full set of milestone reviews, detailed plans and so forth. We also have a rapid acquisition group who can go out, buy something, make some quick modifications, and send it out.

Remember Daniel Kahneman's book, *Thinking, Fast and Slow* [Farrar, Straus and Giroux, 2011], where he describes System 1 and System 2 thinking processes? One system is fast but prone to errors. The other thinking process is slower, takes energy, and produces fewer errors. Our project approaches are similar to this model.

Our traditional approach employs critical thinking and the full set of processes. However, there are also times where there is an urgent need and we have to move quickly and accept the risks associated with that approach.

Harpham: Is there a tension between these contrasting approaches to projects?

Gadeken: Some of our operational organizations would say, "Wow, we got that piece of equipment into the field fast. I want to migrate more of my projects to this rapid capability process."

However, there are downsides to the rapid process. If I buy something from a vendor quickly, what's the reliability of that system? What's my long-term maintenance and support plan for the equipment? We address all of those points using the traditional approach. When we go fast, we skip those steps. That means you will have trade-offs in terms of maintenance, reliability, cost, and risks.

Harpham: I can imagine if you're the requestor all you say is that "I requested this item and two weeks later, it's here. Why can't I do that all the time?"

Gadeken: It's hard to do complex projects that fast unless you're willing to embrace a higher likelihood of waste and problems regarding sustaining that equipment over time. There's also public scrutiny of our projects when we have test failures and other issues with our projects. There's a desire to avoid that criticism by using a robust process—the trade-off is that it takes longer to execute.

Harpham: There's a tension between the short term and the long term. The idea is "we can ship this to you fast but don't be surprised if it breaks down next year."

Gadeken: The trade-off is exactly that. You asked for this equipment urgently and we got it there fast. However, you will lose the long-term benefits to a large degree when a rapid process is used.

Harpham: I gather that the DAU organization periodically accepts students from outside the US military, such as those from other federal agencies. How does that work?

Gadeken: We have a small budget to accommodate people from outside of the Defense Department. Our courses are very popular! One audience we appeal to is the defense industry. We would like to have more defense industry students in our courses because we have a lot of work going on with them.

The industry perspective adds to the approach. In our current class of fifty-six students, we have two students from major defense contractors. We also offer seats to other government agencies, such as NASA and the Department of Energy. We like the diversity in our classes. Within the defense world, we have diversity from civilian and military people.

Harpham: What do students from outside the defense world bring to the class in terms of project wisdom or questions?

Gadeken: There are some underlying project management principles that apply to all organizations. The value we get from non-defense students is that they have often tried approaches that we have not tried. It's a fresh set of ideas and examples. They may suggest different solutions when we look at a case study that nobody in the Defense world would suggest.

Harpham: Mandatory training in organizations can be a tough sell. Do you have the challenge of students saying, "I just want to go build submarines, but my commanding officer made me come here. Let's get this over with." How do you engage students coming into the program?

Gadeken: We have had difficulties like that when we started the program. The Navy didn't want to send people to the program because they wanted to put their people on projects immediately. Over time, we won them over by showing how we added value to their people when they take our training first.

Unlike other organizations, the project management career path in our organization is written into federal legislation. That means that people must come to our class—we don't have a demand problem when it comes to training! However, I'm concerned about having students with the right attitude—that they're here to learn how to be a successful project manager versus someone who is just looking for a diploma at the end.

I engage students by saying, "Here's what we can do together." Next, students go through a variety of assessment processes. We're not giving grades like A, B, or C but we are assessing people. Students go through an exercise and they get feedback that may convince them that they are not fully proficient in the project management field. Honest assessment goes a long way as a motivational tool.

Harpham: Would you say this willingness to change and self-awareness is part of your leadership philosophy?

Gadeken: Definitely. You need someone who is humble and candid enough to recognize their own shortcomings. Even high-potential people rising through the ranks realize that they need to embrace continuous learning. They need to keep learning to be effective and to benefit the people they are leading.

We've started to change our philosophy from training project managers to creating project leaders. Just the phrase "project manager" suggests that you're a glorified technical manager. If you don't have that leadership dimension, you're missing important skills to be successful in this field.

Harpham: What is your approach to personal productivity and organization?

Gadeken: This type of job can be very demanding. Project management is also highly dynamic and full of change. A challenge for me is that it has been many years since I rolled up my sleeves and worked on a technical project after I switched my career into training and development.

Therefore, I have to work to keep up in the field. When I moved into civilian life, I stayed in the Air Force reserves for a time. When I put my uniform on, I'd go to work on a base and work on Air Force projects.

When I retired from the reserves, that option was no longer available to me. My field is now project management/leadership education. I feel that I must keep current therefore I go to as much training and as many professional conferences as I can.

Our requirement is that I do forty hours of professional development per year. I usually far exceed that requirement. I go to professional associations, seminars and push myself to keep learning. Given that I'm training high-potential people, I tell myself that I have to be the most highly trained person in the room to keep up with the students.

Harpham: It sounds like lifelong learning is both a key strategy and a passion for you.

Gadeken: That's why I like my role. I'm helping to train our future project managers and I'm benefiting from that work. I'm learning as much as my students.

Harpham: What are some of the books that had a significant impact on your thinking and work?

Gadeken: At a recent conference I attended, I heard Simon Sinek speak. He has some great books like *Start with Why* [Portfolio, 2011] and *Leaders Eat Last* [Portfolio, 2014]. I enjoyed hearing him speak. His books are great.

I've always liked *Good to Great* by Jim Collins [HarperBusiness, 2001]. I really like his concept of a Level 5 leader. We have a mythology about leadership that claims that leaders are always charismatic and that you're excellent at public speaking. Those are nice to have but they're not required attributes.

My focus right now is studying leadership because our organization has many subject matter experts on other aspects of project management. I need to understand and keep learning about leadership. I believe that a lot of leadership can be learned from studying good leaders in a variety of contexts: business, military, and even sports and politics.

I've always been a student of history and that interest translates to leadership. For example, I study the American Civil War and the leaders involved in that conflict. How did they handle their opponent if they were outnumbered or outmaneuvered? I've actually written an article about project management lessons from the Battle of Gettysburg. I have a class exercise that was directly inspired by the Civil War.

I like to read biographies of leaders and see what leadership insights I can glean from those.

Harpham: I see where you're coming from. I've benefited from studying Ron Chernow's biographies of John D. Rockefeller and George Washington.

Gadeken: Once upon a time, I thought Abraham Lincoln was lucky and that he had outstanding people working for him. When you study the details, you find out his reality was quite different. It just looks like that on the surface because Lincoln was so good at leading different people. Lincoln's leadership achievements are explained in excellent detail in Doris Goodwin's *Team of Rivals: The Political Genius of Abraham Lincoln* [Simon & Schuster, 2005]. He actually put his rivals in his Cabinet and they became his advisors. At the end, it looks smooth but it was not like that while it was happening.

Harpham: Lincoln's example shows the value of leaders surrounding themselves with strong people who voice different opinions.

Gadeken: In fact, you need different perspectives around you. You want people who will tell the truth, even when it's painful to hear.

Harpham: Any closing thoughts on project management that we haven't covered?

Gadeken: If I look at what I'm doing now, I never could have predicted my career path. I was lucky enough to have my career evolve rather than plan it out. If I planned it out, I would likely be in a research lab and potentially, I wouldn't be as happy. I'm glad how things worked out. I made incremental decisions to guide my career according to my intuition.

At one point, a senior person in the Pentagon asked me to come and work for him. In the traditional career path, that would have been a wonderful opportunity—to become a senior executive in the Pentagon. At the time, I took a few days to think about it. I realized that the opportunity didn't meet my definition of success even though that's what the system encouraged.

My definition of success was to be where I could influence people to become better leaders. That's exactly what I'm doing in my current role. Following my own definition of success has been important.

Chapter Summary

- Recommended books include *Thinking Fast and Slow* by Daniel Kahneman, *Start with Why* and *Leaders Eat Last* by Simon Sinek, *Good to Great* by Jim Collins, and *Team of Rivals* by Doris Kearns Goodwin.

- Key qualities for highly successful project managers: a high proficiency in soft skills, such as relationship development and political awareness.

- Recognize the profession. If you are joining project management from another discipline, be prepared to study and learn new methods in order to become successful, especially interpersonal and leadership skills.

- Career success: It is up to you to define career success in your own terms, even if the organization has defined career paths.

- Teaching project management: Take note of Gadeken's approach, which combines self-study activities and case studies based on actual projects.

Shobha Subramonian

Principal Project Manager, SAS

Shobha Subramonian is a principal project manager at SAS in Cary, North Carolina. She is currently the R&D program lead for the SAS Customer Intelligence 360 program, which develops and builds Software-as-a-Service [SaaS] products. She started her career as a developer at the Dow Chemical Co. in 1993. Later, she joined Accenture and continued as a software developer in SAP applications. She obtained the PMP certification in 2006. Afterward, she progressed through project management roles at three different companies, working on and leading various software development projects. Prior to her current role at SAS, she led a project to install Workday to replace the organization's existing HR and payroll systems.

Subramonian holds a master's degree in computer science from Central Michigan University. She is married with two adult children and lives with her husband in Cary, North Carolina.

Bruce Harpham: How did you get started in project management?

Shobha Subramonian: Several years ago, I was working at a Big Six consulting firm. In that organization, I worked as an application specialist—a combination of a software analyst and a business analyst role—working on SAP supply chain systems. I expressed an interest in leadership to my managers. I wanted to lead the work of the team.

© Bruce Harpham 2018
B. Harpham, *Project Managers at Work*, DOI 10.1007/978-1-4842-2668-1_7

We had project managers in the company who led large projects. There was a smaller project that came up that presented an opportunity. There were no project managers at the company available to lead some of the smaller projects. Management asked me if I would like to lead the effort. I was happy to get involved.

I was working on the project's tasks and leading it. It was a small team of about six people. It gave me the opportunity to create a plan, work the plan, and so forth. I covered planning, requirements, design, implementation, and execution of the project. It was a good introduction to project management.

This was in the days when project management was not fully recognized as a distinct role in the way it is today. Sometimes managers led the projects. Sometimes lead developers led the projects. This presented a perfect opportunity for me. I discovered that I was good at project management and that I enjoyed this kind of work.

Harpham: What was the objective of the project?

Subramonian: To implement enhancements to an in-house customer complaints management system. For this project, we gathered requirements from our internal users. We had to convert those requirements into a design, test the features, and implement the enhancements.

Harpham: You had this desire to take on leadership responsibility. Did the project satisfy what you were looking for?

Subramonian: Yes, it did. On the project, I learned that I had to take the different personalities on the project into account. That was a new challenge for me. I had to account for different strengths and weaknesses on the project team and put that insight into action. I had learned some leadership and project methods from observing and working with other project managers. However, I learned that there was much more involved to make a project successful than organization.

Beyond organizational skills, it is vital to bring a team together and understand the talents of the different people. It was a very good experience. There was a little bit of a balancing act because I wasn't really a leader in a traditional sense—I did not formally have that role. I had to be careful not to step on anyone's toes.

Harpham: What methods did you use to inspire the team to work together effectively?

Subramonian: Today, I use the agile methodology, which has practices such as daily Scrum meetings, planning meetings, etc. that automatically and regularly bring the team together and helps the team build closer working relationships.

In earlier days, with waterfall project management, these kinds of team interactions were not inherent with the project methodology. I think it is important to bring the team together to build these connections. We had an open office layout, we had lunch together, and we interacted outside of the project itself. That helps to build relationships with the people you're working with. Having those connections makes the project more successful and easier to manage. Take the time to get to know each person and have conversations with them about their life outside of work, such as their families or hobbies. Connecting on a personal level makes you more approachable. As people get to know each other better, they definitely work better together.

Harpham: Currently, you're involved in research and development projects. You're creating something new and exciting. Walk me through what's it like to do R&D projects in your current role.

Subramonian: It presents an interesting set of challenges compared to earlier projects I worked on. In the past, I had a framework to go by. In contrast, I'm developing the project and framework to run it at the same time in R&D.

There are no standards or guidelines to use because the product we're developing is so new. The environment and the platform are also new. We have to define the rules and the standards. It's exciting and challenging. It can also be pretty daunting at times. When you get the project done, it becomes a model for others in the company to follow.

There are a lot of smart people in R&D, which makes a big difference as we try to navigate this new ground. However, there's a lot of trial and error to make it work. Once we get it to work, it's a very satisfying experience.

Harpham: What is a recently completed R&D project you've worked on?

Subramonian: We recently created a cloud-based, multi-tenant digital marketing product called SAS Customer Intelligence 360. This is something new for our company. We're also using a continuous release process for this product. Up until now, our product releases have been developed over months or years and then we roll out a new version. With this new product, we have customers using the product and we roll out new software versions to them each month.

This is drastically different from projects that we've done before. We had to think of a model that would fit the different stages of the development cycle and still meet a monthly delivery schedule. Our team had to delve into how to deploy this on the cloud, and configure different tenants as per the customer requirements. We drew expertise from people we hired who had worked on similar technologies at other companies. Self-education was a key factor with this project. Our team members went to workshops and training sessions, and worked with AWS [Amazon Web Services] consultants to figure out how to use these services.

Our first release of the software, which was an early adopter release [pre-production or trial software] in June 2015, was very challenging. Getting into the cadence of a monthly release was the next step—that took a while to perfect. I developed a process model where development, testing and related activities are now on a rhythm where we can release monthly.

Harpham: What exactly does this marketing product do for the customer?

Subramonian: It's a digital marketing product based on customer intelligence. The product user [such as a retail store] would use it to gather data from their customers on the Web. Based on this data, the user decides what to market to their customers. The product runs analytics on shopping behavior and other customer activities. Based on that analysis, the marketer is able to come up with campaigns to market more effectively to its customers.

Harpham: How did you move to the monthly project cadence? Did it mean compressing activities or doing them differently?

Subramonian: We had to take on a completely new mindset. I had to manage the scope differently—adopt a much smaller scope. Our previous projects had a scope appropriate for a one-year duration. With a monthly release, a smaller scope was needed. A key question became "What can we do within the month?" For example, adding the ability to create mobile in-app messages to send to mobile app users, or enhancing email messages by adding images or backgrounds. It's a very small slice of what you would normally do on a project.

Today, we have a shippable product every month. Previously, we might have completed development activities in our monthly sprints. Theoretically, we were planning to have a shippable product at the end of each sprint. But in practice, that was not the case, since much more is required to have a shippable product than to just complete development. However, today we are actually releasing the product each month. Learning this new approach to scope management was key. It took a while to develop this approach. Cutting scope down enough in order to be able to deliver monthly was something we learned how to do. The first few efforts to adapt to the monthly cycle were so ambitious that we went two or three months between releases. We planned features that were too large to complete in one sprint. We learned to break these features into smaller components and to get better at managing the scope.

We also had to learn about the cloud technology and how to push out new upgrades. Our team worked closely with customers to make sure the software was meeting their requirements. When it didn't meet their requirements, we took in that feedback to make changes.

Harpham: How do you measure success in this environment? For example, how do you know if the July release was better than the March release or vice versa?

Subramonian: Success for us is primarily customer satisfaction. We roll out our software and customers are using the early version. Our measure of success is: "Does the product meet customer expectations?" Also, we look at how many defects are found in the product. The initial challenge was to actually be able to deliver the product on a monthly release schedule.

The next challenge is to make our software fulfill customer expectations in every respect. That includes delivering new functionality with high quality and reducing defects. At this point, we're still early in the game. Every release is better than the previous one in terms of meeting the release date and responding to customer questions quickly.

Harpham: Let's explore customer satisfaction. In large organizations, project managers are sometimes several steps removed from the end customer. That distance makes it difficult to understand the end customer. What are some of your methods to understand the end customer?

Subramonian: In our organization, we have a close tie with the operations team and the technical support team, and the product management team. We work closely with those teams, which helps us to understand customer feedback even if we are not in direct conversation with customers on a daily basis.

From time to time, R&D managers and directors go out and visit the customer in person. They engage with them in workshops and seek out their feedback. That is all brought back and shared with the project team in great detail. That helps us decide our focus for the next several releases.

Harpham: Earlier, you mentioned the importance of professional development in doing R&D products. Could you share some examples of professional development activities that have made a big difference to your career?

Subramonian: I have attended various information sessions about the product. I also went to workshops on cloud products to understand how they are managed and developed. That was beneficial for me to understand how cloud-based software works. Other people in the team had more in depth training on the technology, processes, and tools.

The more informed you are about the product, the better it is for the project manager. It makes you into a more effective project manager. It's true that we can apply our project management methods regardless of the software. That said, it's more effective when you know the product and the technology. It means you are able to speak the same language as the team.

Harpham: How have you decided how much technical depth and knowledge to acquire as a project manager?

Subramonian: I started my career as a developer and worked in SAP software for several years before going into project management. I worked on projects related to sales and distribution, quality management, finance, materials management, etc. As I worked on different projects, I tried to gain a good understanding of the functional aspects of the software I was building.

The fact that I have a development background definitely helps me. The fact that I'm not fully conversant with the latest technology may present some challenges. However, you have a technical lead and developers on the project who have that expertise. They're happy to share information so that you can understand the big picture. If you have a good relationship with your technical team members, it's easy to have a conversation to gain that understanding.

I also think it's valuable to take training sessions to get an overview of the product. I aim to attend training sessions put on for developers from time to time.

Harpham: What are some lessons and insights you've learned from mentors over your career?

Subramonian: Sometimes I think a project is on track and going well. Then, there's a sudden surprise problem that I didn't anticipate. Communication is the most important activity in project management. It's key to reach all of the people who could influence your project and take it in a different direction or derail it.

Thinking back to my earlier projects, I remember getting close to the end on one of them and then something came up. Someone on the customer side raised an objection on a particular change. At first glance, the objection seemed trivial. I never would have thought that this would derail the project but it did! You cannot overlook or discount even small risks or small stakeholders without consequences.

I learned to put my finger on those situations. For example, keeping more people "in the know" and making sure they are fully backing the project. People don't like surprises! If somebody reaches out to you and says, "Hey, I didn't know this project was happening," you need to manage that.

Harpham: Let's look at the stakeholder management aspect further. Can you share more about the situation where a stakeholder raised a red flag and caused challenges for the project?

Subramonian: I remember working on a project for the SAP quality management system. The client had a few people involved on the project who defined the requirements, and we worked through the design, testing, and implementation. There was one requirement where we noted an exception—that we would not be able to deliver a feature because it had high cost and low value. This exception had buy-in from most people on the client side including the supply chain specialist who was the primary client, and the project sponsor.

However, there was one person—a material flow specialist, from whom we didn't get buy in for the exception. She didn't say much early in the project. As the project kept going, I made the assumption that the issue had been addressed and closed. That was not the case. It became evident during signoff that what we thought was a small issue was unacceptable to the client. We had to stop the project and put in an enhancement.

Just because the client didn't say, "Hey stop, I don't agree," is not enough—it's necessary for us to proactively get their explicit agreement. We needed to go back and do the due diligence on the issue. We didn't hear from them and assumed everything was fine. That was not the case.

Harpham: That could be a project management principle: "Avoid assuming stakeholder silence means there are no problems or risks on the project."

Subramonian: In our minds, we thought it was a trivial issue, so we didn't pay much attention to it. Obviously, this person had a different view. It's important to get that explicit approval from all of the stakeholders. If the stakeholder has the ability to throw a wrench in the project, they need to be considered.

Harpham: What was your perspective on the stakeholder in this case?

Subramonian: I think the stakeholder had the view: "I haven't been asked for my OK. But my lack of comment doesn't mean I approve of the project." They had an expectation that the requirement would be done.

Harpham: That illustrates how a disconnect with a stakeholder can become more pronounced over time. Let's now turn to your approach to productivity. What does your personal productivity system and habits look like? A medical doctor who smokes would likely raise questions. Likewise, a disorganized project manager may raise questions about their ability to organize and execute.

Subramonian: I use project plans and processes quite extensively. However, I aim to keep it simple for my teams—I believe very strongly in keeping organization simple and easy to manage.

I use the organizational tools available at work and the methodologies I have learned over time. Microsoft Project, Outlook, calendars, SharePoint, and JIRA [a product that provides issue tracking and project management functions] are some of the tools I use for communication, scheduling, planning, and tracking work with my teams.

In terms of books, *The Magic of Thinking Big* by David J. Schwartz [Touchstone, 2015] had a big impact on me. One of the ideas that was really instilled in my mind from this book is that you can achieve things with the power of belief. That is, if you believe very strongly that you can do something then your mind finds the ways for you to do it. This has been reinforced with me through my own experiences over the years, and it has enabled me to make significant strides and changes successfully at key points in my career. I've also read *The 7 Habits of Highly Effective People* by Stephen Covey [Simon & Schuster, 2013], which had a similar influence. It highlights how we shape our lives [either consciously or unconsciously] by our choices—and the importance of being proactive.

Harpham: What role have mentors played in your career growth?

Subramonian: I have sought out mentorship by reaching out to successful people. A company that I previously worked at had a formal mentorship program that I found helpful. Each employee was assigned a mentor with whom they would meet about once a quarter. This provided an avenue for employees to discuss all kinds of topics and issues with the mentor, some of which they may not want to discuss with their manager. In other companies, I looked for people who were good to learn from. Some people are more open to mentoring than others, so it takes a while to find the right people.

It's also important to recognize that mentoring can be a very satisfying experience for both people. It's helpful to find people who are experienced in the company and who can train you on what works and what doesn't in the company. The culture of every company is different and that's something you can learn from a mentor. Techniques that work in one company and setting may not transfer over to a new company.

From time to time, there are announcements and requests for people to join corporate projects or initiatives outside their usual sphere of responsibility. I like to sign up for some of these opportunities because it enables me to expand my connections and knowledge beyond my regular work. There are new perspectives and experiences to learn from these groups. It puts you in the position to handle different types of situations.

Last year, I was involved in a quality initiative with a team of people where we looked at various tools and reports to measure and track quality in R&D projects. We eventually added some of them to the project management toolkit. In a previous job while working as a software specialist, I got an opportunity to be involved in a communications project to support the rollout of a new HR system for the company. It was enlightening for me to see the detailed planning and organization that went into crafting the various communications to the different levels of management and employees of the company. This offered insights and understanding of subtle differences in messaging and also helped me to enhance my own communication skills.

Harpham: What is your approach to mentoring other people?

Subramonian: My approach is influenced by the fact I have benefited from mentors and learning from others. I look for opportunities to teach classes from time to time. For example, if you learn a software tool before other people in the company, you have the opportunity to teach that tool to other people to help them become effective.

Harpham: In that case, you're benefiting from being an early adopter?

Subramonian: Exactly. I've done this in a few different instances. For example, I had prior experience with the JIRA tool from previous roles. Therefore, I could guide people in my current department on how to use it effectively. The more everyone knows about the processes and tools we use, the more productive they will become. I created a presentation on using JIRA and then shared it with other project managers in the company. I'm always open to teaching. Teaching helps me to connect with other people and it is always well worth the effort.

Harpham: For the reader who is interested in project management but currently works in a different field, how would you suggest they make a career move into project management?

Subramonian: Look for opportunities to lead a small group. If you do that, it will be a great experience. It will also help you discover whether you like leading people. I had the vision that I would like to lead a project. The first opportunity I had to lead confirmed my interest in leading. It was good to get that confirmation.

On the other hand, there have been people who have gone into project management and left the field. It might not be their cup of tea. It might be different from what they expect. You have to be "the glue" on the project bringing everyone together and make it work with different personalities. You also have to keep the project on track and meet deadlines.

Are you comfortable working toward deadlines and making the entire team work toward a deadline? These are key points to ask yourself when you look at a project management career. Are you happy to plan the work and organize the team? You may become the go-to person for people on the team who have a question. I enjoy doing all of that.

In contrast, if you enjoy being technical or taking direct control over the work, you may want a different role. The project manager often has to look to other people, such as the project sponsor, to make key decisions. You might not have as much power as a project manager as you might imagine.

Harpham: A tolerance for pressure and stress from deadlines and the uncertainty of leading in the project environment comes with the job.

Subramonian: Absolutely, those are important qualities for success in project management.

Harpham: Looking out over the next few years, what are some important trends that you see on the horizon in terms of technology or other trends?

Subramonian: The move to cloud-based technologies is likely to become more important. Rapid technological change requires us to be adaptable. I think it's important to be open to change and keep up with changing needs. At one time, developing a product could take eighteen months. Now, you are developing a product for a set of customers and delivering it in a month.

I'm excited to work on our current product because it is new. I expect more projects to be like this in the future—coming up with new products using cutting-edge technology. I look forward to that.

Chapter Summary

- Recommended books include *The Magic of Thinking Big* by David J. Schwartz and *The 7 Habits of Highly Effective People* by Stephen Covey.

- Ask for opportunities. Subramonian grew her career by asking for leadership opportunities, which opened the door to work in project management.

- Mentorship: Seek out mentors, whether or not the organization has a formal program, to grow your career. Likewise, seek out people to mentor if you are an experienced professional.

- Go first. To grow your knowledge and credibility, look for opportunities to "go first" in your organization, such as being the first to learn new systems and processes.

- Dealing with stakeholders: If a stakeholder or a customer raises an issue, take the time to understand it up front, even if it seems like a small issue to you.

Kristen Fleming

Vice President of Integrated Production, VaynerMedia

Kristen Fleming *is vice president of integrated production at VaynerMedia, a digital agency headquartered in New York City. She oversees and manages a team of integrated producers, whose work includes complex digital builds, event production, video production, photo production, and emerging technology (i.e., virtual reality, Amazon bots, etc.).* **Fleming** *also supports VaynerMedia's domestic and global satellite offices by leading trainings, implementing structures, and finding the right local market hires. Before leading integrated production, she helped build VaynerMedia's project management team. In four years,* **Fleming** *grew the team from one person to 55 people. She led development of current training programs, project management tools, and internal structures. She also performs improv around NYC and brings the art form's "Yes, and..." mentality to all her work. Prior to VaynerMedia, Fleming was at another social media start-up, Big Fuel. She graduated from the College of the Holy Cross in Worcester, MA.*

Bruce Harpham: How did you get started in project management?

Kristen Fleming: I fell into project management. In college, I studied theater and English. After graduating from college, I moved to New York to pursue acting. After several years, I decided the acting lifestyle wasn't for me anymore and decided to change direction. During this time, I was working as an intern at a public relations agency. Through an improv group I was in, a friend at a start-up social media agency noticed that I was highly organized and looking

© Bruce Harpham 2018
B. Harpham, *Project Managers at Work*, DOI 10.1007/978-1-4842-2668-1_8

for a career opportunity. She introduced me to people at the agency and I started there as a project coordinator.

In true start-up fashion, there was rapid change and surprises. A senior project manager resigned within a month of me joining the company. As a result, I was assigned the responsibility of managing that person's projects. It was a crash-course introduction to project management. I found that I was naturally good at project management and enjoyed doing it. I was also excited about social media—especially the dynamic and changing nature of the field.

Harpham: What was involved in this "crash course" experience with project management at the agency?

Fleming: It was a crazy experience. I had about two weeks' notice that the person was going to leave and I had to take over. For example, I had to rapidly learn about all the tools and technology she was using on her projects. I was learning the basics of project management through the experience of working on a variety of projects—projects that ranged from producing social media content to more complex work [e.g., developing a global social architecture for a major electronics brand on Facebook]. I quickly learned what I could control and what my limitations were. By listening to the right team members and trusting their expertise, I gained a large breadth of project experience in a relatively short period of time.

Harpham: What was it like to rapidly transition from a project coordinator role to a project manager role?

Fleming: The biggest shift was moving from a reactive mindset to a proactive leadership mindset. I took a step back from being in the weeds of project details and looking at the big picture. Specifically, I focused on the end goal of the project and led the project team to focus on that goal. It was a trial and error experience to learn the ropes quickly.

Harpham: What is a project management lesson that you've learned the hard way.

Fleming: The hardest lesson to learn is becoming less attached to the project plan. Instead, I've learned the value of providing flexibility for the project's team. That may take the form of negotiating internal deadlines, pulling in a different person to work on a task, or solving content production issues. Having the confidence to adjust the plan has been important.

I've struggled as a project manager in situations where I have been too rigid on the schedule. At the end of day, rigidly adhering to the plan for the plan's sake doesn't lead to success.

Harpham: What does flexibility from the plan look like in your context?

Fleming: Flexibility means being smart with the resources that you have. In addition, it's important to give thought to the next important milestone on the project and balance that against the project's end goal. Let's say you have two deliverables scheduled to run sequentially [e.g., complete A, then do B]. However, those deliverables may need to run in parallel given what the client is asking for.

Harpham: The principle is put the plan and tasks in service of the end goal. The details on how we get there is helpful, but it's not carved in stone.

Fleming: It's a producer mindset. The focus is on the work—always asking, "How do we get the work done in the best way possible?" Adopting that perspective has contributed to my success rather than focusing on myself or things outside of my control.

Harpham: What do you mean by the producer mindset?

Fleming: Project management can be highly task-focused—moving from A to B and checking off tasks. The best project managers are not just strong at the technical work [e.g., schedules and tasks]. In my field, great project managers understand the creative vision, the overall strategy, and the production capabilities of different media. The ability to connect big picture issues, industry knowledge, and technical project management make up a star project manager.

Harpham: What is a project that you're proud of achieving at VaynerMedia? What was the project's objective and what was achieved?

Fleming: I'm proud of quite a few projects. One of my first big projects that I led was for Hasbro's Monopoly game. In 2012 and 2013, we led a social media marketing project for Monopoly. It was the perfect combination of content, nostalgia, and new technology for that time.

Specifically, the campaign involved eliminating one of the game tokens and coming up with a new one. We came up with the idea of producing a Facebook app where users could visit, see video content about the game tokens, vote on the one they wanted to "save" and vote on which game token they wanted to bring in. It was also VaynerMedia's first Facebook app.

The campaign gathered tremendous buzz and attention. Conan O'Brien even made his own token—though not the most appropriate.... Fans also developed grassroots campaigns to try to save certain game tokens from elimination. There was a hardware store that created a social content series to save the wheelbarrow game token. It was incredible to see the reaction and high engagement. Further, the app supported eight different languages, so there was global usage. The project's success in terms of earned media and engagement was awesome for me to see.

From a stakeholder management standpoint, there were many points to consider. I led collaboration with both internal and other creative agencies working on different aspects of the campaign.

Harpham: Was the earned media a project goal or a happy accident?

Fleming: I knew that we were going to get a lot of earned media from it because it's an iconic board game. However, I was pleasantly surprised at just how much attention we got for it. It was exciting to see how many people were talking about it.

Harpham: Did everyone on the project team get a copy of the game?

Fleming: Yes! Everyone on the project team received a copy of Monopoly. I wanted to save the wheelbarrow game token and he made it through!

Harpham: The project reminds me of a reality TV show where the audience votes people off the show. Was that the concept?

Fleming: We used the concept of a "Monopoly jail" for the app. All the game tokens were stuck in jail and users had to break them out. Each token had animated videos showing how they would break out of jail. It was a lot of fun!

Harpham: Let's turn to interaction with partner agencies and their role on different projects. Other agencies don't report to you and yet you have to lead them. How do you manage that interaction?

Fleming: VaynerMedia is known for being a people first company. That means we treat all employees well and that spirit extends beyond the company. It is expected that I work to build strong professional relationships with all the partner agencies or vendors involved. Specifically, I aim to get to know each individual person at the agencies at a personal level. When you take a "people first" approach to the work, people tend to rally behind you and the work. Quality ultimately benefits.

Harpham: So you've managed to fight against the "resource I will do task X, resource 2 will do task Y" mentality that's sometimes encouraged by project management software?

Fleming: There's a lot of collaboration on projects. It's far better to work with the team at an individual level rather than viewing them as anonymous resources.

Harpham: What does "people first" philosophy look like in your daily work?

Fleming: It starts with putting attention on the individual person. For example, I look for subtleties in personality and preferences. I might have a creative professional on the project who knows how to prioritize and doesn't want to be micro-managed. Alternately, you might have a person who cannot prioritize to save his or her life. In that case, the person needs constant attention to be successful. A high level of EQ [emotional intelligence] for the team you're working with is important.

The ability to observe and adjust as a project manager also comes in helpful here. If I approach someone in one way and I observe that it doesn't go well,

I'll take a different approach next time. I tailor my approach depending on who I'm talking to.

Harpham: Experimentation is a big part of your approach to relating well to other people?

Fleming: Definitely.

Harpham: It sounds like the project manager has to be the person that takes the lead in being flexible in their communication style rather than demanding everyone saying, "Do it my way!"

Fleming: I have an idea on how we can get the project done. At the same time, I have experts in creative design, technical development, and other fields. Given that reality, I want to get their input so we can be successful. I don't want to be a dictator on the project—that hurts the work and the team.

Harpham: What is your approach to leadership?

Fleming: My starting point is that I listen to everyone involved on the project. Next, I try to understand where each person is coming from. As I have moved up at VaynerMedia, my success comes from listening and helping the people I work with. I also start from a place of trust. I think people in this industry have a tendency to overdramatize problems or get overly sensitive about disagreements. I take the view that we're working toward the end goal of helping the client and let's keep that in mind with regards to whatever our disagreements may be concerning process or methods. If you know what you're doing, you need to trust your teammates to get their work done and trust their ideas.

Harpham: Listening is sometimes underappreciated as a skill. Let's say you're in a meeting with two other people: Jane is listening well to you and Robin is not. What are some of the differences that you observe in their behavior?

Fleming: My style is usually to defuse a situation with a joke or with humor. If someone is not listening to me, I'll probably call attention to it in a joking way. If the lack of listening continues, I will ask about it directly: if you have somewhere else to be, please head out and we'll catch up with you later. My assumption is always that a person's behavior is not a personal insult to me. They probably have eight other concerns going through their mind. By taking that approach, people don't feel attacked. Empathy is a tremendously important part of effective listening and successful project management.

It's unlikely that Robin would walk into the meeting thinking, "I'm going to show Kristen how much I disagree with her. I'm just not going to listen to her today." Robin probably has a million other concerns on her plate right now. I'll make a bid to get her to pay attention. But if that doesn't work out, I'll encourage her to step out of the meeting so she can attend to her other concerns.

Harpham: It sounds both direct and polite—asking someone to leave a meeting if they are preoccupied with other matters.

Fleming: You want to be as respectful as possible especially when you're responsible for creating the timeline, milestones and getting people to do the work. If you someone loses respect for you, it will make your job much more difficult.

Harpham: What is your approach to leading people from different disciplines? Many project managers started their careers as engineers or developers, and feel comfortable with those professionals. However, they may struggle to relate to and lead other professionals.

Fleming: It's all in the approach you take. I'm not going to claim to be an expert in coding, for example. That said, I know the levels of effort and time required for certain kinds of coding tasks from experience. Even if it's not my field of expertise, it's important to understand enough to ask the right questions. Listening skills also come into the picture again here. In some cases, I play a translation role between different teams, such as a technical specialist and the client account team. I ask good questions, repeat back what I hear to confirm that I have understood the information, and explain to the rest of the team why a given technical issue matters.

Harpham: What's your approach to starting a new project in the first few days?

Fleming: I like to starting with auditing the brief—a summary document—that describes what the project is all about. Next, I bring the key stakeholders together for a meeting to discuss the brief, answer questions, and clarify any ambiguous points in the brief. After that, I build out a project timeline and review that document with the stakeholders. Finally, I schedule the project kick off meeting.

In the kick off meeting, I cover a number of points. I start with roles and responsibilities—who will be performing certain kinds of work. I also cover the project schedule in the meeting.

Harpham: In some meetings, I see people ask, "Does anyone have questions?" And then wait a few seconds for a response and keep moving. In those cases, there could be questions or issues that people are not raising. How do you proactively engage people at this stage?

Fleming: I directly ask individual people in the meeting and ask for their feedback or agreement. Recently, I was in a project review meeting discussing scripts for a video. The director was in the meeting, however, he didn't appear to be engaged. He may have been preoccupied about other video projects. Someone else asked the director if he had any questions and he said no. I wanted to err on the side of caution.

In this case, I asked the director, "I want to triple check with you about these scripts and projects while we have you in the room. We want to make the best use of our time once we all arrive on the set for filming." Specifically, I asked him whether there were any aspects of the project that might lead to unanticipated costs that had not been planned for. With those prompts, the director refocused and commented in greater depth about the project. In fact, he raised a concern relating to one part of the script. We then had the opportunity to work through that particular issue.

A good project manager needs to be listening to everyone and be able to react quickly. Some people may not be listening to the same degree or notice what is not being said [e.g., the director appeared to be too quiet or disengaged]. I knew going into this type of meeting that there was a high likelihood that we would have some production issues to address. As a result, I guided the conversation to make sure he engaged with the project and thought through the production.

Harpham: The prompting questions—What about X? What about Y?—play a role in helping the person to engage in the process?

Fleming: Yes exactly. Those kinds of specific prompts often bring better results than an open-ended question, like: "Can you think of anything that might cause a problem?" A vague question often leads to a vague answer.

Harpham: What inspires confidence in you when you see another project manager in action?

Fleming: Adaptability to changing circumstances comes to mind. I like to see somebody who is confident and capable at using project processes and procedures and knows when to put those aside to move ahead on a project. Social media—the focus of our company—moves fast. We are building massive amounts of content in short periods of time. Therefore, there's a risk for errors if project managers do not steer their ship. If a project encounters problems, good project managers will jump in to develop a solution with their team.

Harpham: How does prior experience working at agencies have an impact on project manager success in your context?

Fleming: Prior agency experience is critical. Prior experience is especially important in certain areas, such as photo and video production. The project manager may not personally know how to do each step of the production process, but they will know the steps of the process and the teams you need to interface with to get things done.

Harpham: Have you seen project managers join the organization without agency experience and how did that go?

Fleming: We move so fast that you need to have a good baseline of knowledge before you join the organization as a project manager.

Harpham: How do you mentor and guide new hires to the organization given that VaynerMedia has been growing rapidly?

Fleming: We have an in-depth onboarding process. Everyone who joins the team is assigned a project manager "buddy." That person is going to be with you for the next three weeks. In addition to company level onboarding activities, we have a specific onboarding process for project managers. New hires are walked through all the templates we use, the processes we use, an overview of operations, and shadow other staff. There are also applied exercises where a new hire is asked to build a schedule or budget and we review it with them. It's almost like taking a class in our agency's project management methodology for three weeks. I like to strike a balance between providing the support and giving people enough rope to figure some aspects out on their own.

Harpham: How did this onboarding process come about?

Fleming: At one point, a large number of people joined the department. I discussed the situation with my manager and we agreed to build out a formal training process. We created a living Google Docs document with details on our processes and capabilities. As our processes change [as is the nature of social media], our document is updated in real time.

Harpham: Rapid growth may bring challenges for project governance. How do you strike the balance between the need for speed and the need for governance?

Fleming: Confidence in the project processes and tools is helpful. A top project manager knows what processes or steps that they can safely skip in order to meet deadlines. However, it's also important to recognize when too many corners are being cut and detect when a project is going off the rails. It's a constant negotiation process to balance that out. Project managers are highly valued here because they bring that holistic project perspective.

Harpham: There's significant discretion then on how and when to apply the project processes?

Fleming: Yes. There's a conversation around those decisions to think through the implications. If we reduce the number of project review meetings or put two activities in parallel, it's on the project manager to propose the solution and discuss it with the right stakeholders. Once we agree on the adjustment, it's up to the project manager to move it forward.

Harpham: Are there project auditors or similar review processes? Would project managers be questioned on why they decided to skip a certain step after the fact?

Fleming: If the decision works out at the end of the day and the client is happy, that's our top concern. After each project, we go through a post mortem meeting to discuss how the project went. Specifically, that means collecting feedback from everyone on the team. I then compile that feedback and look for patterns. I'm looking for practices we want to keep and areas for change. For larger projects, the post mortem process has been highly valuable. It gives everyone an opportunity to be heard. In addition, this process reinforces the organization's values—namely, a commitment to constant improvement and optimization.

Harpham: What are some of the insights you've gained from these post mortem meetings?

Fleming: Following a large video project for a soda brand, we had a post mortem meeting to discuss it. As the project was unfolding, we thought the right solution was to assign additional staff to work on the project. Unfortunately, that approach couldn't have been further from the truth.

What we needed was a small, very senior team to execute and make decisions without going through other people. That was a huge learning curve for us. In actuality, the large number of people on the project made decision-making and communication less effective.

This project also lacked a RACI [Responsible, Accountable, Consulted, Informed] process. There were numerous people spread across multiple functional areas, such as the account team, creative, project management, and the studio. We did not define who was responsible, who was accountable, and so forth, for each deliverable. In particular, the lack of clear roles and responsibilities between our creative team and the studio caused difficulties.

Harpham: It's interesting how the fundamentals—like using a RACI thoroughly—keep resurfacing. This suggests that we don't need new approaches as much as need to use existing methods more thoroughly. Why do you think the RACI concept was omitted from the project?

Fleming: There were several factors at play. A big piece of it is that we still operate like a start-up. And because of that, we prioritize flexibility and speed with less rigid processes. The trade-off is less focus on basic processes like using a RACI. Ironically, it's those basic processes that make an even greater impact when you're moving fast on a high-stakes project.

Harpham: I think of the analogy of road rules and signs on a highway. If you're going to drive 100 miles per hour on the German autobahn, it's important that everyone is using the same processes [e.g., traffic rules and regulation]. In that sense, process and structure enable you to drive quickly and safely.

Harpham: For the reader who is currently not in project management and who wants to move into the project field, what advice would you give them?

Fleming: It takes a lot of initiative on the individual to take on additional work that goes beyond one's regular responsibilities. Look for people you admire and who do good work in your organization and seek out their advice.

This goes beyond asking to meet with someone once. Ideally, this involves shadowing them, asking to take on some of their minor tasks, and observing how they do certain tasks like building a statement of work.

It's a tough field to break into if you lack direct experience. So it makes sense to start small. In addition, I recommend adopting the following attitude: "Look, I don't know how to do this and I want to learn it. Can you teach me?" Put yourself in situations where you're not going to be the leader in the room. You're likely going to be uncomfortable as you learn the new field.

Harpham: It's an important mindset to adopt if you want to thrive in the field—a willingness to learn and be uncomfortable in different situations.

Fleming: Definitely.

Harpham: What books have shaped your professional thinking and growth?

Fleming: I'm drawn to books about successful women in various fields. For example, I enjoyed reading Tina Fey's memoir, *Bossypants* [Little, Brown, 2011]. Other books by women comedians—like Mindy Kaling and Amy Poehler—have inspired me. I'm impressed by their drive to succeed and their exceptional ability to connect with people through their work. Their humor and humility give me ideas and approaches on how to relate to people.

Harpham: What productivity habits and methods do you use to stay organized and clear?

Fleming: My email inbox operates like my to-do list. We use Gmail and it has great capabilities to filter and tag messages. For example, if a message comes in with an action item for me, I will label it as a task as well as which client or project it relates to. I usually have no more than ten unread emails at any time. If I have more than that, it's a sign that I'm having an unusually hectic day.

From a time management perspective, I aim to be realistic and fair to myself regarding what I can achieve in a given day. I look for an hour here and there through the workday to sit uninterrupted and get tasks done. If someone attempts to book a meeting with me during that time, I decline the invitation and explain why. If I don't do that, I could easily have no work time for myself all day. I know that I can't be effective if I'm in back-to-back meetings all day. I find that people generally understand when I push back against some requests citing my need to get other work done.

Harpham: Looking ahead over the next several years, which trends and opportunities interest you professionally?

Fleming: Working with new technologies is one of the most exciting aspects of my work. For example, we're getting into virtual reality and bots for Amazon and Facebook. Taking my project management skills and applying it to completely new technology is interesting. "I know how to build websites and apps. How do I translate that experience to building bots?" Those are the questions I'm looking forward to exploring.

Chapter Summary

- Recommended books include *Bossypants* by Tina Fey, *Yes Please* by Amy Poehler, and Mindy Kaling's books.

- Seizing opportunities: Fleming received a "crash course" in project management when a project manager unexpectedly left. What changes in your organization present similar growth opportunities?

- Pragmatism: Creating the project plan and schedule is helpful but it cannot come at the expense of client satisfaction.

- The producer mindset: To become exceptional in the agency world, great project management skills are part of the story. You also need to understand the creative vision, project strategy, and production capabilities. Look for opportunities to adopt this perspective to continue your career growth.

- Project management fundamentals: Omitting project fundamentals like RACI charts often causes problems. Ask yourself: What fundamental project processes could you apply more systematically to improve your productivity?

- The people-first project manager: To enhance collaboration with your team, be prepared to adjust your communication style and approach to suit the needs of other people.

Hassan Osman

PMO Manager, Cisco

Hassan Osman *is a PMO manager at Cisco Systems (**Osman's** views are his own and do not represent those of Cisco), where he is responsible for leading and managing a team of project and program managers on delivering projects to Cisco's global clients. Prior to his PMO role, he was a senior program manager, where he was responsible for scoping, negotiating, planning, and executing multi-million-dollar projects for customers.*

Before joining Cisco, **Osman** *was a management consultant at Ernst & Young, where he analyzed troubled programs at Fortune 100 companies, and recommended strategic plans to improve their alignment with project objectives.*

Osman *is the Amazon bestselling author of two books: Influencing Virtual Teams [2014] and Don't Reply All [2015]. He holds PMP, CSM, and ITIL certifications, and is a graduate of Carnegie Mellon University and Harvard University. He regularly blogs about project management and virtual teams at TheCouchManager.com.*

Bruce Harpham: How did you get started in project management?

Hassan Osman: I've been involved in various projects for many years. Thinking back to my graduate studies at Carnegie Mellon, there was a summer project where I served as the project manager. I led a team of six graduate students at the Software Engineering Institute at Carnegie Mellon. I learned all the project management basics on this project—putting together Gantt charts, understanding scope, defining goals, and so forth. My early roles were in the information security field, and my success in those roles heavily involved project management.

© Bruce Harpham 2018
B. Harpham, *Project Managers at Work*, DOI 10.1007/978-1-4842-2668-1_9

Harpham: What was the objective of the project you built during your graduate studies?

Osman: The project was called SQUARE—Systems Quality Requirements Engineering Methodology. The Software Engineering Institute sponsored the project to improve software security. The objective was to build security directly into the development process as opposed to viewing it as an afterthought. Our customer on the project was an asset management company that wanted to add security orientated software development processes into their organization. The project also led to several professional publications, including one at the IEEE.

My graduate studies focused on information security policy and management, which helped me understand how to defend companies from hackers. The focus of my studies was more on the management practices and policies, rather than the technical aspects, to address continuous security threats. The challenge was that security is a very dynamic field, and one defensive tactic may be successful for a time until attackers found a way around it.

Harpham: What is a project management practice that you learned the hard way from a failure or a challenge?

Osman: While I was at Ernst & Young [now called EY], I started in the information security consulting group and later moved into project management consulting. My work focused on independent program reviews [IPRs]. My assignment was to analyze multi-year, multi-million-dollar projects and programs to find out why they were failing, and devising solutions to get them back on track.

On these large efforts, I found a common thread behind many of the failures: the lack of an integrated project management schedule. This problem manifested itself as a lack of situational awareness of metrics, including an understanding of how much work was complete, how many milestones were remaining, and how resources were assigned.

I've worked with a lot of Fortune 100 companies in my career. You would imagine that they would follow top-notch practices regarding how they run their projects and programs. However, that's not the case. My lesson learned from these experiences is that it is worth the time and effort to flesh out a detailed integrated schedule when you are working on a complex project.

Harpham: Why do you think that major organizations are failing to follow these best practices?

Osman: It depends on the situation. In some cases, the people involved lack the skills required to execute these best practices. There's an idea that a high-level project schedule shown in PowerPoint is enough to get the job done. That approach can work on small projects or projects with low complexity.

Project managers often struggle with how to act in the face of uncertainty. Many in the field view uncertainty and information in a binary way: either I have full information or I have nothing. In fact, information about a project lies on a spectrum, where you have varying degrees of information certainty along it. A smart way to plan and revise the plan in the face of incomplete information is by doing what's called "rolling wave planning." The idea is to continually revise and update the plan and schedule as you acquire additional information.

Harpham: This misconception is that one creates the schedule at the beginning of the project as opposed to an ongoing effort.

Osman: Exactly right.

Harpham: It sounds like the problem is not a lack of good ideas, methodology, or process. It appears that these good ideas are simply not used in execution.

Osman: A lot of times, people blame the methodology or process for their difficulties. In fact, they should look at the lack of adherence to the project process or methodology instead.

Harpham: What is your approach to managing conflict and upset stakeholders on projects?

Osman: In one of my previous roles, there was a major conflict caused by a vague statement of work. Unfortunately, vague SOWs [statements of work] are not exactly rare. When you set the scope, you believe your mission is to deliver requirement A, but the customer reads it as A+B. It's a contentious situation because you want to balance not losing the customer with not losing money on the project.

I've been in situations where you're sitting across the table from the customer saying, "Here's what I understood. But you're telling me something different." In those cases, your negotiation skills come to play because you need to work through the situation. The best way to approach those situations is to be as honest as you can. Ultimately, you have to remember that you're dealing with other people—they probably have the same sort of fears and similar goals as you do. The customer usually understands that disagreements are based on business realities, such as the project's profitability, and that you're not "out to get them" on a personal level. I find that I'm able to connect with the other person in a disagreement when we both share our situation and the pressures that we're facing. That transparency tends to encourage the other side to work with you instead of against you.

Keep in mind that you're ultimately dealing with another person, rather than a contract. It's a powerful paradigm shift to apply to any negotiation situation.

Harpham: What is the most complex project you've led and what did you learn from that experience?

Osman: I led a $45 million two-year collaboration program at Cisco. I served as the senior program manager on this effort and we delivered this program to a Fortune 100 company in the pharmaceutical industry. I led a dedicated team of fifteen engineers and five project managers [with other staff on a part-time basis] to deliver an audio-video communication solution that would be used by 80,000 users across the world. My assignment was A to Z delivery: initiation, planning, execution, monitoring, closing, and handing it off to Day 2 operations. The project was complex because we had to integrate multiple communication technologies—audio services, WebEx, telepresence, and network services. In addition, we had to deliver this program on a global scale—the United States, the United Kingdom, Australia, China, Japan, and other countries. It was one of the most challenging projects I've led so far.

Even though we had some issues with the program, I'm pleased to say that the customer was happy with the results. That's what ultimately matters.

Harpham: What was most challenging for you on this project from a leadership standpoint?

Osman: We had people who were used to working in silos and had to bring them together to work on the project. In this context, I define working in silos as individuals being isolated in their roles and not interacting with a larger team to think through dependencies that might affect what they're doing. For example, an engineer working on a document to draft requirements without collaborating with other engineers on different technologies—that could be a dependency. It was challenging because I needed to change the mindset and behavior of the team members, and that's not always easy when they're used to working in a certain way.

As a senior program manager, my role was to make sure that the various project work streams were communicating frequently and effectively. Further, each project team needs to understand how their work supports and impacts other project teams. Everyone was under a lot of stress to deliver on the project, so it's natural to focus on your own work and goals.

Harpham: In that context, it's understandable that people will want to focus their effort on what they can directly control as opposed to the program during stressful work periods.

Osman: That's a common problem. Many program managers face this challenge. You are partly fighting against human nature. It's easy to focus on what you can control.

Harpham: That's part of the value of program management. You can point out: "If you take that approach, Jane will fail. If Jane fails, the entire program is at risk."

Osman: Absolutely. The key is to foster a "one team" mentality across multiple projects. We either hang on together or we hang next to each other.

Harpham: In your consulting work and your current assignment, you have the opportunity to see many project managers in action. What are you seeing regarding recurring blind spots for project managers?

Osman: First, the failure to identify the right stakeholders for the project at the beginning. Over and over, people may get into the project execution phase before they realize that there was a person with a huge stake in the project and they were not involved. In some cases, it could be that a senior leader at another division is working on something that requires a project to be put on hold.

For example, we once started a wireless technology implementation project. Several months into the project, right in the middle of installing access points in one of the buildings, we were told that we should pull them all out because an executive in another division had already approved a major renovation project for that building. Had that executive been involved from the get-go, we would have delayed the entire project until after the renovation was complete.

When I studied for the PMP certification, stakeholder management had just acquired greater recognition in the PMBOK Guide. Specifically, I noticed the emphasis on properly identifying stakeholders in the initiation phase. It's important to identify and engage all stakeholders, whether they are a supporter of the project or not. PMI's increased recognition for stakeholder management is helping to address the situation, which many project managers struggle to effectively work with stakeholders.

The second blind spot is scope creep. The challenging aspect is that scope creep occurs gradually. They call it "creep" for a reason. You may not notice the problem until it is too late. There's a tension between striving for customer satisfaction and maintaining your commitment to schedule and scope. If the scope keeps getting adjusted, you're unlikely to hit your deadlines.

Harpham: Regarding the blind spot with stakeholder management, how do you navigate political considerations to engage effectively in a large organization?

Osman: There are two ways to identify and work with stakeholders in a large organization.

First, start off with a top-down strategy. Whenever possible, you want to engage the leaders of a group. Leaders tend to be well connected internally and have a broad perspective. They can help think through how the project will impact the company. I like to start with a simple email where I introduce myself, explain the project objective in one sentence, and ask whether the project will impact their work. The email ends with the request: "Who do I need to work with on your team to make sure we are aligned for success?"

If you're based in an organization with thousands of people, you cannot reach every single person or department. For example, if you are running a technology project, focus your efforts on senior technology leaders like chief information officers [CIOs]. This approach works though there is an art to doing it well.

The second strategy is "inside out." Start with your list of core stakeholders and ask each one for suggestions regarding who will be impacted by the project. For example, I like to ask if they know of any initiatives currently in progress that may affect the project. If so, who should I connect with to discuss that concern? It's a bit of grunt work to get this done admittedly. However, the onus is on the project manager to think through these issues and reach out, over and over again, to stakeholders to make sure all the right people are involved.

Ultimately, the project sponsor will need to make a decision on how much to engage certain stakeholders. Before the sponsor gets involved on stakeholder issues, the project manager needs to do their due diligence to identify the stakeholders.

Harpham: You may start by identifying ten stakeholders on the project and then seek their assistance in identifying additional stakeholders and their significance to the project.

Osman: That's right.

Harpham: Let's explore your current assignment at a Cisco project management office [PMO]. There are different types of PMOs—some set standards, others provide training, and others directly run projects. How do you determine if you're being successful in the PMO context?

Osman: The PMO plays several functions: developing processes and directly leading projects. The organization also plays a role in financial management: understanding revenues and expenses on the projects that we run. I think of my PMO as a "hands on" PMO. We actually deliver the projects through our project, program, and portfolio managers. I demonstrate that we're successful in several ways. The success and skill development of our people is an important measure. Standard project management metrics are also part of our measures: budget, schedules, and profitability.

Harpham: Regarding the people development aspect—what does that look like? Is there a career path to grow professionals from the project manager role to the program manager role?

Osman: We use a "three E's" perspective: education, experience, and exposure. For education, that means ensuring that people get project management training, leadership training, and certifications. For exposure, this means observing [i.e., "shadowing"] and assisting on progressively larger projects over time. Finally, experience matters in order to build skills and confidence.

The book *The Start-up of You*, by Reid Hoffman and Ben Casnocha [Crown Business, 2012], has been a helpful resource in my thinking in this area. The authors point out that the value and depth of work experience varies considerably. For one person, twenty years of experience means "one year of experience repeated twenty times." For another person, their twenty years of experience may have covered a variety of tasks and increasing responsibility.

My philosophy as a PMO leader is to focus on growing people with new experiences and challenges. You don't want to simply repeat what you did last year. Instead, I think you ought to build on past experience as a foundation to reach new heights.

Harpham: The combination of development activities is helpful. In certain areas, a seminar may be the right way to develop. In other cases, the person may need to be challenged with a new responsibility.

Osman: That's right. You want to coordinate all of these activities together with a professional development plan. Take into account where you are today versus where you want to go. Then you can use the three E's—education, exposure, and experience—to move toward your career goal.

Harpham: What are your thoughts on the agile project management methodology?

Osman: In its purest form, I think of agile as a product development methodology. I'm not involved in developing new software or products in my PMO management role. However, I see value in using agile concepts in our process. I like the idea of developing a process, experimenting with it, and using the "fail fast" concept. If it doesn't work out, we learn from the process and can adjust accordingly.

Harpham: It's helpful to keep agile's origins in software product development. It may be difficult to apply it in some contexts. For example, if someone makes a mistake on software code, it can be corrected with relative ease. If a mistake is made with the foundation of a skyscraper, it's much more difficult to adjust that error. Perhaps agile will evolve further to adapt to other contexts in the future.

Osman: Absolutely.

Harpham: You've created an online course on managing virtual teams. Why did you create the course and what is your approach to the topic?

Osman: I saw a need in the marketplace for better understanding of how to manage virtual teams. Over the past twenty years, we've seen a steady increase in virtual team activity across the world. There's a different skill set required to manage a virtual team effectively compared to a traditional co-located team. When you're in the same physical space, you can read body language and better understand mannerisms. Keep in mind that we're a social species—we work best when we're face to face with others. However, that working arrangement is being disrupted with the rise of virtual teams.

In my current role at Cisco, I work from home ninety-five percent of the time. I lead a team that is spread across the east coast of the United States and other global locations. In the past, I've led teams across nearly every time zone in the United States, as well as various international locations. Those experiences have equipped me with a new skill set.

Trust is the biggest challenge involved in managing virtual teams. For example, how can I trust that people are getting their work done? In the course I teach, I break trust down into a simple formula. Trust equals reliability plus likability. That means you can increase trust by increasing reliability, likeability, or both. It's also important to view trust on a spectrum—it's not an on/off switch [trust vs. no trust].

To increase reliability, there are several methods. At the beginning of any project, you want to verify the skills of the project team members. Make sure that they are qualified to do the job at hand. Leading by example is another strategy that I cover in my course. As the project manager, you need to be explicit at what you want, especially in a virtual team environment where you lose a lot of facial and body language signals.

Increasing likeability is another method to pursue. There are a lot of studies that show that people who like you end up trusting you more. There's a tendency to be more transactional—exclusively focusing on business activities— in a virtual team environment because there's no watercooler chitchat. To counter that tendency, I recommend making time for team building exercises and allocating a few minutes on conference calls for social matters. Finally, look for an opportunity to have at least one in-person meeting to build intimacy and cohesion for the team.

Harpham: Viewing trust as a spectrum is helpful. That perspective means that we can gradually improve trust levels over time. Anything else you would like to add on virtual teams?

Osman: Managing offshore teams is a subset of managing virtual teams. To succeed, it's important to look for nuances and look for cultural factors that may shape how people interact with you. In some cultures, there's a view that saying no is rude, so you have to manage around that.

The best way to address this is to use a softer message and approach than a direct no. For example, stating disapproval by starting with: "I see it differently…" and then explaining your point and asking, "What are your thoughts about that?" or "Would that work for you?" to have them agree to your "no" through consensus. Some cultures have to "save face," - a direct no would be too harsh for them to digest.

As the project manager, you have to adapt your communication style to suit the team.

Harpham: The perspective on saying no or raising objections is interesting. Project managers sometimes ask their teams to challenge them or present new ideas. However, if the project team comes from a culture that highly values authority or deference to leaders, that request may fall flat.

Osman: Absolutely. In other cases, developing a consensus is a challenge. I have seen a case where challenging someone older than you is considered rude. For the project manager, it's important to understand these nuances. If you are unaware of these issues, it's easy to significantly add time to the decision making process and slow down the project.

Harpham: Building on the communication theme, let's turn to your book *Don't Reply All* on email best practices. What are some of your effective email practices?

Osman: I was looking to solve a specific problem with the book: we're all struggling with a high volume of email. In many cases, email is the default mode of communication given that people have different schedules and may be working in different locations. Ultimately, improving the quality of email communication is my main concern.

Over the years, many people have stopped reading emails in depth. Instead, they have developed the habit of quickly scanning their emails. I know some people who simply delete emails that are more than a few paragraphs long on the assumption that those urgent matters will result in a call or a follow up. Writing an extremely long email puts the onus on the reader to interpret and understand what you're saying.

Let's start with the "reply all" email feature. This is one feature that you should use with care. You want to avoid sending irrelevant messages. Many people use this feature in a casual way, which adds to email overwhelm.

If you're assigning a task in an email, I recommend using the "three W's": who, what, and when. Every task should have all of those in order to be understood. If you're sending out an email to your team, an action should be addressed to a specific individual [the "who"]. The "what" is an explicit description of what you want to happen. Finally, the "when" should be a specific time and date— the deadline. You can write an action item in a single bullet point as long as you address the three W's of who, what, and when.

Another problem is to write an email to your entire team by stating something like: "Hey team, I need X." The problem with that approach is that you're not assigning a clear owner for the task. In that case, the bystander effect kicks in—where each individual tends to assume that someone else will step in to handle the issue, and therefore, nothing happens.

Finally, having a clear "what" is important. If you write that you want a short report on a topic, you need to be clear. Short might mean half a page or five pages, depending on who reads the email. The message needs to be direct and clearly describe what you want.

Regarding email length, I recommend writing emails that are five sentences or less. When an email gets too long, the recipient would likely get confused because they would be unclear about whether the sender wants them to do something or just be informed about general information. If an email is strictly meant to inform someone, I recommend writing FYI [for your information] at the beginning of the email to clarify that point. The five-sentence rule is a heuristic rather than an absolute guideline. I also like to write a short summary at the beginning of the message. The approach is based on a common Internet abbreviation: TL;DR [too long; didn't read].

In cases where you have a lot to communicate in an email, I recommend breaking the message into two parts. The first part is labeled "quick summary", which is five sentences or less. The second part is labeled "details", which adds all the details and supporting facts you consider relevant. For example, if you expect the reader to take an action or deliver something, put that request into the quick summary section and tell them that the supporting details are below.

Harpham: What are some of the books that have been significant to your professional growth?

Osman: I'm a voracious reader of non-fiction books. I'll mention *The 4-Hour Workweek* by Tim Ferriss [Harmony, 2007]. The book points out how to use the 80/20 principle in your work. You have to be effective first [choose the right, high-value tasks to work on] before you become efficient [optimizing your approach]. That's a lesson that has been powerful to apply.

Harpham: What does your personal productivity system look like?

Osman: My approach has been influenced by David Allen's excellent book *Getting Things Done* [Viking, 2001]. I'm a big believer in the fact that if you don't write down tasks or other important data, they will disappear. If I'm in a meeting with someone and the other person doesn't write down tasks, that's a red flag to me. I'll become concerned that the task will be forgotten. In our world, there's no way to keep up with all the information coming your way unless you use a system of some kind. In some cases, I may write up a meeting summary email to make clear what I expect to happen.

Harpham: What emerging trends and opportunities in business and technology over the next three to five years have your interest?

Osman: I believe that work arrangements will continue to move to a virtual context. I think virtual work adoption will increase dramatically. Technologically, the tools and infrastructure that support virtual work are becoming better and more widely available. Economically, virtual work arrangements are an attractive way for companies to reduce expenses, such as office rental and upkeep. Virtual work also means you have access to talent from across the world as opposed to your local area. This trend means professionals will need to develop their communication skills to higher levels, including developing better skills with phone and email communication. Likewise, delivering a presentation through an online tool like Cisco's WebEx will rise in importance.

Virtual work is also a way to address growing demands for work/life balance. For instance, I am unlikely to accept a traditional job at a different organization because of the excellent flexibility I have with my present role. Virtual and work from home arrangements are also an excellent way to reduce commuting and pollution. It's a win-win for everyone.

Chapter Summary

- Recommended books include *The 4-Hour Workweek* by Tim Ferriss and *Getting Things Done* by David Allen.

- A common failure point in large projects and programs: the lack of an integrated project schedule that brings together all work and activities.

- Process and methodology: Inconsistent use of a project management methodology or process is a significant threat to project success.

- Two strategies to identify critical stakeholders: The top-down strategy involves engaging executives or other leaders to determine how or whether the project will impact their organization. The inside-out strategy is to ask your project team and well-informed stakeholders to assist you.

- Strategies to improve results with virtual teams: Look for ways to gradually develop trust, reliability, and likability. For example, resist the tendency to act in a purely transactional manner when interacting with virtual teams.

Ilana Sprongl

AVP, Enterprise Project Management Office, TD Bank Group

Ilana Sprongl *has over 20 years of experience in project delivery and process improvement for financial, ecommerce, manufacturing, and small businesses. Much of her career has focused on program and project delivery improvements, including the combination of agile and waterfall delivery methods to meet business needs. A skilled public speaker and trainer known for engaging employees through motivation, communication, and rewards, Sprongl is renowned for her ability to simultaneously respond to the need for change while using disciplined change management principles.*

In her current role as Associate Vice President (AVP) in the Enterprise Project Management Office (EPMO) at TD, Sprongl supports the continual improvement of project processes and the project management life cycle. She has also led the development of responsibilities, including TD's first agile-based delivery methodology and a new program delivery framework. Prior to joining TD, Sprongl supported project management activities in the ecommerce industry, aligning software delivery timing with client project delivery to ensure customer satisfaction.

In her spare time, Sprongl volunteers her time and speaking skills to support organizations like PMI. She mentors several PMs and fellow Western University (London, Ontario) alumni, and engages in fundraising activities supporting local healthcare.

© Bruce Harpham 2018
B. Harpham, *Project Managers at Work*, DOI 10.1007/978-1-4842-2668-1_10

Bruce Harpham: How did you first get exposed to the world of project management?

Ilana Sprongl: By accident! In the late 1980s and the early 1990s, project management wasn't yet a career path. Project management offices were starting to become more common. I found myself running small projects to improve business processes. It was the dawn of Microsoft Office and I helped small businesses build out their processes and use this technology. I worked with yoga studios and other small companies. It was a step-by-step process: defining what you will do, making sure that your stakeholders carry out the program, and more.

My first formal project management experience was at a dot-com company in the late 1990s. The company had a major client who wanted to leave because they didn't understand how work was being delivered and the timing. I put in place a project management process for that client using a waterfall process. Subsequently, that process was rolled out across the company.

Harpham: What was the nature of the dot-com company?

Sprongl: It was a software-as-a-service company serving the ecommerce industry. The company has since gone out of business. They built websites for a number of companies selling gifts, flowers, and clothing. This was the first time that I thought about project management as a profession and what it meant for a company to use it. I also learned the kind of support that project managers need to be successful.

Harpham: Client frustration was a driving force for project management in that company?

Sprongl: They wanted to know what they were going to get and when.

Harpham: At what point did you move into the banking industry?

Sprongl: I joined TD in 2010. I joined the online channel to help build the PMO for that area.

Harpham: Was this PMO in existence before?

Sprongl: The whole group was new. At the time, TD had a central EPMO [Enterprise Project Management Office] for the whole company. They had some basic guidance for project managers to use. We built out a much more detailed methodology that was geared toward activities in the online world.

In a standard PM process, you think about going through stage gates, gathering requirements, and so on. That process doesn't consider the reality of a web property: the need to have mockups, wireframes, and related specifications that go beyond a standard piece of software.

Harpham: What was the process to standardize project work? Sometimes these efforts to standardize are perceived as administrative overhead. Or these efforts can be seen as creating consistent results.

Sprongl: It was a bit of both. Some people really loved it—especially in areas where that had not been included in processes before. Areas that were impacted by the changes, such as phone channel, were included earlier in the process to ensure that their teams had the right tools to support the changes. They were happy to be included and consulted. On the other hand, those who had to run the checklist and do all the steps were not always happy. To manage the transition, a change management perspective is helpful. What's in it for everybody involved?

Consider the project manager's perspective. In the old world, the project manager kept track of activities using whatever process they came up with. If they missed consulting or working with somebody, the attitude was: "We'll catch it later."

That approach was contrasted with a new world to get that all done up front. As a result, it feels like it takes longer to make progress in the beginning. To address that concern, we point out the benefits—that subsequent parts of the project run better and you have the right people in the room from the beginning. That means fewer delays, rework, and stress later in the process.

When we rolled out that methodology and subsequent methodology changes, I found that it was better to engage the teams as you build the methodology. When you do that, it is easier for people to understand the benefits and you tend to achieve buy-in more easily.

Harpham: What would that engagement look like? Is the conversation: "We're changing the project methodology. What are your suggestions?"

Sprongl: Generally speaking, I find that you're more successful if you bring a proposal and request feedback rather than presenting a blank piece of paper. For example, here's a new process—a new set of templates or gating procedures. And then you say, "Here's what we're planning on doing. What do you think about it? How will this work for you? Is there anything here that wouldn't work for you? Why?"

I suggest avoiding handing out a blank piece of paper and asking people to design what they want. That approach tends to lead to chaos. It's better to provide a straw man for everyone to poke at. "Here's the model or template we're thinking about. How do you feel about that? Do you think we're missing anything? Is there a step that we need to add?"

When you're going through a process redesign for project management, a lot of things in the old process are just there from tradition. The meaning and the reason behind old processes have long been forgotten. Using the Five Whys technique from requirements management is helpful here. Ask people why they want a given step or activity added. In many cases, the real reason is often not relevant in the current circumstances.

Harpham: What's an example of a process that was based on tradition that was later revealed not to be necessary?

Sprongl: We had one step in a process where everyone staunchly informed us that you can't buy hardware before a business case is approved. Well, that wasn't actually the case. The actual approval was that someone had to approve the spending and any ongoing costs associated with it. Since ongoing spend was typically approved through a business case, people assumed that a business case process was required.

This assumption was preventing people from buying hardware in time to actually start development. Hardware can have a three- to six-month–lead time, depending on what you need to build on. If you have to wait until the whole project cost is detailed down to twenty percent accuracy to make those hardware purchases, you're easily going to extend your project timeline by a year.

If you can get that hardware approval earlier, you have better options. You simply need to think about the implications: Can we repurpose the hardware for something else if the project doesn't go through? If we can't repurpose it, what's the cost to carry it versus the cost to delay the work?

Harpham: What kinds of hardware or equipment do you mean?

Sprongl: My background is almost entirely software development, so it's usually something like special servers or something like that. Most organizations, especially large ones, have larger lead times because they don't purchase one computer—they purchase five hundred at a time.

Harpham: It sounds like this was a major roadblock.

Sprongl: Right. Everybody said, "Oh, it's policy." But that was not the case. There was a complete side step of the real policy and what the policy was designed to achieve.

Harpham: Was there a suggestion that added to the methodology in a positive way?

Sprongl: The Five Whys concept typically occurs in requirements, business analyst training, or requirements management. We took that Five Whys idea and sprinkled it throughout governance and recommendations. The idea is to get to the root cause or issue by asking "Why?" five times in a row to dig deeper into a process or way of thinking.

When I think about reasons for project failure, scope shift is often an issue. People want to spend their budgets before they lose them. I've seen that in every organization that I've been part of. Unfortunately, that means that people start spending without a well-formed plan.

Often, you see cases where the project will start and people think they understand the problem they have. In fact, people jump too quickly to a solution. For instance, they might say, "I need a database to get this information." Well, the minute that you say, "I need a database," then you're jumping to a solution. The better question to ask is: "What information do you need for your goal?"

Harpham: Can you share an example of people jumping to a solution stage too quickly?

Sprongl: The database example I mentioned previously is common. People are looking for a particular piece of data, so the assumption is: "We need a database." However, the data is often already in some system, so you just need a way to get it out. I have seen many cases where someone asks for a database—and that request needs to be questioned. You might not need to build or configure a database. Maybe what you need exists somewhere else in an existing system.

Harpham: Building a database would be overbuilding in that case.

Sprongl: Yes, that's right.

Harpham: How would you approach the request differently?

Sprongl: There are different ways to think about software development projects. How modular do you want to be? How much do you want to be reusable versus throw away with the next version? Do you want to engage a consultant to build something custom? Is there existing software that you can use? Often when people come up with a project idea, they have software in mind.

Harpham: The idea of "I have a shiny new tool that I want to use" way of coming up with project ideas.

Sprongl: The requirements they put together for the requirements of the project are sometimes based on the shiny new tool rather than what they actually need. Unfortunately, that approach often leads to customization of the shiny new tool, which is harder to maintain and use.

A guiding principle we use is: Be clear on what you want, not just what you think you need. It is a concept we use in sponsor onboarding training.

Harpham: Let's explore sponsor training. Executives are usually great in their field of work, but perhaps they are new to the project sponsor role. They want to drive the project to success, but it's new territory at the same time. How do you guide an executive on sponsoring a project well?

Sprongl: At TD, we actually have sponsor onboarding. It's a key part of what we do for sponsors of our major projects. I believe passionately in doing that. Sponsors definitely have responsibilities on their projects that they need to understand. They have to bring the project vision and they are the voice of the customer. They also bring the business value perspective: Is there value in building this software or project?

If they cannot articulate the value and vision, then we have a problem. We might deliver the project, but it might not be what anybody needs. It's important to have that conversation up front before resources are used.

Once the project vision and value is clear, the sponsor's role expands to support. Ultimately, the sponsor is the champion of the project. If you have a sponsor who can't be bothered to attend project steering committee meetings or encourage project participants to do their best, then we have a problem. The sponsor also helps navigate competing priorities. Another leader may have different priorities and want to allocate their resources to their pet project. The sponsor plays a role in addressing priorities and organizational issues. The onus is on the sponsor to make people understand their own work and the benefits of the project.

Harpham: What kind of feedback do you get from people who have gone through this onboarding process?

Sprongl: Generally, we get very positive feedback. A lot of what I hear is people saying, "This is all common sense, but I never really stopped to think about it." After all, we're talking about bright, intelligent people. You don't get to be an executive sponsor anywhere without being a bright person. However, you're so busy with your daily job responsibilities that you don't have much opportunity to think about a project and your role on it.

When an executive becomes a project sponsor, they still have all their other work responsibilities. Projects get added on top of everything else they have to do. Executives usually have very competent teams working with them and so we tend to assume that things will get done. In projects, the question becomes how well the work is done and how it will be adopted, especially since you may have to interact with people who are outside of your regular team.

Until you sit down with the executive and walk them through the project process, they may not fully understand it. It's the difference between them saying, "Yes, that makes sense" to actively understanding what they need to do. When we go through the onboarding session, there's a practical emphasis: "You need to support the project and this is what that means. Here's what it means to run a project steering committee. You get input from peers and experts, but it is still your decision."

Other points to cover include the importance of "lessons learned" and observations throughout the project rather than leaving it to the end of the project. For example: "What did we learn during the initiation phase? Did we engage all of our stakeholders effectively?" Then take that learning and apply it to next phase of the project.

Harpham: Lessons learned can be powerful if they are done well. How do you ensure that lessons learned exercises create value?

Sprongl: It's complicated. The natural inclination is to point fingers, even in a well-run lessons learned session. To address that inclination, we point out that it is a team exercise and to use "we" language in the meeting. Looking at a process or decision and asking how we can do better next time. That's better than saying, "You didn't talk to the stakeholders enough!" The principle is to encourage collaborative behavior.

Historically, I have seen teams conduct lessons learned sessions and extract some good nuggets of insight. Unfortunately, those insights tend to sit with that team. They don't get propagated beyond four or five people. It's important to leverage these lessons across the enterprise.

They are critical to learn from and use to update training. I've found that everybody likes to share "lessons learned" insights, but they don't go very far unless you update training, job aids, and other resources. Otherwise, there's no reminder to put that insight into action.

Our sponsor onboarding process includes the lessons learned from past sponsors. That's an example of connecting lessons learned back to your processes. If you don't do that, the lessons learned insight doesn't add much value.

Harpham: I like the idea of using lessons learned to adjust and improve processes. Can you share an example of how a process was improved through lessons learned?

Sprongl: We built the sponsor onboarding process initially because we realized that sponsors needed better training in how to be effective. Our methodology is under continuous improvement. It's not static. We're always getting feedback. If you see a pain point occurring over and over again in every large project, then there's probably some enterprise-wide problem or issue to address.

Harpham: How have you developed a project management career path at TD Bank Group?

Sprongl: TD has always invested in its employees and employee development. As the EPMO, we're interested in the health and well-being of our project managers. We want people to be happy with their career at the company.

Fifteen or twenty years ago, few people selected project management as a career. Today, there are college and university programs in the field. Many people in the field right now did not start their career with that background.

Most of the project managers I know came up through consulting or business analysis that fell into managing things. Project management itself grew up a little strangely. That's one reason why the project management career path is not well defined. The traditional career path in the field was that you get to "senior project manager" level and eventually leave the organization to do independent consulting.

The career path that we have developed includes senior-level roles. People can continue in project management at our organization and become executives. When you're running the largest projects and programs in the bank, you need to be an executive. It's a cross-enterprise effort that needs a person with the authority to lead multi-million-dollar projects and programs. We have vice presidents who are managing large programs at the bank. That is a relatively new concept. Relatively few executives have their focus on delivering a program.

Harpham: Was that career option available five or six years ago?

Sprongl: Five or six years ago, it didn't really exist in my experience. A small number of few senior project professionals came in on a contract basis, did their work, and left. When those people leave, the organization loses all of that knowledge and experience. There was a knowledge drain impact. At the same time, the organization needed another person to run a large program and there was nobody on the bench internally to do that.

Developing a project management career path is good for the organization—to retain and grow talent. For the employees, we also considered the question: "What if they want to do something other than project and program management?" In that case, another option is portfolio management versus the other path—executive program management. Both of those options go up to the executive level.

Harpham: Does the growth of the project management career path translate into growth in the absolute number of project managers at the organization?

Sprongl: We certainly have more executive-level project professionals than we did a few years ago. I would estimate that TD has somewhere close to one thousand project managers across the organization including business and technology project roles.

Harpham: The 2008 financial crisis and its aftermath had a major impact on the banking industry. Regulatory agencies make more demands. Governments passed new laws to regulate the industry. How has that change translated into the selection and nature of projects in your world?

Sprongl: The portfolio of projects we do has shifted. Across the news, you see regular announcements of new changes in regulations. Any time there is a regulatory change in Canada or the United States, TD has to respond to that change. Typically, that means we have a new project to respond to those requirements. The number of regulatory compliance projects has increased along with spending on such budgets.

Harpham: Has this environment also impacted other projects, such as projects to develop a new app?

Sprongl: I don't think so. Compliance is always engaged in projects at some point on all of our projects. Even back in the ecommerce company that I worked at, there were regulations to consider, such as PCI compliance. We had to address those requirements. Otherwise, you get fined or suffer other consequences. In terms of regular projects, compliance, legal, and other functions are just as involved now as they were before the crisis.

Harpham: Does regulation change impact the speed of the organization?

Sprongl: We need to make sure that we address regulatory changes as required. But it is a balancing act. If we move too fast, we could be burned. That is, have significant extra work to do after we launch something new—to deal with the regulatory impact. It comes down to the question of your risk tolerance. Are you willing to take the risk and potentially damage your brand? Or do you wait, see what happens, and then act as a late adopter? It's a strategic decision for the business to make. There's a reason they call it "the bleeding edge of technology." They say "bleeding" for a reason. Sometimes you can get cut.

Harpham: When it comes to the largest projects—the projects with the potential to impact the entire company—how do you assign the right people to lead these projects?

Sprongl: It's complicated. I don't think there's any cut-and-dried assessment to say, "Fill in this questionnaire and we'll know if you're ready to lead." It's a combination of experience—"Do you have the right experience in that area?"—and other factors like executive presence. In large projects, you are going to interact with executives—the CEO or other leaders. Are you ready to do that activity?

You could have the best project manager in the world—someone who does well with their team, but then can't speak to a leader. In that case, that person would be ineffective in leading that kind of project. However, those gaps can be addressed with a strong communications team. It goes beyond the individual leading the project. You also have to give thought to the support structure involved in the program.

Harpham: The star performer is only part of the equation. It's also important to look at the supports they can draw on.

Sprongl: If we took a really large program, like a train system or a giant software suite, the program manager is going to be responsible for understanding the dependencies. They need to know the budget, the key people on the team, and the stakeholders. That said, the program manager isn't going to know every single detail of the program and the projects. You might have a testing specialist who makes sure that the system works end to end, for example.

The program manager would rely on their team for support. The program manager's role includes digging into problems and solving those issues.

A combative, non-friendly project manager is probably not the person you want sitting on top of a megaproject. On the other hand, they don't have to be the expert at everything. Other people on the team need to be there for support and expertise.

Harpham: What are some of your personal productivity and organizational habits and methods?

Sprongl: The most useful technique is using a task manager. I use Microsoft Outlook. Everything I need to do in terms of my personal work tasks goes into that. If the task has a due date, I get reminders to prompt me to start working on it. It's the little things that you can lose track of. The big things tend to be front and center, so you don't tend to forget those.

The other point is to be honest with yourself about what you're going to accomplish in any given day. People make promises to themselves, like: "If I can get through these five tasks, then I can do something else." Those five tasks might not be realistic to achieve. If it's going to be really hard to get through those tasks, you're setting yourself up for disappointment.

For example, you might say to yourself, "If I get these five tasks done, I'll go for a coffee after work." Well, you got four tasks done. So you're exhausted and you go for the coffee anyway. We've all done that. You need to be realistic about what you can achieve.

In sales, they have a saying: Under promise and then over deliver. Set realistic goals for yourself. Set goals that you can achieve in your work.

Harpham: I've heard the suggestion to only book yourself up to the sixty to eighty percent level. If you go to one hundred percent booked and something changes, the stress level goes through the roof.

Sprongl: That's exactly right. The general rule of thumb is that nobody works more than eighty percent of the day on actual work. There's coffee, conversations, and so forth. Even if you work through lunch, you're still probably only about eighty percent productive. People forget this principle when they set expectations for productivity for themselves and others.

The better approach is: "I will get these three tasks done today and I'll do more if things happen to go smoothly." Make realistic commitments that you can keep. Don't overcommit yourself in the hopes that you'll make up for the time later. It's a commitment to yourself, not to other people.

At the end of the day, you go home with yourself, not your boss. If you keep disappointing yourself, that's not good for morale. Lower morale leads to lower productivity and other problems.

Harpham: I think some people are drawn to project management because they have an achievement orientation: I can check off that I completed this task or project. There's a potential shadow side to that tendency if you push it too far.

For the reader who is in another line of work, perhaps they're a software developer, and they're intrigued by project management. What is the entry point to get started in project management?

Sprongl: In today's world, it would greatly depend on their background. If you were a software developer, you might transition to a technology team lead role. After that, you might look into moving into project management.

For a student still in school, I would say to take some project management courses. After you graduate, look for a junior project manager or project coordinator role. It depends on your situation. Project management isn't a trade and there's no set apprenticeship.

Taking courses is never a bad idea. In fact, I have no PM letters after my name. I started my career before project management certifications were widely recognized. However, today is different—earning those certifications shows your interest in the career. It's a way of saying, "Yes, I'm serious about project management." You can earn an entry-level certification, like the CAPM [Certified Associate in Project Management] from the Project Management Institute, to get started.

I recently did some volunteer work with an organization where I trained them on project management. In that context, their projects included organizing events. I liken project management to baking a cake for an event. What's the scope? I'm making food for a potluck. What kind of dessert? A chocolate cake. Here's the ingredients, here's the timing, and all the other factors. Baking a cake is a mini project.

When you start thinking about your life in those terms, you start to see projects everywhere. Once you see those activities as projects, you can use project management methods to achieve better results. You likely have some experience from your life that can be seen as a project.

Harpham: What are some insights that you've learned from mentors over the years?

Sprongl: I had a manager tell me early in my career, "Control is an illusion." When you think about being a project manager, it's all about control. So, it was interesting to keep that concept in mind. You can suggest and you can plan, but you're not really controlling anything. It made me take a hard look at what I was doing. That observation impacted my entire management style.

We've all seen the dictator project manager. I was probably one of those earlier in my career. My manager at that time basically told me to quit that approach. If you want people to do things, you have to be nice to them. If people don't want to do something, it doesn't matter if you have it in your plan. They have to want to do it.

There's some research circulating around that suggests that people quit their manager, not their company. In my experience, that's true. If you're a command-and-control project manager, people are not going to want to work with you. You need to remember that projects are a team effort.

Harpham: Looking ahead over the next four to five years, what do you see as trends that are impacting project management in your context?

Sprongl: I think the definition of a project is going to shift. We still have megaprojects going on. However, if we look at the research, big projects rarely achieve their goals. Given that, how do we achieve our goals with small, nimble projects? Agile plays into that trend. Small, fast projects are likely to become more important.

Harpham: Any final words of wisdom for readers?

Sprongl: Your team is the project, not just you. It's all about the team working together to get something done.

Chapter Summary

- Revisit policies, processes, and traditions for value. What "business as usual" traditions and processes does your company have? Are these still adding value, or are they merely slowing down your projects? Use the Five Whys technique on your policies.

- Develop a career path for project managers. Sprongl has played a role in developing TD Bank's career path for project managers. It's an excellent strategy if you want to attract top talent for the long term.

- Executive sponsor training: Executives are busy and focused on their "day job." If you want them to succeed in sponsoring projects, consider adapting TD Bank's sponsorship onboarding process.

- Personal productivity: Be honest and fair with yourself on how much you can reasonably accomplish each day.

- Avoid starting with solutions. When you see a request for a specific solution (e.g., "Build a database for me."), challenge whether that is the best solution. There may be better options available to address the customer's goal.

Jason Fried

President, Basecamp

Jason Fried *is the co-founder and president of Basecamp, a Chicago-based company that builds web-based productivity tools that, in their words, "Do less than the competition—intentionally." The company also developed and open sourced the Ruby on Rails programming framework.*

Fried earned a Bachelor of Science degree from the University of Arizona. He is also a columnist at Inc. *magazine.*

Bruce Harpham: How did you first get started in running projects?

Jason Fried: Initially, we ran a web design firm. Clients hired us to perform website development. Primarily, it was companies that already had websites, so the work was mainly redesign projects. At first, I was an independent freelancer, and eventually, I started to hire other people. Ultimately, we built the Basecamp application because we needed a better way to manage the projects that we were producing for clients.

Harpham: Were you dependent on email and similar tools to manage projects in the early days of your company?

Fried: We used email and in-person meetings to get most of our project work done. That's still the way most people run projects. It's an okay way to run for a time. At a certain point, you need a system and consistency to ensure results.

© Bruce Harpham 2018
B. Harpham, *Project Managers at Work*, DOI 10.1007/978-1-4842-2668-1_11

Here's how I like to think about it: everyone knows their own mess, but when you work with other people, you have to get to know their messes too. That's where everything gets difficult. That's why I recommend the value of a shared, consistent system for the project team. That way, you don't have go around to everyone on the team asking for information.

Harpham: What did the pain and disorganization look like in your experience? Does it mean missing client deadlines?

Fried: There were a few different problems that I faced: missed deadlines, things you forget to do, and tasks slipping through the cracks. It could even be where somebody asked you to do something and then you wrote it down somewhere that wasn't reliable and easy to find, like a Post-it Note. Or you wrote down the task and you forgot to tell somebody else what they had to do.

There's also the impact on the client: how the project experience feels for the client. Does the client think you're organized? Does the client feel confident in your ability to deliver on what you say? It's not only the fact of how organized you are, it's also a question of how you are perceived by others. Simply put, do you have your sh*t together? Do clients believe you?

Following conversations effectively is another challenge. With email, conversations happen in fragments. People reply and there's a fragment of the conversation. Most email apps—almost all of them—speak in replies. It's very hard to get the full story about anything unless you go through a significant amount of quotes from past messages, use different colors, and so forth. It's very difficult to understand and have that information "on the record" where everyone on the team can see it. Everybody manages their email a bit differently. Someone may have deleted a reply. Someone may have replied, but not to everyone.

It's important to have one version of the truth when you're running projects. Email is not going to work for that. Email lives in different places so it is not a shared truth. A shared, single version of the truth that everybody has access to is important. That means there are no questions about who said what when. Nobody can say, "Oh, I never saw that" or "That was never sent to me," because you have a record that covers all of that in one place.

It's not just about dropping the ball. It's about having things on the record when you might need to refer to something or to prove something was discussed.

Harpham: I've seen projects where there is fear that an auditor will find some unfilled corporate requirement. People create the meeting agenda and check off that Bob attended. Then, everybody is asked to agree with the minutes of the meeting.

Fried: That's a good process to use for some companies. You're getting approvals and related points on the record. It's important to have a shared resource that covers this information.

Email is not a shared record. It's a distributed record. Fundamentally, distributed records are different: you don't ever know if they are in sync. Chat has the same problem: it's a fragmented record where many conversations may be happening at once. It's difficult to refer back and understand what's going on.

Harpham: How do you mange projects where the project team members are in different locations?

Fried: The answer is that you do nothing in person - everything happens in the system. That doesn't mean you will not have occasional conversations. Rather, anything that is important needs to be put in the system. In that way, everyone has access to the same information. If three out of four people are in one place, that fourth person may feel left out and unable to contribute.

Our company is widely distributed. We have fifty people in the company right now. Thirty-five of them live in different cities around the world. The company grew up that way so it is part of how we operate. Every product discussion, every important discussion, and every tiny piece of work that needs to be documented all happens in Basecamp. That way, we all have a shared truth for our work.

When you do work in person, you have to go back and document it later. You're writing down a different version of what happened because you're translating a memory of what happened. That's why it it's important to have those interactions directly in the system.

This approach can be frustrating for some people who are used to being in meetings and operating in person. You have to think about the long-term benefits. Projects are often fluid—people come in and others leave. If you only discuss projects in person, getting somebody new up to speed is very difficult to do. The new person is unable to understand the conversations and what has been done. By having everything documented, the new person will be able to get up to speed much more quickly on the project.

Harpham: You've advocated remote work arrangements in your writing. As a manager, what is your approach to making remote work effective?

Fried: My view is that there is no difference between remote and local. Even people working in the local office work the same way as people who work in different places. They do it through the system—Basecamp in our case. Then, it's not about remote versus local. It's about how you work with people in your organization.

I understand the traditional argument about valuing in-person work. The argument doesn't stand up for me, because just being in a place doesn't mean anything. Sitting at a desk doesn't mean you're working, it just means you're sitting at a desk. Typing on a keyboard doesn't mean you're doing work, it just means you're typing. The only way to evaluate whether someone is working is by looking at their actual work. The best way to look at their work is to look at what they produce and track their contributions. That means looking at what is assigned to the person, checking that tasks are getting done on time and which conversations they're participating in through the system.

I have been very careful to avoid creating two cultures: one for people who work in the same location as me and another for remote people. You don't want to treat remote people differently. You should treat people the same way, regardless of where they work.

If you're local, there's more chance to have informal conversations and that does tend to generate some local bias. However, that bias should not impact how you evaluate someone. That should be based on their work. Of course, this approach assumes you're doing knowledge or information work. If you're talking about retail sales or a restaurant, that's a different situation entirely.

Regarding the local bias, it's something to reflect on regularly. Earlier today, I had lunch with a few people who are in the same office as me. I can't do that with people who work in different cities. It's very important for the manager to avoid favoring people simply because they happen to be in the same location as you. That requires self-awareness.

Harpham: In reading your book *Rework* [Crown Business, 2010], you have some interesting perspectives on estimates. What is your approach to creating project estimates?

Fried: First of all, humans are generally terrible at making estimates.

It's important to state realistic expectations up front. When we did projects for clients, my view was to fix money and time. Therefore, scope became the variable factor. We would always hit the budget and schedule because we had flexibility regarding scope.

I would ask clients, "What do you want to do?" On hearing their request, I would often respond with, "I don't think we can do all of that in the time we have. However, I think we can do the following…"

If you want more scope, we can increase the time and money. We kept money and time fixed. Without that, there's no end. Without an end, it's difficult to make decisions. Of course, the project could end when you run out of money. However, that's a problem because the project is in limbo and the client is probably unhappy with the "result." My feeling is that you should always have something that is finished. If we get to the end and we don't deliver what we promised, that's on us as the project manager.

Harpham: Your observation is an interesting contrast to what I see on some enterprise projects. The scenario could be a $5 million enterprise project and the sponsor wonders to herself, "Well, I spent the money, we're eighteen months into the project, and I don't have any improvement to my systems. However, the project manager is still telling me that the project is on track but I don't have an end product."

Fried: It's basically impossible to anticipate every variable that will come up over a two-year period. That's why almost every long-term project exceeds the budget and schedule. Estimating a project over a two-year period is unrealistic. We would never take on projects like that as a general rule. If we did take on such a long-term project, I would never say, "This will be done by this date."

I would look out a few months and make a schedule estimate at that range. That tends to work much better. The secret is to make short-term estimates on your projects. Finish that amount of work and then make an estimate for the next chunk of work.

At our company, we only plan work out in six-week increments. We know there is a whole lot more than six weeks' worth of work to be done but we only plan for six weeks. Even with that restriction, we get it wrong sometimes and have to adjust scope. If you're trying to plan out a project with a two-year schedule and achieve something complicated, like an ERP [enterprise resource planning] implementation, it's just not going to work.

Many in the industry cheat or lie when it comes to promising these big projects. The consulting firms know it's impossible to deliver a complex technology project on time, on budget, and on scope. Unfortunately, the client doesn't know that. The client thinks that they're hiring a large consulting firm and that the consultants know what they're doing.

I should also add that I haven't run large multi-year projects. But I have heard horror story after horror story about these projects. I have intentionally focused on short-term projects because that's the only way I can be responsible to an estimate.

Harpham: Interesting to hear about the six-week planning rule. It almost seems that the further one plans into the future, the higher the "fantasy quotient" on the plan.

Fried: Exactly right. The further you attempt to plan into the future, it gets much more difficult to be accurate. It is pure fantasy to plan out years into the future. People aren't able to plan out what they will be doing in their own life in two years, so why would that approach work on a project?

Returning to the example of the multi-million-dollar ERP project, they may get it done. However, it's not done well. For instance, they may achieve their schedule but sacrifice quality. The system may be implemented but you may have to redo it to get the functionality you truly want.

In almost every case, shorter timelines on projects are the better way to go. In that way, you get into the routine of delivering smaller amounts of scope with reliability. You can then repeat that process until you complete the whole effort.

Harpham: What is your approach to designing "quick wins" on projects?

Fried: Let's take the client perspective. Recently, I was the client for a house construction project.

My architect and the contractor were the firms that I hired to do the project. As a client, it's very enlightening. I realized that you want to see progress on the project as a client.

Showing any progress is great. For example, I was excited to get an update from the project team. The contractor's update simply provided new pictures of the project—even when it was nothing more than a hole in the ground for the foundation. Technically, that wasn't a milestone on the project that the client needs to know about. However, that's absolutely what the client wants to see—evidence of progress. By designing for small wins, it's easy to show progress to the client on a regular basis as you progress through the project. Delivering quick wins builds confidence, trust, and momentum between the project manager and the client.

If you write a check to a design firm for $20,000 and you don't see anything for a while, you're naturally going to be suspicious. You have no right to be suspicious but you will probably have that feeling anyway.

However, if you receive updates from the design firm, such as, "Here's some early ideas for the logo and this is where we stand in the design process," that makes a big impact. Show the client that you are doing work and making progress on the project. I know a lot of design firms are afraid of showing work that is unfinished, because they're worried about creating a bad impression. However, you can easily address that possibility by explaining it to client: "This is a preliminary concept for the project. We are still developing multiple ideas and we wanted to share an example of what we are doing."

In contrast, if the designer disappears into the proverbial cave to do their work and doesn't communicate for a month, the client will start to freak out. In this case, the client has no idea if progress is being made. The client doesn't know if the designer has encountered problems or anything else about the status of the project.

It's about the process, sharing the work as you go, and writing frequent updates. Clients should get updates once per week if not multiple times per week. Share pictures of the hole in the ground or the equivalent for your work. I remember feeling wonderful that I could see progress on the house. Silence is bad on projects.

Harpham: There's an unspoken assumption with some project managers to stay quiet until they accomplish something large, such as completing a milestone. Yet, silence increases anxiety for the client or project sponsor.

Fried: Silence makes the client's concern worse and worse. Once distrust builds up, it is very hard to recover from that. Show your work and explain what you're doing to the client.

Harpham: The key is to show progress and provide updates even if progress made seems small?

Fried: Exactly. Project managers feel the need to deliver awesome results and that is the ultimate aim. Everybody understands that there's a process and many steps to go through. Bring the client to the cutting room floor so that they can see the process.

Harpham: In your book *Rework*, you write "Meetings are toxic." Can you elaborate on your perspective? For many project managers, meetings are an indispensable tool. How do you minimize meetings but still achieve the progress and connection you need to keep moving forward?

Fried: Allow me to be self-serving, but Basecamp is the answer for me. The problem with meetings is that they're live events. In most cases, a meeting is a discussion about a topic and you generally don't need to have a live meeting in order to have a discussion. In some cases, it is helpful to pull a bunch of people into a room. But most of the time, it is better for people to write up what they're thinking and add their thoughts over the course of a day rather than putting me on the spot in a meeting room. The added benefit is that you have everyone's thoughts on the record.

People think about a meeting as an hour of time. It's not. If you have six people in a room, it's a six-hour meeting. You pulled away six people to talk about something that could have been written up and discussed asynchronously in most cases. We use meetings as a last resort if there is no other way to address the issue. Meetings are also difficult to organize when you have people in different time zones or if people are out of the office on a given day. When you write up the topic and allow people to respond on their schedule, you have the benefit of getting their input.

I know that some people may object to this approach. They may say that it is slower to discuss the topic over a day. In a minority of cases, the answer is yes. Most of time, it is incredibly inefficient to pull a bunch of people into a room to discuss something that doesn't need to be discussed right now.

Harpham: If I'm a project manager and I adopt this practice, I could go from twenty meetings per month to four meetings. Is that reasonable?

Fried: Yes. Cutting down the number of meetings you have by twenty-five percent or fifty percent would be great. The people who are doing the work, they need the time to get the work done. As a rule, I don't want my people to work more than forty hours per week. That's enough. Forty hours is enough.

If every person has about forty hours of work time to get their own work done, that's enough. It's not enough if the company claws back twelve hours per week in the form of meetings and other activities.

I think of meetings as "company time" that takes away from an individual's ability to get their work done. If you put ten hours of meetings on somebody's schedule, they may well have to spend fifty hours at the office to get everything done. That's how you end up with people working longer hours. They are unable to perform well because they're tired and burned out.

A big-picture perspective is needed when it comes to meetings. On the short-term perspective, you may well think that it would be easy to organize a meeting to discuss a topic. If that is your approach on every topic and situation, you're taking time away from the true work people have to do.

Use meetings occasionally. Assume that most topics and issues can be covered over time. If everything needs to be discussed ASAP in a meeting, you have a deeper problem: your time management or expectations have problems.

Harpham: The forty-hour workweek is a key premise then. If you're routinely working more than forty hours, you may have a management problem.

Fried: Yes. If we take the forty-hour per week rule seriously, then you have to ask yourself what activities are you taking on? Are meetings adding value or taking it away?

In a lot of companies, meetings are a primary way to take away time from other activities. If you start with the principle of "My people work non-stop—whatever it takes to satisfy clients," you will face consequences. You're likely to be sloppy with your time and other people's time. I think of time and attention as an extremely limited resource.

It's interesting—companies typically have CFOs and they're careful on how they use their money. People have to create budgets and fight for money. Yet, they waste people's time like it's free. That's one of the broken ideas in modern business: the notion that time and attention are not treated as precious resources.

Harpham: Let's turn to the origin of the Basecamp product. What's the origin of Basecamp and how was it different from other project management applications on the market?

Fried: Basecamp is best suited for small companies. It is best for companies who think about project management as a communication problem. Basecamp is about communication, sharing thoughts, and getting feedback—rather than producing Gantt charts. Most people who use Basecamp are not project managers. They're people who need to run a project. It might be a designer or a business owner running projects and they decide that they need to get organized. Basecamp isn't a good fit for Boeing, where you're building an airplane or a satellite. If you're doing client services projects, it is a great tool for that context.

Harpham: What drives customers to use Basecamp?

Fried: Most of our customers come to Basecamp with some kind of homegrown system. Typically, that's a reliance on email, meetings, chat and so on. They're coming to Basecamp from a loose system, which works well up to a point. Typically, they come to Basecamp once they get to a certain number of employees—often once they hit five or six employees.

If you have two or three employees, a lot of companies manage to operate with an informal approach. Yelling across the office works at that level. As you get larger, you need a systematic approach.

Our customers generally don't switch to Basecamp from Microsoft Project or a similarly complex system. Usually, they have some kind of improvised approach. Once you have a few plates spinning and a half dozen people at the organization, you start to realize that improvised systems don't work anymore, because the owner or manager doesn't know what's happening. Even worse, the manager becomes a bottleneck on productivity because staff can't get fast and easy answers on what to do next.

I hear customers say, "I need a system to organize my work" rather than "I need a project management tool." People are frustrated with disorganization! Some simple structure goes a long way toward addressing these frustrations. Adopting a single place to understand what people are working on. A way to make announcements, a way to ask questions, and so forth. They're looking for a way to work. Basecamp is good for your organization if you have five to ten employees with no particular system in place. It doesn't tend to be a good fit if your company is over one hundred people who are trying to switch from an established project methodology to Basecamp.

Harpham: For readers who may not be familiar with Basecamp, can you give an idea of the product's scale?

Fried: We have two million companies with Basecamp accounts today. Inside those companies, there are dozens or hundreds of people who use Basecamp. We don't charge by the "seat." We allow an unlimited number of users per company to use the product for a fixed price.

Harpham: What is your leadership approach?

Fried: I recently read a wonderful book called *Turn the Ship Around! A True Story of Turning Followers into Leaders* by L. David Marquet [Portfolio, 2013].

The author is a former US Navy captain who commanded a nuclear submarine. The Navy assigned him to turn around the worst-performing submarine around in the Navy. Improvement was objectively measured in several ways, including the number of sailors who want to sail on the submarine again, down time, and repairs needed and other factors.

Traditionally, the military is focused on orders—giving orders and following orders. That's how a lot of companies operate. That's how we used to work in fact.

After reading this book, I changed my perspective on leadership. He changed the way people worked on the submarine. He realized that if he gave orders to everyone all time, then only one mind on the ship was truly working hard—his mind. Therefore, he was also the bottleneck because everyone had to come to him to get orders. Instead, he changed the perspective: I will no longer give orders except for a small number of cases, such as firing a weapon that could kill. Instead of coming to me for permission, I want you to come to me with intent.

Instead of asking, "May I turn the ship thirty degrees starboard?," the sailors changed their approach to say, "Captain, I intend to turn the ship thirty degrees starboard." If the Captain agrees, you have to follow through and you're taking the responsibility to carry out that action. In this case, you brought the idea to the company and you have the intent to do it. These approaches are very different—asking permission versus working with intent.

I don't ever give permission to do anything in our company any more. If you ask me for permission, the answer is no. Instead, you come to me with intent for what you plan to do. Then, I will cheer you on or ask you a few questions about it. The questions may help you to realize what you planned was not a good idea or an idea that needed to be refined. I don't want people to ask permission because that puts responsibility on me rather the individual.

Harpham: What do you keep as "reserve power" to yourself?

Fried: My emphasis is on the company vision and experimental ideas that an employee may not feel comfortable to explore. Recently, we launched a change to our pricing structure. I wanted to make a change to pricing because I felt the pricing approach we had was too complicated. Once a year or so, I will say, "Here's a big initiative I want the company to do." How that gets done is partially up to me and partially up to other people.

Harpham: What is your approach to personal productivity and running your day?

Fried: The best tool I have is the word no.

The only way to be productive is to have fewer tasks to do. I seek to avoid overburdening people with too many tasks, because I realize that approach doesn't work. I set the example that I work on one activity at a time. I push back hard against people who like to multitask and switch between activities. I don't use to-do lists, so I limit myself to one or two activities at a time. That approach forces me to focus. Over the past eight weeks, we've been working on the new rollout. That's all I have been focused on. There are thirty to forty other projects going on in the company, but I don't follow them in detail because my focus is on the rollout.

Once upon a time, I had the view that everyone should know everything that's going on in the company. However, I found that a weekly check-in is enough. Each Monday morning, everybody writes a short report on what they plan to work on in the coming week. That's enough information from management to understand the company.

Harpham: What are some of the important trends in technological or economic change that have your attention?

Fried: I want to help companies become calmer. There's a real anxiety piling up inside many companies. I hear about it constantly.

There's a sense that every task is ASAP and notifications are constantly going off. This is a toxic trend that we're pushing hard against with Basecamp. I want to be able to promise our customers that if they use Basecamp, their company will be a calmer, saner place. What are ways we can reduce notifications? For example, there is a new Basecamp feature called "Work can wait." It allows each person to set their own work schedule on any given day. Outside of those set work times, Basecamp will not send any notifications, emails, or other messages. All of that will be held until the next workday.

Chapter Summary

- Recommended books include *Turn the Ship Around!* by L. David Marquet, *Rework* by David Heinemeier Hansson and Jason Fried, and *Remote: Office Not Required* by David Heinemeier Hansson and Jason Fried.

- Client perceptions: As you manage the project, ask yourself how you come across to the client. Does the client think you're organized? Does the client have confidence in you? What can you do to show progress (e.g. sharing pictures showing progress on a construction project)?

- Support remote work. Fried's company has successfully used remote work arrangements for years. The right tools are only one part of the story. It's also important for managers to avoid "face-time bias" (i.e. showing favoritism to local staff over remote staff) in people management.

- The six-week planning rule: Fried recommends keeping detailed planning to a six-week horizon, and then use that experience to deliver the next part of the project.

Tom Atkins

President, Tramore Group

Tom Atkins, *CMC, PMP, ICD.D, is president of Tramore Group. He is an experienced executive and senior program manager. He advises public and private sector organizations on strategy, operations, and improving the effectiveness of enterprise-wide project management. He is past chair of the Board of Directors for the Rouge Valley Health System. Tom has completed executive programs at the University of Toronto's Rotman School of Management and UCLA's Anderson School of Management.*

Bruce Harpham: How did you get started in project management prior to establishing Tramore Group?

Tom Atkins: I've worked on many projects in different organizations. In 1994, I started TWA Consulting Services. In 1995, I acted as the lead consultant on the operational due diligence related to forming Symcor Services Inc. [Note: Symcor is an outsourced financial services company based in Canada that provides various services to Canadian banks, such as check processing, statement production, and related activities. Symcor is owned by the Bank of Montreal, Royal Bank of Canada, and Toronto Dominion Bank]. The scope of that project also included developing the vendor strategy and providing strategic advice related to establishing Symcor.

Harpham: How did you come to work on large projects, such as advising on the formation of Symcor?

Atkins: In brief, I was engaged by the Bank of Montreal, Royal Bank of Canada, and Toronto Dominion Bank to lead the operational due diligence to set up Symcor.

© Bruce Harpham 2018
B. Harpham, *Project Managers at Work*, DOI 10.1007/978-1-4842-2668-1_12

Harpham: So you received the call out of the blue one day to lead this project?

Atkins: The Symcor project opportunity resulted from a previous job I held. In the early 1990s, I was vice president and general manager for the Financial Line of Business at Unisys Corporation in Canada. During my time with Unisys, I dealt with the CIOs at various financial institutions. I led reviews of the cheque-processing operations and image processing viability at two of the Big Five banks among many other projects.

Harpham: It sounds like you have developed great depth in working with Canada's leading banks. How did you develop that expertise?

Atkins: In 1977, I was national accounts manager to the Big Five chartered banks [Royal Bank of Canada, TD Bank, Bank of Nova Scotia, Bank of Montreal, and CIBC] for Xerox Canada Inc. In the course of that role and later roles, I learned about the industry in depth.

Harpham: What happened to TWA Consulting Services?

Atkins: In 2000, the company was sold to Sierra Systems Group [SSG:TSE]. After that sale, I ran Sierra's business in Southern Ontario, including the GTA. Much of the work we did in that company involved delivering large and complex programs, such as Sarbanes-Oxley compliance for CIBC and Bell Canada. We also implemented new financial and human resources systems at the UN's High Commissioner for Refugees in Geneva. Most of the programs and projects we worked on at this time focused on large organizations in Southern Ontario and the Greater Toronto Area.

Harpham: Why did you decide to sell your consulting firm to Sierra?

Atkins: In 2000, we received several offers for the company and we decided to accept one of those offers.

Harpham: How did you come to form Tramore Group, a consulting organization focusing on program and project management?

Atkins: In late 2006, a little over a year after I left Sierra Systems, I decided to form a new business. I considered different areas we might work in. Many large organizations were not particularly good at delivering large, complex projects and programs. As a result, I saw a need to provide consulting relating to effective delivery of projects and programs.

Harpham: In the first year of the company, was the focus on the financial sector?

Atkins: No, the focus was on large corporations and public sector organizations. That includes banks but it was not limited to banks and financial institutions.

Harpham: When Tramore Group comes in to assist with large projects and programs experiencing difficulties, what does that look like to you?

Atkins: It starts with a large organization allocating a budget in the order of $5 million to $100 million or more to undertake a program. Then, the organization would often spend the budget and not end up delivering on the scope. Once we receive a call for help, our first step is to assess the situation and understand what has caused the initiative[s] to derail. For that, we typically assemble a team of senior consultants with experience in program and project management and work with key subject matter experts. The result of the assessment is then presented to a senior executive team at the client empowered to make decisions and recover the initiative[s].

Harpham: Why do you think such project and program failures continue to happen?

Atkins: In large organizations, we often see an expense control mentality. That approach works very well in many cases, like regular business operations. However, that approach doesn't tend to work well when delivering a large program. The default approach is line item management. For example, a senior leader might make decisions on who to appoint to lead these programs based on the cost of the individual, rather than on the basis of the individual's capability and experience.

From a cost perspective, appointing a current employee to lead a program or project is less expensive than bringing in an independent contractor or a consulting firm. As a result of the expense control mentality, you end up with people that lack experience in doing the work. The lack of experience often extends to the project sponsor.

As a consequence, variances on projects tend to be misunderstood. Variances may not be measured at all or only detected when they are very large. When cost over runs occurs, it is rarely attributed to poor estimation and planning. Instead, there's a view that cost over-runs are just a normal part of the process.

Harpham: It sounds like part of the problem lies in failing to appreciate the difference between normal operations and project/program work.

Atkins: They are very different activities. Executives at large companies are exceptionally well trained at running the day-to-day operations of their business. They tend to be concerned about client satisfaction, employee satisfaction, achieving service levels and responding to market pressures. They tend not to be focused on the need to rigidly manage the initiative's schedule, rigorously police the budget, and relentlessly contain the scope.

Harpham: Can you elaborate further on "relentlessly contain the scope?" What does it look like when that is done well?

Atkins: It starts with having a business case that defines the initiative's objectives, including its financial feasibility. Second, you have to have a change control process that is embraced by management or whoever plays the project sponsor role. Those managers must insist that no additional budget or scope is approved without going through the process. This process defines the impact of the proposed change on scope, schedule, and budget. It should also identify how benefits vary as a result of the proposed change.

Sometimes, the discipline breaks down. Management may say, "Listen, we need this change. Just add it." In that case, there's often no true understanding of the impact of that decision on cost or schedule.

Harpham: There's a perception that a small change doesn't warrant a process-based review?

Atkins: Or it could be a change that is viewed as important to do. In other situations, the change may appear simple on the surface. However, a proper impact analysis may show a material impact to cost or schedule. That analysis generally involves elaborating the work required to fully implement the proposed change. Without a proper process, often we see the cross impacts are not identified when the change is proposed, which results in significant variances identified in late stages, such as the testing phase.

Harpham: Regarding implementation of this discipline, do you see cases where the project manager may not feel confident about challenging a manager or executive when that leader fails to follow the process?

Atkins: That's one of many causes. Sometimes, you may have people who look at the project as "ticking off" completed tasks. They don't really know how to think about the project as a whole. They may not recognize a change as an addition to the scope. Or they might not understand how estimates are constructed. For example, an activity may require X work effort and it turns out that 2X is required to get it done. Some people may simply assign additional resources to complete that activity without thinking through the impact to the overall budget or the additional complexities that a 2X estimate may imply.

Sophisticated organizations understand their internal costs for day-to-day operations. However, many large companies don't recognize that their internal employees are a resource that costs money. Or they don't recognize all of their employees in that manner.

Harpham: What do you mean that companies do not recognize their employees as a cost?

Atkins: Consider the case of a large company with full time technology professionals on staff. That developer's work on the project, such as developing software, is likely to be reported correctly. I see a gap in most the other project activities performed by employees that provide daily advice and input on the project design for instance. These other activities are not understood or recorded as part of the project cost. As a result, there is not a true understanding of the project's total costs to the organization.

Harpham: Would this mean that the project's costs are often significantly understated?

Atkins: Project costs are complex to understand, so consider all that goes into it. Consider the cost of taking the appropriate time to create estimates. Consider a program with a $100 million budget. It would not be uncommon for the project to spend $25 to $30 million to complete the detailed requirements and design, understand how the benefits are going to be achieved, to socialize the initiative internally and all of the other activities required for a successful delivery. This diligence will result in a reliable estimate that is plus or minus ten percent or so. If you take a high-level approach to estimating, you wind up with estimates that are plus or minus fifty to one hundred percent or more.

Imagine this process as a funnel. At the top of the funnel, we can call the top stage "ideation." In that stage, you might hear something like, "We would like to introduce this new business function and apply it to 1,500 locations." At this point, the high-level estimate might project that it will cost $50,000 per location. Given those estimates, the project makes sense in terms of costs and benefits.

The next step down the funnel adds greater detail and precision. Activities at this stage may include high-level requirements, design, a project charter, and services and products from vendors. With this additional work, the revised estimate may be three hundred percent higher than the prior estimate. After completing this additional work, the project manager may discuss the idea with P&L owners, business owners, and other decision makers. The decision maker's response is often "We'd like you to investigate this further. Here is some seed money to take this to the next level. Go out, talk to some vendors, and get a better understanding on the program's cost."

If you issue RFPs [request for proposals], you will have additional information on prices and costs. Prices offered in an RFP are often different from negotiated pricing. Even though this is the case, you will have a better idea on the likely costs relating to vendors.

At the same time, you will probably realize that you need additional support to integrate the program into your existing systems and processes. That work may require purchasing additional professional services. As the projected cost increases, the need for project and program management controls tends to come up. The program manager role then has to coordinate the contributions of technology groups, the business groups, corporate support areas, and so forth. All of those groups need to participate in order to build a successful program. As this work progresses, your estimate is likely in the plus or minus fifty to seventy-five percent range.

Later, you drive down to detailed requirements. At this stage of the process, you may realize that you have to build three or four solutions for a given function to work. You didn't think about that fact until you started on the detailed requirements. As the details are developed, the cost tends to increase. However, the accuracy of the estimate improves. With these requirements in hand, you can start to think through how you will fulfill them. If you need development or testing, you may look at doing that activity internally, outsourcing it overseas or to another company. Your estimate is now in the plus or minus thirty percent range.

Subsequent steps of the planning look at people. For example, how much executive oversight is required for this program? What governance model will we use? Which vendors will we use and what will they cost? With continued work to develop these points, you may be able to get an estimate with a ten percent accuracy level.

To review: at the ideation stage, the estimate may be accurate to within three hundred percent. The next level of detail may yield an estimate accurate to within fifty to seventy-five percent. With detailed requirements, you may check to a thirty percent accuracy level. Once you select the team, hire vendors, hire professional services staff, and so forth, you can get to a ten percent accuracy level.

Harpham: Do you see a corresponding increase in the benefits side as you develop and better understand the cost structure of the program?

Atkins: The benefits we're pursuing are reasonably well understood at the beginning of the process. The manner in which the benefits are harvested is better understood as you go through the planning work. Further, you will better understand what exactly drives the benefits. Finally, you also develop the method to measure the benefits as they occur.

You may generally understand the benefits you're seeking at the beginning. However, you may not know what exactly will trigger those benefits until later. In addition, with an experienced project management team and proper planning process in place, the team is enabled to identify alternatives to harvest benefits earlier than originally thought.

Harpham: Have you seen cases where the return on investment breaks down [i.e., costs exceeds benefits] as the planning and estimating work continues?

Atkins: Yes. This tends to happen because the costs turn out to be much higher. The estimated benefits don't tend to change. For instance, we thought we could harvest ten dollars' worth of benefits by spending five dollars. That's a good business case. However, as we elaborate the project and develop a good picture on the costs. At that point, the project may take longer than initially assumed and have ten dollars in costs for ten dollars in benefits. That's much less attractive.

Harpham: How do you approach project scenarios where the benefits become too costly to obtain or the return on investment is unattractive?

Atkins: There are various strategies to consider. One option is to reduce the scope of the program to reduce the cost while seeking the same benefits. This exercise can justify the cost of the program.

Harpham: Do you see organizations regularly going back to measure whether or not the project achieved the business case in terms of ROI or benefits?

Atkins: The best practice is to measure the benefits periodically while the program is underway. That's important because there is a need to confirm that the benefits you're chasing are still attainable at an acceptable cost. If the costs climb higher to attain certain benefits, then you need to have a discussion about whether it makes sense to continue to spend money. That conversation does not happen often enough.

When that conversation does happen, we rarely see programs cancelled. However, the program may be changed significantly and go through a re-planning exercise. A new approach may be needed to optimize the business case.

Harpham: You mentioned that these conversations about costs and benefits during the program don't happen often enough. Why is that?

Atkins: I often see project teams focused on delivering the project with a heads down mentality. There is often an assumption that the project's benefits will still be there. It's incumbent on the business leader to think through the business needs and whether it still makes sense to continue with the project. Remember, it is the party receiving the benefits that has the best understanding of whether those benefits can still be harvested.

Harpham: What kinds of changes could prompt this type of reassessment?

Atkins: Here is one type of change I see happen at large organizations. Let's say the program has a budget of ten dollars per year for four years. In year one, the business may say, "We need to cut that budget to eight dollars this year because we have a challenge to meet." In response, we will say, "Sure, we can do that. However, two dollars' worth of scope will need to be moved into next year." As a result, the project's budget is stretched out over a longer time period. If you do that kind of change multiple times, the project may be completed a year later than originally planned. That means losing on the benefits for a year because the project completion was pushed out a year, plus potentially adding extra costs for keeping resources engaged longer. That change also means your original benefits, the time you anticipated receiving those benefits, and costs need to be reviewed to see if the investment is still attractive.

Harpham: What is your approach to guiding someone through the consequences of a trade-off decision in that scenario?

Atkins: As an outside consultant, our approach would be to suggest that this reassessment ought to be done. It is up to the client to decide if they want to apply the effort required to analyze the impact on the business case and the benefits by stretching out the investment. We have had clients that say, "No, we're comfortable with the decision. Please move ahead." And others that say, "We'd like to better understand the implications of this decision. Please advise us accordingly."

Harpham: What do you see as the differences between a successful project manager and a successful program manager?

Atkins: At the project level, it's very important to understand all of the stakeholders and what their success criteria are. Further, you want to understand what the stakeholders need to contribute to the project and what they expect from the project. It's an exercise in tracking the schedule, the scope, and the budget at a reasonable level of detail. Governance and communication processes need to be developed such that the stakeholders effectively contribute to the project, understand the direction the project is going and if the project is on track to meet its objectives. Managing changes through a proper change process is another key responsibility. The project manager will help the stakeholders to understand the implications of their change decisions. Risk and issue management need to be understood, including the probability that risks will occur.

At the program level, you face similar types of challenges—but they're on steroids. You may have ten or twelve projects running underneath you with project managers doing the work I just described. Most complex programs have work streams that report to the program manager and other work streams that work across the program [e.g., end-to-end testing, organizational change management, and communication].

As a program manager, you have two different activities to run. Most of the time as a program manager, you will have a program delivery office supporting you. That delivery office will be led by a senior project manager: that person functions as your second in command. The program delivery office manages activities, such as change logs, the master schedule, the overall budget, and communications. Your job as the program manager is to spend eighty percent of your time with the rest of the organization and only twenty percent of your time with the program team. In contrast, the project manager has the opposite ratio: eighty percent of time spent working with the project team and twenty percent spent with the rest of the organization.

Complexity is a key reason for the differing points of emphasis between program and project managers. When you are delivering a program in a large company, there are usually multiple business units and corporate support areas [e.g., compliance, risk management, procurement, etc.], functional units [technology and operations], and so forth. As a program manager, it is your responsibility to engage with leaders in other units two or three months in advance of when you need them to do something for the program [e.g., assign a person from your group to support this part of the program].

Your job as a program manager also extends to risk. For example, thinking through the assumptions that may have led to a risk occurring. If a risk occurs, the cause may be due to an individual who is not getting the job done right. In fact, the problem could be due to the individual's working style rather than the substance of their contribution. Clashing work styles hurt productivity. In that case, you may want to make recommendations to adjust the team.

The program manager's job is fundamentally strategic in nature. They need to think about what the program needs next month, two months out, three months out, and more. Once that thinking is done, the program manager needs to arrange the appropriate resources and communicate to support that work. The day-to-day execution of project activities belongs to the project manager[s]. All the projects under the program are controlled and coordinated by the program delivery office.

Harpham: You raise a good distinction in terms of focus: mainly, external focus for program managers versus internal focus for project managers. The other distinction I noted concerned the time scale: many project managers focus on the week as a fundamental unit, while program managers are typically working on a longer time scale.

Atkins: Successful program managers are always looking one to two quarters out. This longer-term time horizon may not fit well with the agile approach in the program context. In such cases, there may be some "agile" accelerators that can work in waterfall programs, like co-location and daily stand-up meetings. However, I find that large transformational programs tend to need a greater emphasis on planning than is typical in an agile project.

Harpham: What does planning look like in these programs?

Atkins: Detailed activities might be planned out over a time horizon of ten days. Over the next several quarters, there would be reasonably detailed high-level plans. Next, there would be a high-level roadmap describing the next two to three years for the program. Some very large, complex programs—such as the cheque-imaging programs we've seen in large Canadian banks—don't lend themselves to agile. To understand the undertaking, you have to develop a plan with a reasonable amount of detail all the way to the end before you start building solutions. In this specific example, the plan will enable the program team to sequence the delivery in a way that best meets the initiative's strategic objectives and enables the organization to potentially harvest benefits sooner. In that specific example, keep in mind that there's not much change in how customers write or use a cheque.

Harpham: Certainly, cheques ["checks" in US English] are a very well established financial product.

Atkins: Correct.

Harpham: Let's explore agile further. There's a view in some areas of the field that agile might be a magic bullet that will solve project problems. What aspects of agile are ineffective or inappropriate in large programs?

Atkins: Determining what aspects of agile work in large programs is something we're learning right now. Some of our teams are using agile enablers, such as co-location and daily stand-ups. In our company, we trained our entire workforce in agile and have pursued certified Scrum Master training. We're seeking to understand the skills and techniques and how others might be using [or claiming to use them].

What we have found from our experience is that the core principles behind the Agile Manifesto should always be present in any good project management practice. Good project managers apply most of the principles, if not all, daily. In addition, it is part of our approach to project management to focus on the delivery of the initiative. Our teams try to minimize any additional disruption to the organization that may compromise the ability to deliver successfully. Changing methodologies, especially mid-stream as some organizations have been doing, tend to introduce an extra level of complexity and risk to the delivery.

Harpham: How do you present agile methods to upper management?

Atkins: The sale to upper management largely comes from consulting organizations that do not have a good understanding of agile methods and are not experts in project management. Unfortunately, the pitch to use agile often amounts to "use agile because it's better, cheaper, and faster." After all, who doesn't want to execute projects and programs better, faster, and cheaper? In that sales pitch, the focus is on successful results and the point that a great amount of discipline and new process is required is lost. By "discipline" I mean for instance knowing how to effectively manage risks and issues informally versus formally as in traditional project management practice.

In more extreme cases, for agile to work effectively, an organization may need to restructure entire teams before the new methodology starts to work. Take, for instance, DevOps from agile. DevOps suggests that development [Dev] and infrastructure [Ops] teams should be broken from their silos and morphed into mixed discipline teams, so that code can be developed and delivered to production faster. In DevOps, this new mixed development team will end up reporting to an individual, which goes against some of the existing audit and/or security controls. As a result, audit and security needs to be revised so satisfactory checks and balances are in place. All this work ends up increasing the complexity of an initiative, causing a great amount of disruption, and/or in worst cases, paralyzing the organization, which will compromise the organization's ability to deliver successfully.

In reality, agile comes down to a different way to approach and manage the project work, which may or may not be suitable to all corporate cultures or project initiatives. Most of the work required to successfully manage an initiative using waterfall does not go away and cannot be ignored simply because agile is in place. The work will still exist and will be completed formally [planning] or informally [risks and issues management], and the informality of key processes is where the biggest challenge lies in organizations that opt for agile.

Harpham: Can you elaborate on the impact and significance of legacy systems to projects?

Atkins: Legacy systems tend to be large and complicated. They tend to require a lot of coding, a lot of testing and crystal clarity on your plans if you plan to modify or replace them. Projects involving legacy systems lend themselves more to a waterfall methodology at this point. That means going through the process of requirements, design, building, testing, and so forth.

We are seeing programs executing in a hybrid fashion. Some work streams operating in an agile-like manner with other work streams in the same program operate in a traditional waterfall methodology. Early indicators suggest this way of working has the potential to deliver a program at a lower cost and shorter duration than using traditional waterfall in all work streams. But there is little evidence yet to prove this conclusively.

Harpham: What have been some of your lessons learned in working on projects and programs?

Atkins: Here's one mistake I see often: using business analysts who lack the appropriate capabilities to lead an exercise in developing requirements. If you start with bad requirements, you're going to have a lot of rework later. In fact, there may be so much rework that it sinks the business case.

I remember having a conversation on a large program with the chief operating officer of a large financial institution. I said to him, "You have two business systems analysts [BSAs] working on this program in the role of a business analyst. However, BSAs at your company are conditioned to receive a request for a function from the business and look into how it can be developed using the existing technology platforms." In this program, the business unit was replacing the "heart" of the business with a new system. It was a situation where you start with a blank piece of paper and ask, "How can we do this in the most efficient manner? If we could do this program any way we wanted, what would we do?" The BSAs didn't have the necessary freethinking and approach to get this work done.

Harpham: How did the situation with the large program play out?

Atkins: I walked the executive through the costs. At first, the COO was only thinking about the cost of the BSAs. He pointed out that it only cost two months wages of the BSAs to see if they could get the job done and he wanted to give them a chance to succeed. However, the COO missed the fact that there is an impact to the program regarding delays and rework. The run rate resource costs for this project were over $200,000 each month. When I laid the costs out in detail, I asked, "Are these the costs that you want to pay to use these BSAs in this situation?" His decision was to add new business analysts within two days who were better suited to the work. This is the value of looking through the right lens with the right data at hand. This COO was a very competent executive and evidence-based decision maker. The decision was easy with the right data.

Harpham: What activities, questions, and actions characterize a highly effective business analyst who is leading requirements development?

Atkins: It starts with making sure that the requirements sessions are properly attended—that all appropriate groups and departments are represented. Their job is to facilitate the meeting, to extract the requirements from the attendees using good process and to document those requirements. Typically, you have two or more sessions to define each functional requirement. In the second session, you would play back the requirements that you documented and ask, "Did we get it right?" Once you receive confirmation on that function, you move on to the next function.

It's also important to guide people through an effective process in developing requirements. You need to understand how the functions are supposed to work and be comfortable in challenging participants to look at the problem through different lenses to identify the most effective alternative.

Harpham: A key part of success in requirements is: "Did we invite the right people to participate and did we make sure that they showed up and participated?"

Atkins: Correct.

Harpham: Let's shift focus to the consulting world. What is your approach to managing your team of consultants at Tramore Group?

Atkins: We start with hiring people that are senior enough that they are largely self-managing. We have a rigorous hiring process. It is much more rigorous than what I've seen anywhere else.

Harpham: Do you see contrasts between hiring at client organizations versus your hiring approach in hiring project management talent?

Atkins: Most organizations have hiring managers who don't know anything about project management. For example, the project manager reports to a business manager who doesn't know project management. As a result, the business manager "hires in their own image" and gets the wrong person.

Our process is simple. It starts with a proper intake process. We interview potential hires almost daily. The interview process has several steps, including peer interviews with our working practitioners. If they clear that stage of the process, the next step is an interview with one of our senior program managers. After that interview, we conduct reference checks, criminal background checks and identity checks before we make the decision on whether to offer employment.

Harpham: Part of the "secret sauce" is paying above average attention to talent.

Atkins: Correct.

Harpham: How have client needs and demands to the firm changed over the past five years?

Atkins: Some of the time we're brought in, the program is already underway and not performing well.

Proactive engagement tends to happen related to large, strategically important programs that have executive attention. In those cases, the executive understands the value of outside assistance to implementing the program.

Over the years, the success of our consultants in recovering troubled initiatives has led to a growing number of engagements where we have consultants leading initiatives from early stages, such as "ideation."

Harpham: In some cases, you're being called in when there's a fire?

Atkins: I am not sure if it is "a fire," but a little less than half of our engagements are remediating existing projects.

Harpham: Turning to the senior people in your firm, what strategies do you see them use for managing themselves and staying productive?

Atkins: It starts with proper training and coaching. For the team and the team leader, we have huddles where senior people who are not involved in that engagement sit with the team every few weeks. This provides an outside perspective on their work.

Harpham: At an individual level, what do their productivity strategies and methods look like?

Atkins: Constant communication is a recurring pattern within the consulting team, with the client and so forth. The details and nature of that communication work adjusts depending on the nature of the project and the organization we're working for.

Harpham: Looking ahead over the next three to five years, what are some trends that may impact the programs you're involved with?

Atkins: The pace of transformation and change is greater now than ever before. The pace of change is increasing quarter to quarter and year to year. The need for companies to change and transform is becoming a critical aspect of competitive advantage. We're already having senior executives at various organizations asking us for direction on ways to increase the pace of transformation while making sure to get it done right.

The biggest single change will be between those organizations that invest in transformation and those who are concerned with managing their costs. I would guess that those companies that are focused on managing costs at the line-item level will fall behind in terms of their competitive position. The chasm between these two approaches—the transformation focus and the cost management focus—will widen very quickly. This is not to say that cost management is not important. It is. There will be a greater focus, however, on seeing project and program leaders as value-added advisors—as important as strategy consultants and subject matter experts.

Chapter Summary

- Building connections: Atkins started to develop relationships with large banks and other organizations during his career with Xerox and other companies. That knowledge and experience supported later opportunities.

- The expense control mentality: This tendency, suitable for regular business operations, tends not to work well in programs and on projects.

- Project management discipline: Omitting the change control process may buy some speed in the short term, but it may come at the cost of a negative impact to the schedule, scope, and budget.

- Steps to develop a program: Estimating the work and budget required for a $100 million–program requires extensive work. Expect to spend significant resources upfront to define the requirements, design, and related activities.

- The differences between successful project managers and program managers: There is a significant difference in complexity between these roles. The project manager will tend to focus 80% of her time on the project team and 20% on the rest of the organization; the emphasis is reversed for the program manager who spends 80% of his time on the broad stakeholder group and 20% with the project team. The project manager is focused on the days and weeks ahead while the program manager focuses on a longer time horizon such as months and quarters.

- Choose your business analysts carefully. Choosing ineffective or inexperienced analysts to do requirements development can cause in significant re-work resulting in cost over runs and schedule delays.

Cornelius Fichtner

President, OSP International LLC

As president and founder of OSP International LLC, **Cornelius Fichtner**, PMP defines the strategic direction of the company and works with project management trainers and coaches to design and develop new products. Fichtner came to project management by accident. He started out as a software developer but quickly realized that he preferred talking to people to writing code. He moved into what was then called "organizational planning" and became certified in the field. It took him about three to four years to make the switch and completely leave software development—all the while leading increasingly complex and important projects.

Fichtner has been working as a project manager in his native Switzerland, in Germany, and in the United States since 1990. He received his Project Management Professional (PMP) credential in April 2004. He has led projects for a management consulting company, a national retailer, an Internet startup company, and one of the oldest financial service providers in the United States. Fichtner also holds the Certified Scrum Master (CSM) credential.

Bruce Harpham: What was your first exposure to working on projects?

Cornelius Fichtner: The first project I worked on was at a paper mill in Switzerland. I was based in the IT department. I had just come out of school, finished a commercial apprenticeship, and started my first job as a software developer.

© Bruce Harpham 2018
B. Harpham, *Project Managers at Work*, DOI 10.1007/978-1-4842-2668-1_13

At one point, my boss said, "Hey why don't you go over to Mr. Smith and help him with something small." Well, I was done with the "something small" eighteen months later.

Mr. Smith wanted a program that would calculate the production cost of every single type of paper produced by the paper mill.

Harpham: This sounds like creating a management accounting system from scratch.

Fichtner: It wasn't quite that elaborate. The application was meant to answer questions like: "How much does it cost to produce an A4 paper at this weight?" and many variations on that theme. There were many types of paper to be analyzed through this program. I didn't really know that I was doing project management.

As I progressed through my career as a developer, I realized that I was basically talking to machines all day. That wasn't enough for me. Reflecting on my experiences traveling abroad for a year, I found that I really enjoyed interacting with and meeting new people. Therefore, I decided I needed a new job and became a management consultant.

At the time, the work was called "organizational planning." In reality, I was doing project management. More and more, I learned about projects, developing project management offices [PMOs] and related efforts. Later on, I was involved in a PMO for a supermarket company in Switzerland. The CEO was a big supporter of project management because he realized many people were involved in projects and did not really know what they were doing. The mission was to teach everybody to succeed on their projects, no matter how small.

Together with an external consultant, we developed a one-page project management methodology. Everything fit onto one page! Based on that document, we taught hundreds of people to manage projects. We taught them to use this structured approach to plan, execute, and implement their work more quickly.

Harpham: What was that process to train people on project management?

Fichtner: I was also involved in teaching people how to use various computer software programs. For example, I taught people how to use Harvard Graphics—something like a cross between Microsoft Paint and Adobe Photoshop—before I got involved in teaching project management.

My approach in teaching project management then was to say:

> "Here are the tools that will help you get your work done."

> "Here are ways to communicate with upper management."

> "Here are ways to schedule your work effectively."

It was more about giving them tools than teaching project management per se.

Harpham: Simplicity and first principles guided your approach to teaching project management?

Fichtner: Yes, that's right. I continued to use the simplicity concept in other organizations.

Years later, I was working in a project management position at a financial services company. In that case, the company's headquarters required us to implement a project management methodology across our division. Just for kicks, I printed the project management templates that they asked us to use. It filled an entire binder! I'm not kidding! Every single project was required to fill in these forms.

Harpham: In the project world, some people have the assumption that the templates will save us. What did you do when you saw this binder of material?

Fichtner: I knew what I had to do. I went to my boss and said, "Our projects are an average of three to six weeks in duration. There's no way we can do these templates. I will develop a methodology for us that is one page long. I will take everything from the binder and I will condense it down to one page. And in order to help us gain approval from headquarters on this, I will provide explanations on our local, internal processes that cover all the templates that I'm cutting out."

In the end, it was a one page document with a few variations to cover different types of projects. The longest document was two and a half pages. My vision was: "I have to cut this down to one page. Our developers, our business analysts, our project managers—they will *not* fill in these templates. No way."

We then worked with the bank's auditors on our new process. We had a list of every single template that was required. We explained in detail how we are capturing each requirement in other systems and do not need to duplicate the information on the template.

Harpham: What was that conversation like with the auditors?

Fichtner: It was no problem because we came prepared. We told them, "Look, here is the situation. This is the size of the project. This is the overhead that the binder full of forms will create for us." They agreed with the proposal.

Harpham: Having worked at a bank, that sounds like a fast approval.

Fichtner: In the short term, it was a successful response to the overwhelming process that headquarters requested. Ultimately, I decided to leave the organization because they had an overzealous approach to audits. I heard that people would lose their jobs over misspellings or other minor problems.

Harpham: Deeper problems were at play then?

Fichtner: Yes, that's right.

Harpham: What other industries and organizations did you work at next?

Fichtner: After the paper mill, I had a sabbatical. I came back and worked for a vacation tour operator in IT. Then, I went to the management consulting firm for about four to five years. At the consulting firm, I really learned project management without knowing it. That was also the first time that I downloaded and read A Guide to the Project Management Body of Knowledge [PMBOK Guide]. It was probably version one or two.

Harpham: What was it like to learn about the PMBOK Guide for the first time?

Fichtner: Fantastic! I immediately recognized the value of the PMBOK Guide as a way to structure projects.

Harpham: What was next for your career?

Fichtner: I went to a web startup company—we made websites for various clients. I led website development projects for a few years.

Harpham: It seems like you've made a number of industry changes smoothly. What was it like to switch from paper mill to financial services, and so forth?

Fichtner: Throughout the various industries, I was in the IT department in each case. I wasn't making paper in the paper mill. I wasn't advising clients on vacation choices. I had a steady focus on IT activities in these various industries. Initially, I joined the management consulting firm because they wanted a software developer with growth potential.

From that point on, I moved into a consultant and project manager roles. I wasn't focused on the industry—I was looking for an interesting job. From my perspective, I never really changed industries. I was always IT focused.

Harpham: Would that mean a focus on web technologies? Or would this be database development?

Fichtner: As the years went by, it became more and more web-focused work.

Harpham: You found a common thread that you could take through several different organizations?

Fichtner: Yes. It didn't matter that I was previously at a paper mill. I knew how to build good websites and that was all that mattered.

Harpham: At some point, you moved to the United States. How did that come about?

Fichtner: Simple. I married a US citizen. My wife is from California. We got married in Arizona and then lived in Switzerland for ten years. We enjoyed it very much and then decided it was time for a change. We looked at England, Australia, and other places. In the end, it was a fairly simple process to visit the US Embassy in Berne and get my green card because we had been married for so long.

Harpham: Let's move to the chapter of your career when you start your own company. I believe you had some PMP exam training through a professional association.

Fichtner: After we came to the United States, I was with the web development company. I decided shortly after arriving in the US that I wanted to leave the company. Oddly enough, the company moved me from Switzerland to the United States and they laid me off after having me in the US for six weeks.

I realized I had enough savings to keep us going for about a year. I asked myself: "What do I need to do to become competitive?" I decided to obtain the Project Management Professional [PMP] certification and I joined the Project Management Institute [PMI]. I also became heavily involved with PMI. By the way, I found my job at the bank through my PMI connections.

Through PMI, I started organizing continuing education seminars for my local PMI chapter. After receiving my PMP certification, the PMI chapter asked me if I would like to get involved in the chapter's PMP training group. Two or three times per year, I would teach part of the PMP exam course run by the chapter.

Harpham: Did you have a certain area of focus that you taught?

Fichtner: No. I would teach any of the knowledge areas with the exception of earned value. That was the only one that proved a challenge. I had never used earned value in my work. It was a question of knowing what you're good at, so I focused on other topics.

Harpham: When did you get involved in podcasts?

Fichtner: My wife gave me an iPod in 2004. Suddenly, things started to come together. I had always enjoyed teaching. A few years earlier, I had thought about looking for a teaching job or one in training. Around the same time, I had become PMP certified and I was teaching PMP preparation. I also started to listen to podcasts—news, science, comedy, you name it.

I realized there is a lack of project management information in podcasting. I launched *The Project Management Podcast* in 2005. Training, project management and podcasting all started to come together. By mid 2006, I had *The PM PrepCast*, an audio series that would help you prepare for the PMP exam.

Harpham: Did you have your trademark sign-off, "Until next time," at that time?

Fichtner: Absolutely. That started with the first episode of *The Project Management Podcast*.

Harpham: How did the first paid product come up?

Fichtner: My podcast listeners actually asked me to create products. I created the first paid product after running the podcast for about a year. I sold it for $29 and then raised the price to $49 and beyond. Also, I got very negative feedback from other trainers who stated that I was devaluing the PMP exam.

Harpham: What did you tell them?

Fichtner: I told them, "Do you remember the Industrial Revolution and the weaving loom? I am *your* weaving loom and I'm not going away."

Harpham: Yet I still see project management training courses in the $1,000 price range and higher.

Fichtner: Yes, those are still there. Interestingly, I receive feedback from my students that say they learned more and passed their PMP exam from my course compared to a traditional in-person course. This kind of feedback from students makes a big difference. I share these student emails with the team to encourage and inspire them.

Harpham: At what point did you bring other staff into the company?

Fichtner: At some point, I realized that I could no longer support our customers and do the rest of the work. I knew that I needed a customer support representative. It happened within a year of launching our PMP training product.

Harpham: For a period of time, you ran the company on a part-time basis?

Fichtner: For the first year or so, everything was run part-time while I was working a full-time job at a financial institution. After about a year, I made the transition to self-employment.

Harpham: As you have watched project management methodology and *PMBOK Guide* evolve over the years, how do you keep up with it? And do these new editions add value?

Fichtner: The *PMBOK Guide* will never be perfect because it is only a guide to what everybody does. Project management evolves—we've seen that with the rise of agile. The *PMBOK Guide* will never be done or finished. People come up with new ideas and new needs.

The ever-evolving art of project management is documented in each new edition of the *PMBOK Guide*.

Harpham: So the world shifts and we adjust with it?

Fichtner: Yes, the *PMBOK Guide* documents what we are doing in the profession and our changing insights. It's not that the *PMBOK Guide* tells you how to do project management. If you are new to the profession, the *PMBOK Guide* will give you a wonderful overview and understanding of what we generally do in projects. In order to deeply understand projects, you have to lead projects, make mistakes, and learn from them.

Harpham: Speaking of mistakes, project management has a concept called "lessons learned." Unfortunately, lessons learned are sometimes written or discussed in vague or unhelpful ways, such as "mistakes were made" or "the project failed due to software problems."

What's a mistake you made on a project where you took that lesson learned away and applied it afterwards?

Fichtner: It's more a case of death by a thousand cuts in my case. There's a saying, "How do you recognize a good project manager? It's the woman or the man over there with all the knives stuck in their back." They've failed so many times and lived to tell the tale.

Little things that went wrong, rather than huge mistakes, stand out to me. For example, poor word choice in a status report that upset someone. I learned to choose better words to avoid that. There are many examples like that. Thankfully, I did not have an experience like, "Oh no, the bridge crashed! We're in big trouble!"

Harpham: What is your approach to coordinating virtual teams? I understand that your staff and contractors are in different locations and countries. How do you bring the team together in that case?

Fichtner: We are fully virtual. Everybody works from home. Our staff are all over the world—Canada, USA, South America, Israel, the UK, and the Philippines.

In the last few years, we have used an agile approach on our projects. We have a daily stand-up meeting. IT services and other groups that perform operations also use this practice even if they are not running projects. One person on each of these calls becomes the responsible team leader to make sure that tasks are being completed.

On the project side, we simply bring everybody together daily. We have clear agile artifacts: road maps, release plans, the definition of *done*. Even though we have multiple projects underway at the same time, it's interesting to bring together people on different projects. There's usually some shared insight or learning from people commenting on different projects.

Harpham: With this virtual company, how have you developed your leadership philosophy?

Fichtner: I'm still thinking about it. I've always been a servant leader. I have always tried to serve my customer when I was running projects in a customer facing role. Now, I simply see myself as serving the employees and contractors on our team.

I read the book *The Strategic Project Leader* by Jack Ferraro [Auerbach Publications, 2014]. It was great. Everything he talks about and writes about there aligns with my thinking on leadership. I developed a service-based approach to leadership and projects. It's about helping *you* to become successful—that's always been my mantra.

Harpham: *Getting Things Done* by David Allen [Viking, 2001] helped me get started with productivity and running projects. It's one of the few business books I've read more than once. It has great techniques, like the "two minute rule" and "the weekly review." What are your productivity habits and methods?

Fichtner: I've experimented with various productivity systems and approaches over the years. Frankly, I've found that a pen and pad of paper works best for me. The act of writing a to-do list and then cross out completed items is satisfying.

Harpham: In 2016, I still see environments where there are project "war rooms" where there are sheets of paper on the wall showing project status, stakeholder information, software development, and other activities. There's still something valuable about seeing information laid out in paper. Likewise, authors Robert Greene and Ryan Holiday both use notecards in their research.

Fichtner: That makes sense.

Harpham: Which resources have made a difference to your thinking and your career?

Fichtner: I run a web-based business. Everything that I have learned and done for my business has been through digital media. I run a podcast so listening to and studying podcasts has been extremely helpful. I can listen to podcasts and get business training while I go for a walk.

The number-one podcast that helped me with my Internet business is *Internet Business Mastery*. It explained how web-based businesses work, how to accept payments and everything else. Jeremy Frandsen and Jason Van Orden, the hosts of the podcast, focus on mindset and understanding yourself. They explore questions like, "What do you really want to get out of this business?" and "Are you looking for freedom from the nine to five? Or something else?" Going through that thought process was good in starting and running my business.

I also listen to a few podcasts purely to stay informed on Internet marketing. One is called *Internet Marketing Insider*. The other was *Internet Marketing Podcast,*—that one is no longer being produced, however. Those helped me to develop marketing in the Internet world.

The other business podcast that I regularly listen to is *HBR Idea Cast*. HBR [Harvard Business Review] brings on high-level people to discuss important business questions, such as "How do you find the right talent for your company?" I also listen to TED Talks. I find them to be interesting and applicable because they help me to take a broader perspective on my business.

Outside of the above podcasts, there are dozens of other ones that I listen to. I like *Show Runner* on how to run podcasts. *Quirks and Quarks* from the CBC about astronomy and science. There are many others. I listen to an enormous array of podcasts on different topics.

Harpham: In addition to the great material, I also find that TED Talks are a great resource for public speaking.

Fichtner: I fashioned my presentation at the 2015 PMI Congress in terms of my slide design—one picture and a few words—based on the TED Talks style. TED Talks are certainly a world class speaking school.

Harpham: For reader who is in another profession who wants to switch into project management, what are some first steps to explore a move to project management?

Fichtner: Humans have an innate ability to manage projects. Tell a seven-year-old that he or she is going to have a birthday party and that they have to set it up. Without much help, they will start working on it in a haphazard but relatively planned way.

By the time you are in your early twenties, you already have a good understanding of project management. If you want to transition to a project management job, apply project management to what you're doing right now. Everything you're currently doing will improve from using project management methods and processes.

If your boss gives you a new task, think about it from an initiation perspective. Write a small project charter—it could be one page or half a page. Take project management best practices and apply it to your tasks even if you are doing operations. Learn what makes you more successful and build on that.

Harpham: Looking ahead over the next five years, what trends on the horizon will impact the profession and how people practice it?

Fichtner: I'm reminded of the old saying: "What is the stock market going to do? It will fluctuate." It's very much the same with our profession.

Ten years ago, nobody would have thought agile would become this popular. It's very difficult to predict the future.

If I had to take a few guesses, here's what comes to mind: Agile may decline somewhat in popularity in the coming years because it has been on the rise for several years. Something else may come along and replace it. Agile will be integrated with traditional project management. I'm not saying that agile is going away, but it will fluctuate in how it is applied.

Benefits management is a hot topic right now. If you look back fifteen years ago, people were talking about benefits management and asking similar questions then. Now, it's coming back as an area of focus.

The PMI Talent Triangle has implications for project manager training. The Talent Triangle suggests that project managers need skills in three broad areas: technical project management, strategic and business management, and leadership. This model will shape the courses and training materials we use.

At the same time, there's a danger. Dr. David Hillson, the risk doctor, pointed out to me if PMI wants project managers to take on leadership and strategy, who's going to lead the project and do the work? There may be a risk that we're pulling project managers away from the actual work and pushing them into other areas.

There is also a demographic issue: project managers are getting older. Every PMI chapter I know asks the question: "How do we engage the younger generation in the profession?"

Chapter Summary

- Recommended resources include *The Strategic Project Leader* by Jack Ferraro, the *Internet Business Mastery* podcast, and the *HBR Idea Cast* podcast.

- Leverage simplicity. Fichtner used a one-page project management system to guide smaller projects and train staff on project management.

- Transition between industries: As a project manager, you can apply your skills across several industries. Fichtner used his technology and project management skills in financial services, paper production, and other industries.

- Starting a project management business: Fichtner started his business on a part-time basis for about a year prior to leaving his full-time job.

- Using agile: Fichtner and his company are a fully virtual company that operate using the agile framework.

Brennan Dunn

Founder, Double Your Freelancing

Brennan Dunn *is the founder of Double Your Freelancing, which helps teach freelancers and consultants how to earn more money and work with better clients. He's the creator of Double Your Freelancing Rate, Double Your Freelancing Academy, and a number of other courses for consultants. His free pricing course, Charge What You're Worth, has helped thousands of freelancers and consultants. Dunn previously founded a project management software company called Planscope and a web design agency.*

Bruce Harpham: How did you get started in project management?

Brennan Dunn: I started my career working at web design agencies. At a certain point, I transitioned my career into freelance web development. At this point, I became both the project manager and the specialist ["the doer"] delivering the work to the client. About a year into my freelancer career, I faced a turning point: scale up the business or start turning away clients. Eventually, I built up an agency with eleven employees. At that stage, project management became more complex and interesting to manage.

There were multiple concurrent client projects to manage. At the same time, we had to carry out sales and marketing activities so that we would have projects to work on in the future. In order to sell future projects and plan accordingly, I needed to understand approximately when our current projects would be completed. Understanding the projects became more difficult as I moved into a management role, as opposed to being in the weeds of delivering to clients. At this scale, I started to learn much more about how to manage projects effectively.

© Bruce Harpham 2018
B. Harpham, *Project Managers at Work*, DOI 10.1007/978-1-4842-2668-1_14

Harpham: So the transition from individual freelancer to managing an agency was a turning point in your project management journey?

Dunn: My overall responsibility was to make our clients happy. I also had to give thought to scheduling considerations and client expectations. For example, if I committed to a client that we would kick off a new project on December 1st, then I had to make sure that the team was available to work on the project by that date. In terms of client management, making sure we received timely feedback as we worked through the project became an important concern. When it was just me and the client, it was relatively simple to get feedback and keep moving. In larger projects, that becomes more difficult.

After I exited the agency, I decided to create a project management software application called Planscope. I was unhappy with the agency's internal processes to manage projects.

Harpham: There are quite a few project management software applications on the market. What was special about Planscope?

Dunn: At the agency, we had a billable hours business model. Tracking work hours for each professional and producing invoices was difficult. In many cases, the client would get an invoice and have questions about it: "How did the work output correlate to the hours billed?"

A key priority for Planscope was to ensure that each time-sheet entry related to a project task. For example, let's say you build an application for a client that has a billing feature. With Planscope, you could see the billable hours associated with creating that billing feature.

In addition, we kept running into a battle between scope and budget remaining. Our projects typically took three to six months to create. Clients would request changes or new features once they started to work with a prototype. We were happy to add additional scope. However, there was often a conflict between adding new scope and having no change to the budget. In that scenario, you may end up not getting to the finish line.

To address this challenge, we built a simple reporting system that reported project progress versus budget remaining. This reporting mechanism would serve as the canary in the coal mine to show the relationship between progress on the project and remaining budget. With that insight, we can ask what steps we should take to address the situation before the project encounters serious trouble.

Harpham: How were change requests addressed in this environment?

Dunn: Our projects typically looked like a customized social media website— like a Facebook clone for cat enthusiasts. Some clients would have an idea, raise funding for it, and then come to us to build the project. Initially, they would ask for one product at the beginning of the project. Then a month or two into the project, they would start to play with the product and start asking for new features or functionality.

We practiced an agile development process that had minimal upfront estimation and planning. Therefore, we were happy to look at changes as they came in. However, clients struggled with decisions on whether to apply their budget to their original idea or move budget resources to develop new feature ideas. We were doing our job as consultants to educate clients on the trade-off decisions they were considering during the project. However, I felt that a project management tool would clarify this process even further.

Harpham: Did Planscope provide improvements for client communication?

Dunn: Other features included sending out a daily status update email to the client. This update would tell the clients which tasks were worked on in a given day, a list of items to be reviewed by the client, and so forth. Prior to using Planscope, my agency had to do this kind of reporting by manually writing an email.

Harpham: For these large projects where the client had a big idea like a Facebook clone, defining scope is challenging. You've developed a road-mapping process to address this situation. What goes into that process?

Dunn: Many agencies do some type of road-mapping process at the early stage of a project. Another way of defining road mapping is paid discovery: clients pay for assistance in developing their general ideas into a more specific concept. It's a short, small, consulting engagement with the goal of you and the client on the same wavelength about the project.

I kept encountering the issue where we struggled to sufficiently understand the client and their ideas early on. In particular, it was painful to reassign someone from a revenue-generating project and have them sit through a series of meetings with a prospective client. From a business standpoint, it wasn't in our interest to operate in that way—putting a lot of staff time into unpaid activities, like meeting clients to gather information and prepare proposals. I wanted to transform this time into a revenue-generating activity and use it to generate something valuable for the client at the same time.

Rather than looking at this activity as the client paying for a project estimate, I took a different approach. I would say to the client, "You have an assumption regarding a business problem that needs to be solved. You have an idea on how that can be solved. Day in and day out, we build solutions that solve problems just like this. I propose that we sit with you to define the best way to get to the end goal that you have in mind."

Many new freelancers think their job is to be reactionary: whatever comes their way from the client, they should agree and build it. Over time, I've developed a different attitude. I'll say to clients, "I've been down this path of action with other clients and I don't think that is best way to go for these reasons… Here is what I suggest instead."

Last week, I consulted with a client in the Midwest related to marketing automation processes. With a non-disclosure agreement in place, I went about learning as much as I could about the business. The questions I covered includes: How do they make money today? Who are their customers? What is the average lifetime value of a customer? How does the client currently upsell or cross-sell? How do they get past customers to come back and buy again?

Many of my clients do not have all of these data points on hand when I first ask. In the road-mapping session, we're achieving several aims. We're defining what the project is going to look like. Further, we want to determine how we can use the project as an investment in improving the business.

Rather than saying, "Hire me to code an application for x hours," the conversation changes to "How can we make this project into an investment for the business?" That happens when the consultant deeply understands the business prior to making any recommendations. After the road-mapping session, the client receives a deliverable – a detailed report that defines next steps. This report could be brought to another person for implementation, if they wish.

For my own business, the price of the road-mapping session roughly corresponds to the estimated price of the full project. For a $60,000 project, the road-mapping session might be $2,000. When I was running the agency and routinely delivering projects in the $250,000 to $500,000 level, the road-mapping project was typically priced around $5,000.

In addition to the value contained in the road-mapping session and the deliverable itself, there are other benefits for client. They have the opportunity to work with the consultant for a relatively short period of time and learn whether they can work effectively with you. For the consultant, the road-mapping session often shortens the sales process. If a client is thinking about spending $50,000, $100,000, or more with you, and you're an unknown to them, they will tend to take a lot of time to make a decision on a project like that. In contrast, if the client has a positive experience on a short project, they tend to move faster to the larger project. It's tough for a client to go from spending $0 with you and move to $500,000. For the kinds of clients we work with, a $5,000 road-mapping system is effectively an "impulse purchase," especially given the value we deliver.

Here's an analogy. If you want to go from New York to Los Angeles, you wouldn't simply get in your car and drive west. You need to have a plan and know which roads you will take. At the same time, you may adjust your approach as you travel, but do you need a plan to get started on the journey.

Harpham: How do you work with clients to determine the ultimate goal of the project? For instance, the client may request, "Please build a social network website." How do you determine the underlying goal?

Dunn: It's important to assess the client. You don't want to end up with a portfolio of projects that didn't go anywhere, even if you made money on each one. You want successful projects that you can point to and use as case studies in your marketing. I've had clients with a business track record move into a completely new and unfamiliar area—like launching an Internet business. In those cases, they may have "TechCrunch expectations," where they imagine starting an Internet business is somehow easy.

Helping the client to prioritize their ideas is one way to discover their goal. I remember one client who wanted a website with complex community features like private messages, moderators, and permissions. However, the website had not yet been built and there was no community of users. In the road-mapping session, I showed them why these social media style features didn't add much value at this stage of the business. I've seen first-hand how difficult it can be to build certain types of Internet companies, such as two-sided marketplaces that bring together buyers and sellers. Ultimately, the biggest risk for the client is a bad goal, like putting all their hope into getting acquired by Facebook rather struggling with non-functional software.

However, if they wanted to pursue the "get acquired" goal, then the project needs to adjust. A functioning app is not enough. The project also needs to include a product that will attract attention from investors. In fact, I've helped some clients put together pitch decks in order to seek funds from investors. After a few rounds of funding and continual improvement to the product, the end goal of getting acquired becomes more feasible.

Harpham: Did you think of your business as a technical company or in a different way?

Dunn: I didn't see the agency as an "app development company." Clients typically don't say, "I want to spend $500,000 to get an app." Instead, they want to pursue a goal like building a new line of business around the app. The more we are able to learn what they ultimately want to achieve in the business—the end goals, then I can come in with better ideas to help them connect the dots.

The client's end goal for the project drives the metrics we care about. If they're seeking to get acquired, the important metrics may be how many new users are signing up and how much time do they spend on the site? If we're building the project to become a profitable business, then we look at different metrics, like conversion rates, customer lifetime value, and so forth.

Our job is to use our technical expertise and skills to define a way for the client to achieve their end goal as soon as possible. If the client simply says, "I want an app and you're an app development company—let's do this project," that is not the kind of project I want to work on.

Harpham: In your work training and consulting with freelancers through Double Your Freelancing, what are recurring mistakes you see in how they run projects?

Dunn: The biggest misconception consultants and freelancers have concerns what they will spend their time doing. For example, a web developer moving from a corporate job to an independent consulting career may assume that she will get to spend all of her time creating websites—exactly what she loves to do all day. In fact, there are many other functions you have to perform. You have to do project management tasks, such as managing the client's expectations and change requests, as well as sales and marketing.

I typically see people struggle to define and manage client expectations effectively. Many independent consultants may sell a project, but they don't have a defined onboarding process that sets out the next steps. An onboarding procedure defines for the client how the project will be done, how communication will work, and what is required in terms of feedback. If these points are omitted, the client starts to get concerned and may start micro-managing the consultant like an errant employee. That's bad news for the consultant because it means unstructured interaction from the client and less autonomy in how you do the work. There's nothing worse than the client who expects you to deliver, but then disappears and is unavailable for feedback or updates. When the client disappears like that, it's easy to build something that doesn't meet their needs. That can lead to costly disputes over the project.

Most project failures don't relate to technology or product malfunctions. Instead, poor communication causes failure over and over again.

Harpham: What does your onboarding process look like?

Dunn: Day one, I start with the road-mapping session: a small, self-contained project to define the problems and goals. This could take three hours or longer, depending on the situation. Next, I produce the road-mapping report that details the business case for the project and the relevant data points, and outlines next steps. Functionally, the road-mapping report doubles as a project proposal. When the client accepts the proposal for a larger proposal, I set up the foundation for the project.

My current practice is to use Laura Elizabeth's Client Portal template to act as a central repository of project information. It's a simple web template that defines several points for the client. It explains how project communication will work. It provides information on my availability for the project. It also includes links to the project file in Trello—my project management application, the staging website for the project materials, and all the assets involved in the project. I make one of those for every client I work with. Creating and delivering this resource to the client is a key part of the onboarding procedure.

I also define how communications and meetings will work. Rather than ad hoc meetings, I schedule a recurring weekly meeting with the client. At that meeting, we cover any and all questions related to the project. I also have a procedure that defines what to do for urgent requests. Further, I explain how I will provide project updates to the client. I don't let the client assume how the project will work. If I make assumptions about their involvement in the project, it's a recipe for disaster.

Harpham: Do you get resistance from clients regarding the onboarding process?

Dunn: I make it clear how I operate. If the client wants a 24/7 "coder for hire"—that's not me. Early in the process, I explain how I work. The process of setting expectations starts at the very beginning when I receive an inquiry from a potential client. By marketing myself as a consultant and operating accordingly, most clients respect my process. They understand that I am focused on their business goals and there's a process to manage the details of communication and interaction.

Harpham: The idea is to reduce back-and-forth communication by having a single repository for project information for the client?

Dunn: With this approach, it's a simple reference for clients to use. It's better than resending emails or anything like that.

Harpham: Using templates and standard processes over and over again gives you added mental capacity to add value in other ways.

Dunn: Consultants face the challenge of being perceived as high risk by the client. That doesn't mean we're high risk in terms of failing to create working software or whatever you're building. Instead, the perceived risk is that the consultant flakes out, fails to communicate, or otherwise fails to act professionally.

If I receive a project inquiry from a potential client, I don't immediately move to schedule a call with them. I send each prospect an intake questionnaire first. Only after completing that document will you receive a link to book an appointment on my online calendar. After your calendar appointment is confirmed, you will receive a PDF file that details the agenda for the meeting.

Instead of the consultant coming to the meeting like a job interview, I set the terms for the discussion. It's a structured twenty-minute discussion. It's well-structured because the agenda and the intake questionnaire have been completed ahead of time. If you don't provide this kind of structure, many clients will default to treating the process like a job interview.

The secondary value of using this process is to create confidence with the client. This process signals that you've done projects before and that you are taking a systematic approach. Some consultants and project managers struggle with this because they may not think they have "the right" to impose a structure. At the end of the day, the client wants to feel like they're in the hands of a professional who is guiding the process.

Harpham: Perceived risk for the client or project sponsor matters. If you drive the process according to a clear playbook, it puts the client at ease.

Dunn: Exactly.

Harpham: How did you come to develop these processes and structures?

Dunn: You may have seen websites like Clients From Hell, where freelancers moan and complain about clients. For example, reports of a client making an absurd request or otherwise treating the freelancer poorly. In many cases, much of the fault lies with the consultant. Failing to set expectations, use a process, and communicate effectively causes tremendous problems.

Regarding the onboarding procedure, I developed it while I was running my agency. There was a clear business need for me to develop a procedure. Here's the problem I encountered. We would sell a project and then assign different people to work on it. I noticed that the end result of the project would be significantly different because each person had a different approach. I had to standardize the process so that projects would be delivered in a consistent way. Otherwise, the agency is little more than a loose collection of smart people who are not held together with common processes and methods.

Harpham: Did you draw on other resources or people to develop these processes?

Dunn: My lawyer was a key source of inspiration in fact. Organizationally, a law firm and a web design agency are similar in that both sell professional services to clients. He gave some helpful advice regarding the onboarding procedure for new clients.

Harpham: What is your approach to effective delegation on a project?

Dunn: At first, our invoices to clients had details like: "Andrew worked ten hours on your project this week." We moved away from the resource-for-hire model. Instead of selling hours like that, we adopted a weekly billing process [e.g., invoice x dollars for a week of work effort]. That meant that the client received the full-time attention of a senior developer, part of a junior developer, quality assurance, and project management for a set fee. That approach gave me greater flexibility with staff assignments on projects. Internally, I would then look at ways to assign tasks that fit with each individual's expertise and experience.

Harpham: Let's turn to the closing process you use on projects. How do you close out the project?

Dunn: There are several aspects to closing. On a weekly basis, I review the work delivered in the current week and plan ahead for next week. On a monthly basis, I run a retrospective meeting. During that meeting, the focus isn't on the technical content of the project.

Instead, the meeting agenda has three columns for us to address: happy, neutral, and sad. Each person on the project—whether on my side or on the client side—can add items to each of the three columns. For example, they might add a comment about liking the weekly meetings under the happy column. Or write a comment about the staging website in the sad column. If someone else agrees with one of these comments, they can "+1" to the comment to give it more weight.

At the end of the meeting, we analyze the neutral and sad columns for improvement opportunities. The idea is to address these issues and prevent them from becoming a recurring problem in the future.

At the very end of the project, I hold an offboarding meeting. You don't want to simply hand over the keys to the software or product and say, "Have fun!" Instead, we work through post-project issues with the client. For example, do they need support or training in hiring a new person to maintain the system? During the sales process, I highlight the offboarding phase as part of the value we're delivering. We're not going to deliver a website or an application and then disappear as soon as we turn it on. The offboarding process also sometimes functions as a sales opportunity. For example, the client may realize that they need additional assistance with user engagement or maintenance.

Finally, I schedule follow-up actions on my calendar. This is a process that I learned from my real estate agent who sold me my house. She called me two weeks after we moved in to see if everything was going smoothly. A month after that, she called again to ask about our feelings with the neighborhood. A year later, she called again to congratulate us on our one-year anniversary of moving into the house. I adapted this process for our clients. It was a great way to make sure that clients feel supported and to generate testimonials and case studies to use in our marketing.

My real estate agent knows that people often sell their house after a few years, and that people ask their friends for suggestions. By staying in touch, you are more likely to be recommended and receive a referral.

Harpham: I'm impressed by your observation and willingness to adapt strategies from other professions. Some people do not have that open perspective.

Dunn: Whatever your discipline or profession, there are underlying processes. So much of success in the field comes down to learning and mastering sales, marketing, fulfillment, and customer service. You can learn those skills from other people in different professions. You don't have to restrict yourself to learning from peers in your discipline.

Harpham: This follow-up sequence and offboarding is a way to prevent the scenario where the project ships and the project team immediately disappears.

Dunn: In that scenario, people feel left in the cold and unsure on what to do next. We don't want dead, offline websites in our portfolio. We want successful projects and clients. I realized that when we deliver the project, that's the beginning of the journey for the client. We want to help them to succeed in the long term, and that means giving thought to their situation beyond the project itself.

Harpham: What does your personal productivity strategy look like?

Dunn: I have a simple stack of software tools. I use Trello for much of my task management—business and personal items alike. If I happen to get a new idea while I'm on the go, I open the Notes app on my phone to write it down and then transfer it into Trello later.

Every Sunday evening, I plan out the coming week. Specifically, I review the tasks in Trello and then put those tasks onto my calendar. Everything of importance goes on the calendar: exercise time, client projects, working on a new product, and so forth. My reliance on the calendar means that I conserve my daily allotment of willpower. If you look at your to-do list every time you finish a task, and then deliberate on what to do next, that process erodes your decision-making ability. In contrast, if you stay focused on the calendar, which you planned earlier in the week, it makes the whole process much easier.

Harpham: Any other productivity or task management techniques to share?

Dunn: Years ago, I sometimes had struggles in this area. I solved these issues in part by keeping a weekly task list in paper. If I had to rewrite a task multiple days in a row because I wasn't getting it down, it forced me to confront the situation. Was that task actually important? If not, perhaps I should simply delete it.

Harpham: That rewriting process forces you to reflect on what tasks you have on your plate and what is adding value.

Dunn: Exactly. If I postpone a task ten days in a row, the repeated postponement tells me that the task may not be valuable.

Harpham: Looking ahead to the future, what are some technology opportunities that interest you?

Dunn: For my current work focus with clients, marketing automation is a top focus. I'm going a step beyond that to work on personalization and segmentation work in marketing. One of my clients has enterprise clients, small business clients, and freelancer clients. If a prospect comes across a blog post on the client's website discussing the enterprise service and then clicks over to the marketing page, the product information will be tailored to the enterprise audience. Likewise, a user that reads a blog post aimed at the freelancer audience will be served the freelancer information on the product page.

On my own website, I have this type of customization in place, depending on someone's discipline. If someone reads about freelancing as a web designer, the product pages will reflect that fact. If you do work in creating websites, web apps, and related areas, this is an important area that will become more valuable over time.

Regarding software to use to run a consulting business, task management services are popular right now. For the clients I work with right now, they don't want that level of detail. I've seen some tools, like ClientFlow, that are attempting to solve this problem. Over time, I think we will see more Software-as-a-Service tools that assist with onboarding and optimize for client success. There's a tension in these products between giving the detailed view needed for the project team to execute and presenting a client-friendly overview of the project.

Many people are obsessed with finding the latest and greatest project management software tool. However, I think people need to step back and think, "What's a better way to manage clients?" Forecasting analytics is another interesting area for the future. Prior to exiting Planscope, I did some work on this front. The idea is to track your project progress and better understand your clients—how long they take to make decisions. Understand the accuracy of your estimates, and so forth. For web design agencies, improved forecasting and planning based on project data will be valuable.

Harpham: Which books have been valuable in shaping your thinking?

Dunn: A few books come to mind in different areas.

Agile Retrospectives: Making Good Teams Great by Esther Derby and Diana Larsen [Pragmatic Bookshelf, 2006]. This book gave a great introduction to retrospective meetings and it helped tremendously. I used this process within the project and with clients. It helps bring the team together and come up with concrete tasks to improve the organization.

Selling the Invisible: A Field Guide to Modern Marketing by Harry Beckwith [Texere Publishing, 2001] is another excellent book. If you're selling professional services or some other intangible, this is a helpful book.

The Strategy and Tactics of Pricing: A Guide to Growing More Profitably by Thomas Nagle and John Hogan [Routledge, 2010]. Though it is aimed at marketing executives in large companies, I found it quite helpful. It is a great overview of different pricing methods, such as cost-based pricing, how buyers perceive value, and related issues. It's not for everyone and it's not written for a consulting audience. I got a lot out of this book that helped me to improve my business.

Finally, I think there's a lot of value in reading *Plato's Dialogues*. They show how to learn about somebody's beliefs and ideas through a questioning process. My background from college is in the classics. I've learned a lot from that field.

Chapter Summary

- Recommended books include *Agile Retrospectives* by Esther Derby and Diana Larsen, *Selling the Invisible* by Harry Beckwith, *The Strategy and Tactics of Pricing* by Thomas Nagle and John Hogan, and *Plato's Dialogues*.

- The origin of Dunn's project management app, Planscope: Dunn was inspired to create the Planscope app after struggling to find effective tools and methods to run projects at his agency.

- The proactive consultant mindset: In his work with many freelancers and consultants, Dunn has noticed that top performers proactively define their relationships with clients in terms of communication structure and frequency and overall expectations. You can't assume that your client knows the right way to work with you.

- Adapt lessons from other professions: Dunn has adopted best practices from lawyers and real estate professionals to improve his productivity. Look beyond your discipline for new strategies and tactics to improve your performance.

- The road-mapping strategy. Not sure how to approach a vaguely worded client request? Consider Dunn's process to use a road-mapping service to define the goal before getting involved in the project's details.

Tracy Ford

Director of APM Practice, General Electric

Tracy Ford *is the director of the APM Practice of GE Digital's Global Services organization. She manages a global team of engineers that deliver GE's APM and SmartSignal products to customers. Based outside of Chicago, Illinois, her team supports customers all over the world with all types of equipment. They are on track to triple the number of assets connected year after year. A 25-plus-year GE veteran, Ford has worked at various GE companies, including GE Renewables and GE Energy. She holds a master's degree in computer information systems management from Union College in Schenectady, New York.*

Bruce Harpham: How did you get started in project management?

Tracy Ford: I've been with General Electric for twenty-five years. I started in GE's Software Technology program that was based out of our Global Research program for new college graduates. I got started by analyzing data packets flowing through networks and the traditional, waterfall project management methods. Later on, I earned a master's degree from Union College and took on new assignments within GE: system analyst roles, project manager roles, financial transaction quality roles, product manager roles, and product quality roles.

My current assignment is the Asset Performance Management [APM] practice leader in the Chicago area. I work with a global team of over thirty GE employees and forty-plus contractors. I have a team in Brazil, a team in the Middle East, and other locations. My focus is on the project management and implementation of the APM product, a leading offering for GE Digital. I often face the challenge of delivering the promises made by the sales team. I have to

© Bruce Harpham 2018
B. Harpham, *Project Managers at Work*, DOI 10.1007/978-1-4842-2668-1_15

be a top-notch project manager to deliver on those requirements. In fact, I've recently hired a number of project managers to the team to supplement the team's existing engineering strength.

However, you can't walk in from the street and start working as a project manager here. In my view, you need training from an organization like the Project Management Institute [PMI] and a lot of PM experience to be successful. My day-to-day work involves overseeing sixty-five projects around the world and ensuring that we're meeting the customer's requirements.

Harpham: What were some of the first projects you worked on?

Ford: I started working on projects as I went through the company's software technology program. I learned about the project life cycle in terms of the waterfall model. It was helpful to break projects into discrete parts—requirements gathering and the subsequent steps. I remember liking the process because it was very prescriptive. On the other hand, there's a problem with that approach. The waterfall approach can be quite time-consuming to work through. By the time you get to implementation, the customer requirements have changed or the technology is obsolete.

In 2001, I started to work on large IT projects at GE as an IT project manager. In those projects, much of the programming was done by contractors. At the same time, there were tough demands from internal customers to deliver the project. In my experience, GE internal customers can be the toughest customers because they expect a lot from their GE peers. About a year after starting that role, I pursued PMI training. I found PMI's model helpful especially in terms of risk management, understanding the critical path process and getting clear on roles and responsibilities. Learning the PMI approach to projects gave me a great structure to work on. I had originally worked on IT because it is logical work. I like the clarity and the ability to follow a checklist. Project management has much of that structure and logic.

Harpham: What was the objective of these early projects?

Ford: One early project was called the "EP configurator." [The energy products configurator was a tool for customers to configure the type of GE product needed to solve their energy needs.] This system helped GE end customers enter specifications and figure out what type of GE power turbine they should get. In essence, this tool was to help the customer understand what type of turbine they would need. This system would also provide information to GE's proposals team, which would work on the request with the customer.

I have also worked on full-scale ERP implementation projects. As the acting manager for the sourcing group at the GE Global Research Center, I worked on an ERP implementation project from the business side.

Looking back, one of the projects I'm most proud of is an ERP implementation for an online parts ordering system for GE Renewables. That project was extremely challenging. The project had high visibility. This system was directly used by the end customer and internal GE groups. It involved making hard decisions to meet the deadline. For example, I had to say no to certain requirements in order to meet the schedule. The question became "What can you get done in the time frame we have?"

I started my career using the waterfall approach to project management. Today, I'm a proponent of the agile methodology. If you take a long time to implement technology, it's going to be obsolete by the time you finish. The potential for instant feedback in agile is highly attractive.

On my current projects, it's important to get our customers set up on our website as soon as possible. That way, they can see our systems and capabilities even if the system had not been fully deployed and configured. At least, they can see and touch the system to start to understand it. That way, they can give us feedback. The last thing I want to do is spend three to six months implementing a project in isolation and have the end customer say, "Oh, this system doesn't do what I wanted it to do." Obtaining feedback early and often from the customer is important.

Harpham: ERP projects are interesting because they can have high impact and deliver value to senior management. On the other hand, these projects can burn huge amounts of money if they flounder and take years to be fully implemented. What has your ERP project experience been like?

Ford: Interestingly, we're in the middle of another ERP implementation right now. Oh, my goodness. At this point, I'm on the business side rather than running the project. It's almost a case where I know too much to be a normal stakeholder on the project. We're moving from SAP to Oracle at the moment.

Turning to the ERP implementation I led, there were a lot of moving parts. I negotiated with the project sponsor on expectations. He wanted it to be the Big Bang and he wanted every capability in it. In other words, 100% functionality and features on Day 1 rather than a gradual release. His view was that we're only going to receive ERP project funds once, so we've got to build as much as we can. He wanted to delay the end date of the project in order to build more scope. I went against that view.

Instead, I argued that it's more important to launch a simpler system sooner rather than delaying and launching a more complete system. An earlier launch will give us critical feedback from users on what to do next. Once you get the ERP system live, you can transition to a quarterly process to release updates and changes. My view was to launch the system with the critical features and add more during the quarterly releases. We were trying to do things with Oracle iStore that it wasn't meant to do out of the box. We definitely pushed the capability of iStore to the limit.

For example, we were trying to make Oracle eBusiness Suite into a point-and-click purchasing experience that Amazon provides. When a customer comes to make an order, we wanted it be a pretty good user experience. ERP systems have a lot of great modular functionality. However, they don't necessarily come with an attractive front-end user interface. We had to strike a balance between making modifications to the code and maintaining compatibility with future releases of the ERP product. If you make numerous modifications to the ERP and the vendor releases a new version, your modifications may stop working and you may need to re-do all of the customization work to restore that functionality.

Fortunately, this re-work problem is likely to decline in significance in the future. The rise of micro services in the digital world means minimal upkeep to maintain compatibility with future services.

I sought feedback from small and large end customers. I wanted the system to increase GE's parts business and make it easy for customers to find the parts they needed. Making sure that we understood the persona of the different people who would use the service was important. For example, a person in a purchasing group would likely make purchases on a regular basis and want to just search by part numbers. In contrast, an asset manager may have occasional orders only and won't have the part numbers. To this day, aspects of the system are still being used.

Looking back, I did see some areas where there were struggles. I didn't think through and close all of the holes for pictures of products. The lesson: it's easy to get focused on the promise of a shiny new tool and we forget that there needs to be a process to update and maintain the system after the project team walks away.

Harpham: It's the classic struggle where the project team hands a product off to the operations team to run.

Ford: Exactly. "Who is responsible to maintain this system?" is a key question.

Harpham: What is a project management practice that you learned the hard way from a mistake or challenge?

Ford: Delivering projects in large organizations has been difficult in some ways. In one project, I was based at GE headquarters in New York State. The project had a global impact on GE offices around the world. Therefore, I needed GE stakeholders in Europe to participate and buy into the project. In practice, I struggled to engage them effectively.

I remember saying, "Hey, we need the European office to test this!" or do some other task. Everything on the project was done through conference calls: there was little travel for the project due to concerns around expense control. In this case, traveling to the European offices would have made a positive difference for the project outcome and engagement. We never truly got the European team on board with the project. I tried to cajole and convince the European team with calls and emails.

Unfortunately, I wasn't able to meet with them face to face. The lack of contact made it difficult to communicate the project mission and vision effectively. I think they perceived this project as just another project that GE headquarters was shoving down their throats. When I faced problems like lack of engagement, I would escalate the matter to the Europe management team. While the escalation would get the immediate task completed, I got the sense that it was done begrudgingly.

My lesson from this experience: push for face-to-face meetings with stakeholders whenever possible despite the expense. It's critical to meet in person because you can pick up details that do not come through in other ways [e.g., they're saying yes with words, but signaling no with body language]. Even more important, these meetings give you the opportunity to understand what's blocking them from supporting and participating in the project. In a face-to-face meeting, I think other teams are more likely to open up about their concerns or tell us about risks that might cause the project to fail. For example, the team may be short staffed due to a maternity leave and they're upset about the possibility about being asked to take on additional project tasks. You are not likely to get this information on a conference call but you are likely to get it while networking after face-to-face meetings.

From a timing perspective, you want to gain that understanding and personal connection early in the project. In our case, the engagement issues were discovered very late in the project, during user acceptance testing, when it is hard to adjust the project to meet their specific needs.

Today, I have a rule for my project managers: have at least one face-to-face meeting with the customer. This may seem obvious, but we are a digital company that is creating cloud based projects, so we could actually complete them without ever going to the customer's site! The project manager and lead engineer could visit. That could be at the project kick-off or at the design review stage. It's vital to build the relationship with the customer through that process. You will also understand who will own the results of the project at the end.

Harpham: What were some of the warning signals you noticed that tipped you off that the stakeholder was disengaged?

Ford: I noticed a lack of response or delayed response in answering emails. There were test cases that they were supposed to go through: they didn't get them done. Every "ask" had to be escalated. There was so much going on the project that I didn't stop to ask about this situation. I kept thinking, "OK, I'll just continue escalating to get these tasks done."

I also noticed disengagement in meetings and conference calls. For example, I would invite three people from Europe to a call. However, only one person—or none!—would actually show up. Getting customer data for testing was also difficult. Every step in the process could be seen as an early warning or an indicator that there was a deeper problem of disengagement.

Finally, a contributing problem was the lack of a single point person to represent the European group on the project. If you give a task to multiple people—even if the task is "attend this project conference call"—everyone assumes somebody else will do it. I use the saying, "If it's everyone's responsibility, it's nobody's responsibility." You need somebody who is "on the hook" to get the work done or provide an answer.

Harpham: If a task is assigned to "the technical team," then it is unclear who I contact when there is a problem or if I have a question.

Ford: Yes, that's right.

Harpham: Let's turn to mentorship. What is your experience with mentorship in your career?

Ford: There are some people in GE that I look to as mentors and I reach out to them for advice. At this stage, I'm looking for a sponsor to support my goals rather than a mentor. In my view, a sponsor is someone who takes direct action to support and advance my goals. In contrast, a mentor tends to play the role of a sounding board and helps you to develop ideas. I've been in the GE Digital unit for under two years and I'm still looking around for who might be a good fit as a sponsor.

I have also acted as a mentor to some of the junior people I've worked with, such as the interns who have worked in the department. While I'm naturally drawn to mentoring others, I have a large team of direct reports to manage, so it is difficult to make time for this activity. With each role I've had, I've picked up different tactics and strategies from different people I've worked with.

From a people perspective, I do wonder about our growth rate. This business is growing fast. There are constantly new projects to work on. With our extreme growth we are hiring a lot of people and there is limited time for onboarding activities. Are we all getting enough time to be mentored or serve as a mentor to others? It is definitely a delicate balance between strategic growth and mentoring team members!

Harpham: What are some of the insights you've learned from mentors over the years?

Ford: I recall the following concept: "What would you do if this was your money [or your business]?" At one point, I was working on a project where we were looking at project software in depth to see how it could improve our work. The manager at the time went around the room and asked everyone the following question: "What would you do if this was your business?" It's an important point because it shows he wasn't looking for a yes-man response. He wanted to hear what everyone thought about the issue. When he asked that point-blank question, most of the team reconsidered the project and decided not to do it.

I've also learned about the people aspect of business transformation. In 2008, I was working on a project to implement a new configuration management system for GE's wind turbines. In order to do that, we had to put barcodes on about one hundred components on each wind turbine. That was a challenge because it meant asking manufacturing facilities to take on additional work. My mindset shifted when a manager said to me, "Tracy, you need to think about how you're going to bring them flowers." The meaning? From the other person's perspective, how does the planned change benefit them? In this case, the benefit for manufacturing staff was reducing defects in the manufacturing process. We also made their daily work easier—giving them a scanner rather than recording data in a paper booklet. I had to visit the manufacturing facility and get to know their process in depth. With that understanding, I could go into depth on how I could make life easier for them. The part barcoding and scanning project was fully implemented. The manufacturing staff supported the successful project implementation.

Harpham: Empathy and thinking through what's in it for the other person is an important point. After all, when you are deep in the project, the value of the project will be clear to you and you may assume everyone appreciates the project in the same way.

Ford: Yes, that's right. About seven years ago, I joined Toastmasters because communication skills were not my focus when I started my career as an engineer. Reading your audience, anticipating their questions, and responding smoothly are some of the benefits I gained from working with Toastmasters. Your speaking and listening skills have a major impact on your success or failure.

Harpham: What has been your approach to learning from your experiences?

Ford: I generally ask two questions about projects and other activities I work on: "What went well?" and "What could I do better next time?" I think you can learn to do better from each and every project you work on. In my current role, I focus on implementing our projects quickly and find ways to improve quality at the same time. We have to be a learning organization in order to deliver all of these improvements. I've also started running "Breakfast and Learn" sessions to accommodate the schedules of our global team members.

In the Breakfast and Learn sessions, we cover details related to how to do the APM implementation and automation tools, proper documentation for project managers, Predix basics, etc. It's a combination of project management methodologies and Predix/APM technical details.

We're also looking for ways to improve our knowledge management processes. That's where you get even greater value out of lessons learned efforts. For example, I look at our lessons learned and seek to translate that into an improvement. Is it a training issue? Or a missing step in a process? There are also cases where I simply consider something to be an anomaly that is unlikely to happen again.

Harpham: You've recently hired several project managers for your team. What are some of the traits, skills, and other qualities that you look for when hiring project managers?

Ford: I want somebody who has an engineering background or a relevant industry background. For example, a lot of our projects are in the oil and gas industry and in the power industry. Therefore, I want somebody who has dealt with projects in those industries. I also expect new hires come in with a certification or formal training in project management. That knowledge is an important foundation, because then we can immediately get down to discussing concepts like the critical path or Gantt charts.

I'm also interested to know how they handle difficult customers or solving difficult problems that come up on projects. Alternately, how they would approach communicating bad news on a project, such as showing that it will be late. I like to ask about those issues to find out what language they use to communicate when faced with those issues. I've actually had interviewees say, "Well, I had a dumb customer on this project who just didn't get it." That kind of language is offensive! Oh, my goodness! This is not a person I would want on my team if they are going to treat people like that.

Project management can be the hardest job in the world. You have to be able to improvise solutions. There are no cookie-cutter projects. I got my team T-shirts that say: "Implementation Engineer: Because 'Badass Miracle Worker' Is Not An Official Job Title." You've got to be like MacGyver to get our projects completed. When you are connecting many different types of assets from many different industries in a wide variety of technology environments, it takes a certain "art" to make it all work. There is no one-size-fits-all for solutions, but GE Digital gives us the tools and technology to get the job done.

I'm also interested in understanding a candidate's methodology and methods. How do they like to start a project? That gives me an idea about their approach to a project and their experience.

Harpham: If a new project arrives on your desk, how do you start the project work?

Ford: We use a checklist to get the key information for the project. For example, I get in touch with the inquiry to order [i.e., sales] team to ask about the proposal, and what the customer expects, and review related documentation. I also ask about the customer's history with GE and their expectations. For example, I may be asked to lead a project kick-off meeting next week, which causes a scramble to make it happen.

The next steps will involve getting in touch with other stakeholders within GE. I may call in the managed service team to get them on board [if we will be managing the assets after they are live and collecting data]. I'll often get in touch with the analytics team as well. It's important to get all of the teams aware of the coming project and what is expected.

Recently, I have led the process to use a formal project charter on all of the projects we do. It is a great way to get everyone on the same page [literally] by boiling a very large proposal document into a simple one- to two-page document with scope, assumptions, roles, responsibilities, and high-level schedule.

In the first few days I have a project, the goal is to have the process unfold like the baton pass in a relay race between the sales team and the project team. I start with a standard project plan in Microsoft Project for each project. Based on feedback from the sales team, we add and remove items from it.

Harpham: What are some of your productivity habits and methods that you use to stay organized and focused?

Ford: Well, my husband and I both work and we have three children at home. Pursuing balance is a never-ending task. I start by getting up early in the morning. I grew up on a farm, so that gave me the habit to get up early—5am every day, even the weekends— and work hard. The habit of getting up early and planning my day out before everyone else gets up makes a big difference.

I use Microsoft OneNote to organize my tasks and information. I'm working hard to get away from using paper to track information. I may write a few quick notes while I'm on the phone, but then I will write up a quick summary in OneNote after. With seventy people—a mix of GE staff and contractors— on my team and sixty-five projects, I can't keep that all in my head. That way, I can easily respond to questions from my manager about projects I run. The team has been growing fast. In 2015, we had about a dozen people.

For project management activities, Microsoft Project is my tool of choice. For example, I had a request last Saturday to produce a project plan for a project in the Middle East. In that case, I went through the process of creating the project plan myself. After all, it would be cruel and unusual punishment to ask one of my project managers to work on a Saturday. By knowing MS Project well, I can also review project plans and discover potential problems. For example, not including appropriate dependencies in your project plans can impact your ability to see the critical paths on projects.

Harpham: What books have made a positive impact on your career?

Ford: I really like the book *10-10-10: A Life-Transforming Idea*, by Suzy Welch [Scribner, 2009], for making decisions about priorities. As a mother of three with a very demanding work schedule, you need to make priority decisions constantly. I can't attend all seven meetings that might be on my calendar for the same time period. The book poses these questions to decide on priorities: Is this going to make a difference ten minutes from now, ten months from now, or ten years from now? It's a great process to decide between two options or appointments. For example, I may decide to miss a child's sports game [of which there are many each year], but ensure that I attend their concert because there's only one of those each year.

Earlier today, I happened to re-read part of The One Minute Manager by Kenneth Blanchard and Spencer Johnson [William Morrow, 2003]. It's a great book and I am re-reading it to refresh my memory on the practices.

Harpham: How has your approach to leadership developed over time?

Ford: Early in my career, I had a task-oriented approach: getting the project done and asking what the next task is. I didn't give much attention to networking, relationships, and making sure everyone is on board. Today, I've realized that relationships make a tremendous impact. Without the relationships, the work becomes much harder. I'm focusing on getting out to customers, co-workers, and team members each quarter to make sure that the relationships remain strong with those important people in my role.

Harpham: Looking three to five years into the future, what are some opportunities and trends that are interesting to your work?

Ford: The digital transformation is top of mind for me. I have been focused on the tactical and engineering aspect of this transformation. I need to get more engaged with the adoption for the customer and the outcomes we're creating. My part of GE Digital used to be a separate company called SmartSignal [predictive analytics software]. SmartSignal was acquired by GE in 2011 and has a great product. The next step is to put the business transformation in place through automated quick deployment of the solution. That's what generates real business improvement. We want to shift from running a project and sending out alert notices to customers, to delivering real value for the customers.

I'm also interested in increasing collaboration with consulting organizations and partners, to help GE Digital grow faster. These partnerships will improve the value we deliver to our customers faster.

Chapter Summary

- Recommended books include *10-10-10* by Suzie Welch and *The One-Minute Manager* by Ken Blanchard and Spencer Johnson.

- Stakeholder engagement: Ford recommends pursuing face-to-face meetings to fully engage stakeholders; otherwise, you may run the risk of disengaged stakeholders slowing down the project.

- A daily question to ask at work: Ford learned the value of asking the question "What would you do if you owned this business?" from a manager she worked with earlier in her career.

- Toastmasters: Ford found Toastmasters to be an excellent organization to develop her communication skills.

- The Job Interview Question: Ford often asks prospective new hires how they would handle a difficult customer situation. Candidates who refer to the customer with insulting or abusive language prompt red flags!

Annette Lyjak

Senior IT Manager - Technology Project Management Office, OMERS

Annette Lyjak *began her professional career with American Express. From 1999 to 2017, she worked on financial systems as a Business Systems Analyst in project, program, and risk management. She has spent over 15 years in a variety of roles, specializing in the technical delivery of credit card systems and services to American Express clients around the world. In 2017, Lyjak moved to OMERS (Ontario Municipal Employees Retirement System) Administration Corporation as Senior IT Manager for the Technology Project Management Office. Lyjak has been PMP certified through the Project Management Institute since 2008. She graduated from York University (in Toronto, Ontario, Canada) in 1998 with an Honours Bachelor of Arts in cultural and critical studies. She recently passed the Certified Information Security Manager exam through ISACA.*

Lyjak is looks for opportunities to improve the overall quality in project delivery. She has been highly effective in the areas of new product development and operational risk. Another passion is progressing the careers and experiences of women in technology and business, where she has served as an active leader in organizational programs.

Bruce Harpham: How did you get started in project management?

Annette Lyjak: I always had a knack for project management, even before I learned the term for it. Shortly after graduating from university, where I studied the cultural and critical studies program in fine arts, I went on a two-month trip through Europe with a friend. I planned the entire trip—the schedule and

© Bruce Harpham 2018
B. Harpham, *Project Managers at Work*, DOI 10.1007/978-1-4842-2668-1_16

all the details. I had a natural tendency to plan activities, which has served me well. In total, we went through eleven countries in two months. Some of the countries we visited were England, France, Italy, Czech Republic, and Poland. My focus in my studies was art and architecture, so I was really excited to see all the buildings and art I had studied up close and personal.

I started my career working at Toronto Dominion Bank [TD Bank] as a student. Later, I was a full-time employee in the insurance department, where I worked on implementing a new insurance system. The project brought me on as a new user to test the system. It was my first experience working on a technology project and seeing what was involved with that kind of work.

Shortly afterwards, I landed at American Express in a business systems analyst job in the technology division. I was planning on doing my MBA in fine arts. However, I caught the travel bug from backpacking through Europe—and American Express promised a lot of travel. So I chose to obtain my "MBA" from American Express "university," where I have been afforded with the opportunity to learn through doing projects, creating solutions, creating brand-new departments and methodologies, while getting to see this amazing world we live in.

Harpham: When you were first exposed to projects in the stakeholder role, what was the nature of the project?

Lyjak: In the TD Bank context, I was going through user acceptance testing as one of the end users. We were working on a mainframe computer application that did processing related to lending and mortgage insurance premiums. I had a number of test cases to work through as a user. Most of the time, I was working on insurance administration related to mortgage insurance and related insurance products.

Harpham: What was your focus when you joined American Express?

Lyjak: The company introduced a brand-new financial platform. I was the business systems analyst for this platform. I got to learn the SDLC [systems development life cycle] framework, the different systems at the company, and how to implement a new system from beginning to end. I learned how to discover requirements and translate those into test cases. I actually wasn't fond of writing test cases and that's one of the reasons I moved to project management. In a way, I was operating in an agile manner about twenty years ago.

At that time, my approach to agile meant that small project teams were assigned. Everyone pitched in to help each other to get work done—including writing requirements, developing test cases and plans, and setting up the environment. However, I left the coding to the coders. They're the experts. We worked very closely together with them implementing changes and me trying to break their code. I ended up moving toward a traditional or waterfall project management approach to cope with the increasing complexity I faced on the projects.

Harpham: That's an interesting transition. I typically hear of organizations starting from a traditional waterfall approach and then moving to agile later on. Can you explain that situation further?

Lyjak: Back then, the developers, the project manager, and the analysts supported the software project implementation and the ongoing support. We didn't hand it over to somebody else to maintain. Production support was integrated with our unit.

Harpham: The general enthusiasm for agile needs to be nuanced depending on the industry. In the financial services industry, risk management is a paramount concern. You can't tell a bank customer that their bank account is offline for a day because a system update failed. If an email service goes down for a day, it would be frustrating, but not to the same degree.

Lyjak: Absolutely, risk is a top consideration in the financial industry. It guides much of our approach on projects.

Harpham: What was challenging about test cases and related activities that prompted you to change your focus?

Lyjak: Playing to your strengths was a popular concept at that time in the business world. Books like *Now, Discover Your Strengths* by Marcus Buckingham and Donald Clifton [Gallup Press, 2001], promoted this viewpoint. I thought about my strengths in the professional world. While I considered myself effective at test cases and related activities, I didn't love it. In contrast, I felt I was a natural leader. I liked to organize people to achieve a goal, so I decided to explore that strength by transitioning to project management.

An opportunity came up during this time to serve as a relationship manager for the Canadian division of American Express. The role involved managing projects end to end from a funding standpoint. I was accountable for all projects within a given portfolio/business line and ensuring that all these projects were delivered in a timely manner with quality results. In a way, I skipped a level. I went from a lead analyst role to a program management role. My leader at the time took a risk in promoting me to the role. He realized that I was a people person and had leadership potential. My business analyst background meant that I knew how to come up with requirements and then my leadership ability would support me through subsequent steps of the process.

My relationship manager role involved end-to-end project delivery, working with technology teams and translating everyone's needs into requirements. For smaller projects, I served in the project manager role myself. For example, smaller projects would include updating web copy and limited functions were required to install partner gateways. That was how I gained much of my project management experience. At this point, I thought it would be helpful to pursue the PMP certification.

Harpham: Let's say there are ten projects on the list at different levels of complexity. You would assign eight of them to other project managers in the organization. You would then manage the two remaining smaller projects yourself?

Lyjak: Yes, that's right.

Harpham: In this program management role, did you play a role in influencing or deciding which projects would get funded? It's common for organizations to have more project requests than they have funding.

Lyjak: I had monthly meetings with the executive stakeholders to review their portfolio of projects. On an annual basis, I participated in the project selection process. There might be fifty project proposals on table to be reviewed. All of these required high-level estimates from the technical teams so that we could make good decisions about them. Using a cost and benefit analysis, we generally chose the projects with the greatest positive impact.

Harpham: In executing these projects, how often did the initial cost and benefit estimates turn out to be inaccurate at the end of the project?

Lyjak: Fortunately, that didn't happen. You can detect if a project is going off the rails early in terms of costs and benefits. That's why running smaller versions of the project concept as a pilot is a common approach to mitigate the risk of failure. If the project is in danger of blowing past its budget, it may be shut down.

Harpham: Scrapping a project is interesting because it appears to be somewhat rare. Many people are afflicted by the sunk cost fallacy in making project decisions, including deciding whether or not to continue the project. Have you seen many projects cancelled?

Lyjak: I have seen a few projects get cancelled. They usually don't get to the stage where you have spent an exorbitant amount of money. From a technical standpoint, you may discover that the project will be very difficult to deploy. In that case, it may not be worth pursuing. In other cases, a project may be cancelled if other priorities with a higher value come up.

Harpham: What are some of your personal lessons learned in project management that you learned the hard way?

Lyjak: There's so many! When I became involved in projects in the operational risk area, a wise executive told me, "You can never under communicate." It's true! I found that when I do not provide timely updates with meaningful information, I have run into problems. In those cases, other people may escalate to your manager because something isn't getting done. Poorly written updates frustrate stakeholders.

When a project goes quiet, that worries me. It's a sign that something is wrong. They may be in over their heads. When I see situations like that, I dive in to find out what's happening and help the project team improve their communication.

Harpham: What goes into an effective project status update?

Lyjak: Status updates need to be calibrated to the importance of the project. With a low-risk project, there's more flexibility on how status updates are done. Such updates tend to have less detail because there's no benefit to creating detail if the project is small or low risk.

For a high-profile project, I have different expectations for the status update process. For example, I want to see details on risk tracking, milestones, and further details. If the project concerns an urgent fix to a production system—something that impacts how our credit cards work for the customer, we may have daily status updates to the stakeholders. In addition, the status update may be delivered as a live conference call as opposed to an email.

Status updates need to be customized depending on the type of project you're running. You take several factors into account when you decide on the depth and frequency of status reporting, including project budget, complexity, and customer impact.

Harpham: The recurring cadence is an important part of the process. For example, let's say you had a relatively quiet week where you made incremental progress on various tasks but nothing was delivered. You don't want to go silent for a week.

Lyjak: Right, you never want to go "dark" on a project.

Harpham: If project communication to stakeholders stops, panic and uncertainty may increase.

Lyjak: It's easy to get into a bad habit of not communicating. One week without project communication may be fine. However, that process may easily continue. If the project continues to be silent, you may start to receive inquiries that could have been prevented.

Harpham: Let's turn to the product implementation projects you've worked on at American Express. You worked on implementing pre-paid mall cards. Can you give us an overview of the product and your role?

Lyjak: This product is a gift card. For example, you would buy a $50 American Express prepaid card and give it as a present. The recipient can then use it to make a purchase. When I was implementing the product several years ago, it was a rapid expansion across the United States. The product has grown rapidly over the years and now is available in several countries.

For a year, I took on a cross-training assignment with the new cards development department. It was an easy transition for me to succeed in this department because I had extensive project management expertise to draw on. At the same time, there was plenty to learn regarding how new products are brought to market. For example, I worked with public affairs, translation, and legal as stakeholders in this project. It was also interesting to work with companies and stakeholders outside of the company, like banks and retailers. In most technology projects, the focus is on internal stakeholders. I crafted and created product overviews, which tapped into my creative literary side.

Harpham: How did you adjust to working on a project that has a direct impact on the end customer?

Lyjak: I started by researching the product and how it worked. If a customer bought this product, how would they use it? I approached the challenge by reading up on it and asking questions from people with past experience on similar products and projects.

Harpham: What did you find most challenging personally on this project, given that it was different from your past projects?

Lyjak: It was a different world for me. I had to learn about the different dependencies and connections between systems and people that were involved. The work was an end-to-end process—from product concept, technology required, marketing material, legal, sales, customer support, and so forth. For example, I worked on the copy involved on the product. I also interacted with the art department, which created the look and feel of the product. The product was customized in appearance based on the co-branded relationships we had arranged with various retailers. It was fun to work on that because it was tangible. You could see the card and hold it in your hands.

Harpham: What do you mean that this was a cross-training assignment?

Lyjak: On a previous project, I worked on the Travelers Cheques product. Through the work, I got to know the VP of that group. He encouraged me to work with his organization. We worked out an arrangement to "loan" me from my home department and go work in this other department. It was a win because gave me an added opportunity to see how the business and product development operates. Prior to this role, I was entirely focused on the technology group at American Express.

Harpham: I've heard this kind of arrangement described as a "secondment"— being loaned temporarily to another department.

Lyjak: Yes, that's a way to describe it.

Harpham: It sounds like your connection with an executive played an essential role in landing this opportunity. What was the relationship?

Lyjak: The person was a key project sponsor and I had only worked with him for a short time. During that time, we developed a good working relationship. He liked my work and how I resourced my team to ensure that their skills sets matched to the project goals.

Harpham: This suggests the importance of always delivering to a high standard on projects. If you make a good impression on someone, there are benefits to your career that go beyond the project.

Lyjak: You never know what opportunities will be available to you. That's why you need to put your best foot forward.

Harpham: Turning to risk management, this concept has a dual meaning in your environment. There's project risk on the one hand, and risk in the financial industry sense on the other hand. What's your approach to risk management?

Lyjak: I have seen an evolution in how people think and interact with risk. Years ago, people would just shut down when they heard the word "risk." There was little understanding that risk can also be seen as an opportunity. I learned two important principles about risk. First, that each individual risk needs to be assigned to an owner. Second, risk is also an incentive to encourage us to find creative solutions.

Harpham: What is an example of a creative solution that you developed in response to a risk?

Lyjak: There are different ways risk can impact a project. For example, risk may impact the project schedule, the budget, and scope. These risks can be independent or appear in combination. Identifying the risk is only the first step in the process. The second step is to look for a mitigating control or strategy that addresses it. For example, you may decide to crash the schedule or add more resources to the project in order to achieve the goal.

When you raise a risk to management, you should have a solution in mind. If cost is a concern—that is a common issue—then I will work with the project team to explore ways in which we can reduce costs by leveraging activities, like piggybacking on an active test environment—looking to other technology solutions that still meet the basic needs without all the bells and whistles. I find that leaders appreciate individuals who help get things done effectively and efficiently. I recommend trying to anticipate the needs of your stakeholders, verify those needs, gain agreement, prioritize them, and plan accordingly.

Harpham: Waving a yellow flag on the project to proclaim, "We have a problem," and leaving it at that, doesn't lead to a good result.

Lyjak: It doesn't work well. A lot of people look at risk management as a way to push accountability to somebody else. If you truly want to transfer risk, pay an insurance company for the privilege. As a project manager and a decent human being, you can't simply raise an issue and throw it over the wall.

Harpham: The point you make about insurance companies is a good one. When you buy insurance, you are making the risk their problem. On the other hand, you don't get that benefit for free. In the project context, some think that it is enough to identify a risk as opposed to developing a solution.

Lyjak: It helps to think about other options. For example, if you need another department to act on a risk or dependency and they are not acting on it—maybe they are too busy to take a call with you, then ask yourself, "Is there other work we can do to move the project ahead while we wait?"

Harpham: Project management tends to foster a linear thought process—complete A, then B, and move on to C. It's a powerful way to move a project forward. In other situations, a lateral thinking approach is needed to solve risk issues. What's your approach to developing and using creative approaches?

Lyjak: It starts with talking with a variety of people. That gives you new data and perspectives on the problem. It's also important to look for schedule flexibility: Could we do a future task today to maintain progress while something else is delayed?

Flexibility is encouraged by practices such as the daily scrum meeting from agile. I don't think there's a secret sauce to having creative solutions. It comes down to being well informed on the project and well connected with different people on the project. I stay informed about the project by having regular status updates—usually a weekly status to get a cursory perspective—and will be involved at project-level status when required. I tend to deep-dive on projects when they are risky. Risk can be based on the total cost of the project, experience of the project team, and conversely, our stakeholders, scope, and the time required to implement.

Harpham: It is also a question of looking for proactive opportunities to do some other work. You wouldn't want a project team to sit idle for a week because of a delay by somebody else.

Lyjak: Yes, that's right.

Harpham: Risk management has recently become an area of focus for you. When you see other project managers in action, what are some of the common risk mistakes that you see?

Lyjak: The most common issue is failing to escalate a risk for action in a timely manner. I think that people are often afraid to point out a risk because they think this will make them look bad. I take a different perspective. It's positive and valuable to bring a risk into the open. Otherwise, it will be much more difficult to succeed. There are sometimes weaknesses in risk management during the planning phase.

A lot of assumptions can be made during the definition phase. Sometimes these assumptions are not accounted for, which can lead to issues. This is especially true for assuming another team is going to do the work because they have always done the work before. This is an assumption. You need to verify with the team that they will take on this activity for your project. Otherwise, you could be surprised that the team has recently been reorganized and that activity/function is no longer supported or hasn't been transferred to a new team to support. The earlier you identify a threat to the project and bring that to your leader, the better. The next step is to work with your leader to develop a resolution to the risk. Your leaders and stakeholders need to be briefed on the project's risks if you are going to be successful.

Harpham: There's a "shoot the messenger" anxiety for people bringing risks to light?

Lyjak: That's right.

Harpham: If a peer were to ask for your advice on how to bring up and manage a risk issue, what would you suggest?

Lyjak: I would suggest starting by gathering the facts so that we understand the risk. Which people are involved internally and beyond on this risk? Only once we understand the scope and nature of the risk can we start to look at partnering to develop a solution.

Harpham: The risk may initially be presented as a vague intuition. However, you cannot escalate a risk based on that feeling alone. Further investigation is required to define the risk before you present to an executive or another person.

Lyjak: That's right. Someone I work with recently brought me a risk item where a regulatory obligation needed to be met with limited time. Sometimes we cannot control when a new regulation is issued. There was some information but not all the homework was done on it in terms of the requirements and complexity of the solution. I asked them to do further research on the risk before we did anything further on it. If I was going to take the issue to a senior leader to escalate, I knew I needed to be well prepared in order to do that. Alternately, of course, I'd love to avoid escalating the issue and solve it directly by coming up with different options. However, some risks are beyond our control, so you really need to leverage your leaders' and their leaders' support.

Harpham: How has your approach to leadership developed?

Lyjak: It starts with going beyond administration in terms of how I think about my responsibilities. I bring strong technical experience and credibility to my role as a leader regarding working on systems and implementing systems. I've always appreciated a leader that has my back. That means a leader that gives you freedom in your decision making, and based on your performance trusts your decision-makings skills to back you up.

This leadership approach is something that I try to do for my team. I think people appreciate a leader who will go to bat for them and protect them to a degree.

As a leader, I also give thought to the career development of people working for me. If I know somebody is interested in taking their career in a different direction, I look for those opportunities for them to grow.

A colleague came to me when I was helping to develop a new technology risk organization. I shared with her what we were trying to accomplish with this new organization and she seemed really interested. I was still working on what the organization would like, so it was early days. I worked out an arrangement with her leader to loan her out to me. I eventually hired her for a permanent role. And after a couple of years in the role, she was promoted. She couldn't have come at a better time. She helped me get the department off the ground and she excelled in her new role. We both took risks on each other and it paid off. It's also important for me to be accessible to my team as a leader, including having one-on-one meetings on a regular basis.

Harpham: What are some of the insights that you've learned from mentors?

Lyjak: The "you can never under-communicate" principle was an important lesson. Using that principle won me respect from my peers and leaders over time. It's about putting forward an appropriate, short, timely, and meaningful message for your audience.

Harpham: What does your personal productivity system look like?

Lyjak: In terms of tools, I use Microsoft PowerPoint constantly. Business stakeholders like to be briefed through such presentations. It's helpful to present diagrams and other visuals to explain the technical projects that I'm leading. Sending a Microsoft Project plan file to an executive, in contrast, is probably not going to be received well. I use that for my own work and organization instead. For day-to-day work, SharePoint is a great product to coordinate and share files within the team.

Microsoft Excel is the unsung hero of professional work. Excel is simply great! I recommend project managers and others use Excel to manage data and stay organized. It's also a great tool for organizing and analyzing financial data.

Conference calls and virtual meeting software are helpful to work through issues on projects. I like to use more conference calls, stand-up meetings, and similar approaches on high-risk projects to ensure everything keeps moving along well.

Harpham: What books have been influential for your career?

Lyjak: Several years ago, I took a development course from a management consulting company called Above & Beyond. Tracey Levison—one of the course leaders—recommended the book *The Artist's Way* by Julia Cameron

[J.P. Tarcher/Putnam, 2002]. My undergrad is fine arts, cultural, and critical studies. On the surface, that subject matter appears to be very different than what my career entails.

The book really helped me to further influence my spiritual path to higher creativity. Creativity is fluid and it's up to you how you tap into your creative spirit in your day-to-day life. I may not create the next Guernica by Picasso or Fallingwater by Frank Lloyd Wright—who I did my undergraduate thesis on. My livelihood is in deploying technology solutions. There are so many opportunities for me to be creative in the architecture of a solution, the strategy in which I choose to deploy a project, how I communicate and present information, etc. If you are struggling with your work and finding it mundane, I highly recommend The Artist's Way to help you tap into your creative potential and make the most of your situation—and/or find your path.

Harpham: Which technologies and business trends have your attention and interest over the next few years?

Lyjak: Big data analytics is top of mind for me right now. The potential to generate new and better insights through data has been helpful in my current work in operational risk. There's been a lot of hype and promotion about big data, however, I think this technology will mature and offer greater value over time. Related to big data is the need to capture and manage data effectively. Otherwise, there is no material for the analysis. In my work, I have used big data to identify potential risk areas.

Chapter Summary

- Recommended books include *Now, Discover Your Strengths* by Marcus Buckingham and Donald O. Clifton and *The Artist's Way* by Julia Cameron.

- The right opportunities to learn: Involvement in a brand-new financial platform gave Lyjak a great opportunity to learn about project work.

- The communication rule: Lyjak learned this rule from an executive she once worked with—You can never over-communicate.

- Internal networking: Lyjak grew her career through effective working relationships with executives. Each project gives you the opportunity to make a positive impression and earn opportunities.

- Two practices to improve risk management: First, each risk must have an owner. Second, work to find creative solutions to the risk; identifying the risk is not enough.

Bob Tarne

Engagement Manager, IBM

Bob Tarne, *PMP, CSM, PMI-ACP, is an engagement manager for the IBM Systems Group, where he specializes in leading business process improvement initiatives following lean/agile project management techniques. Prior to joining IBM, he was a managing consultant at PM Solutions, where he was responsible for improving clients' project management practices. He has also worked as a project manager for Sprint and Owens-Illinois.*

Tarne's career began in the US Navy, where he served as a cryptologist for seven years. He is an IBM-certified executive project manager and agile thought leader, a PMI Certified Agile Practitioner (PMI-ACP), a PMP-certified project manager, and a Certified ScrumMaster (CSM).

Tarne holds a BS in electrical engineering from the University of Illinois and an MS in business from Johns Hopkins University's Carey Business School. He has been an active PMI volunteer since 2000, which includes roles as the chair of the PMI IT & Telecom Specific Interest Group and a founding member of the Agile Community of Practice.

Bruce Harpham: How did you get started in project management?

Bob Tarne: My first career out of college was in the US Navy. Initially, I was in operational roles in the intelligence field. As an example, I lead a team of analysts that monitored communications from around the world as part of a 24/7 operations watch center. Since my undergraduate field was in engineering, I had the opportunity to go into a group that did engineering-focused work. I worked with the National Security Agency in a group that put electronics

© Bruce Harpham 2018
B. Harpham, *Project Managers at Work*, DOI 10.1007/978-1-4842-2668-1_17

on spy planes. My department worked closely with a number of government contractors that performed the work while we provided oversight. Once a system was completed, we also monitored how it performed in the field. I started picking up the techniques of project management while in this role.

At the same time, I was going to graduate school at Johns Hopkins University, working on a master's degree in business. I took a few project management courses during my studies for that degree. In fact, one of my instructors liked my final project so much that she kept it as a sample for future classes on how to do the assignment. I thought that was a sign that perhaps project management was meant for me.

Harpham: What was this prize-winning assignment?

Tarne: It was a common assignment for a project management course. I had to come up with a hypothetical project plan to execute a project. I remember that I couldn't do anything directly related to my work because it was classified. My hypothetical project was a deployment of cable television to a rural area using wireless technology.

Harpham: How did you navigate the transition from the US Navy to the civilian world?

Tarne: My graduate school experience helped in the transition—it was a practical program where I was working on projects with other people in various industries. I also worked with a recruiter who specialized in placing military officers into civilian roles. I had good advice and support on how to make the transition effectively. My first civilian role was a project manager in the IT department of a manufacturing company. I was responsible for all software projects supporting the sales and marketing department. One of my big projects was an in-house sales-force automation application. This was before the days of cloud computing and applications, such as SalesForce.com.

Harpham: Why did you decide to exit the US Navy and move on to other activities?

Tarne: I was at a point in my Navy career where I was at a field station in the United States. In order to follow the ideal career path, my next position would be on a ship. That would mean long periods of time away from home. My wife and I had just had our second child. It seemed like a good time to transition and jump into the civilian world.

Harpham: What is a project management lesson you learned the hard way?

Tarne: I had a project a few years ago that comes to mind. I was using an agile methodology, but one of the executive sponsors was not that big on agile. They hadn't seen success with agile and they didn't know if it would work. In practice, this meant they acted as a micro-manager on the project. I was in the position where I was being told what to do, how to run the project and do things that were against the principles of agile. I recall one of the daily stand-up meetings. Typically, a stand-up meeting lasts fifteen minutes. In this case, a senior manager came in and asked detailed questions of every team member. The meeting lasted an hour. All the details had been captured in our agile project management tool, but this manager still asked for verbal updates and used up a lot of valuable time. As another example, management required people to work sixty hours per week on the project rather than at a sustainable pace that agile principles recommend. Over half the people on the project left the company during or soon after the project ended.

Harpham: What was driving the requirement for the long hours?

Tarne: The project was getting behind schedule. There was more work to do than what the team could get done. The customer had a firm deadline for the project. That translated into long hours. Bottom line, I wasn't firm enough in my commitment to agile project management methodology. I should have told them that extra hours or adding more people to the project wouldn't solve the problem of too much scope. I ought to have told the client that we need to do less scope or that we need more time. Putting more people on the project was not going to solve the problem.

I didn't stand up to the client. Lo and behold, the project got into trouble and ended up being late anyway. In hindsight, if the project was going to be behind schedule in any case, I should have stood up and said that we can do this better.

Harpham: There's a mental model at play with the sponsor: "If I add X number of people to this project, that will solve the problem."

Tarne: Yes, that was the mindset in this case. If I believe in the methodology, I need to convince my management that using the methodology is the right way to go.

Harpham: In this case, adopting "the customer is always right" attitude would not have been helpful.

Tarne: In the end, the customer didn't get what they wanted from the project. There's a difference between the customer being right about their end goal and being right on the best way to achieve the goal.

Harpham: If we look at the Project Management Institute literature, achieving customer satisfaction is a high priority. However, we need to recognize that the project manager is bringing certain expertise and professional judgment to the table. That may involve pushing back on the customer from time to time.

Tarne: That's a fair point.

Harpham: What stands out to you as a challenging project that you've led during your time at IBM?

Tarne: I've done a number of projects that been quite interesting in their own way. It's important to choose the right people for the project and avoid the problem of having too many cooks in the kitchen. Studies have shown the ideal team size is less than ten people. On one of my projects, we started with a good-sized team, but as the customer asked for more features we added people rather than extending the timeline. In addition, I like when project teams agree to focus and avoid working until ten p.m. every day.

Last year, I was leading a project to bring the Business Process Management technology to a customer in the financial industry. In addition to running the project, I got to teach the customer our approach and methodology. It was fulfilling to do that coaching and mentoring work.

Harpham: What does coaching and mentoring look like for you?

Tarne: In agile, coaching is a best practice. The first step is basic training on agile. Usually, I start off by sitting down with the project manager on the customer side. I educate them on the steps and process, such as defining what a retrospective is and how to run a retrospective session. I will get to the point where I put them in the position to run the activity while I sit in the background. Then, I give them feedback on how they did. I point out what they did well, suggest what they could differently and points to reflect on. One of the biggest challenges I see when an experienced project manager first starts to practice agile is the need to think they still have to control everything. In agile, if you picked the right people for your team, you need to give them the freedom to figure out how to solve the problem and only step in when they run into a roadblock.

Harpham: What would the relationship be between you and the customer project manager?

Tarne: Usually, they are on a peer level. I generally come in with the IBM team to work on a project. There is a customer team that we work with in order to deliver the project. The customer team has a project manager and that person is a peer. We're jointly responsible for delivering the project.

Harpham: Interesting that you mentioned joint responsibility. I find that when a task is assigned to two people, it is ambiguous who is expected to do what. How do you manage that?

Tarne: At the beginning of the project, I sit down with my peer project manager and make sure we have clear expectations for who is responsible for what. That tends to be prevent the "oh, I thought you were doing this" situation.

Harpham: Do you find that people tend to engage well with that process?

Tarne: Sometimes there is some resistance to the process. Sometimes that resistance is due to the fact that they don't know what their responsibilities will be. The stakeholder may have more on their plate than they expected to have. If a person is truly overloaded, then it becomes a discussion with the person's manager to understand what changes can be made.

Harpham: When it comes to new technologies, I sometimes find that developers may ask if the project manager is technically credible. How do you bring new technology to the table where there may be few or no subject matter experts on the client side?

Tarne: At the beginning of the project, it's common that the client does not have the expertise. I bring my team into the effort because we bring the expertise and deep knowledge of the technology we are working with. In many of our engagements, knowledge transfer and training is a big part of our work to help the client understand the technology. In some cases, the client will bring in people who want to gain specialized experience with the technology being introduced.

In other cases, I have come to the end of the project and the client has not prepared to take over ongoing responsibility for the project. In those cases, the customer had to issue a change request to keep us around longer while they found an internal person to get up to speed.

Harpham: Perhaps they get used to having you around and forget that you will eventually leave and work on a different client.

Tarne: Sometimes these transition issues are overlooked or the client has difficulty finding someone to take it in. It's not good but it does happen from time to time.

Harpham: Let's turn to your volunteer contributions. How did you first get started and what keeps you interested in project management volunteering?

Tarne: I went to my first Project Management Institute conference in 1999. One of my co-workers was working on earning the Project Management Professional [PMP] certification. That got me thinking that PMI would be a good organization to join. I was excited by the conference and returned the next year. At the conference in 2000, I went to a session organized by the IT & Telecom interest group. At the time, I was working in telecommunications at Sprint. I was running a team that was responsible for quality assurance for our billing system. I picked up their newsletter, spoke with some people at the meeting, and went home. Later on, I reviewed the newsletter and noticed that the special interest group had a vacant position on their board. I looked into it and joined the board a few weeks later!

At the same time, PMI was starting up its volunteer education programs. I was in the first class of what they now call the leadership master class. This one-year leadership program helps people to become better volunteer leaders. Eventually, I became the chairman of the PMI IT & Telecom Special Interest Group. I became heavily involved in the annual conference, running events and doing outreach to others in the industry. It was to fun to meet people from around the world. At a certain point, PMI changed its structure and there was no longer volunteer leadership positions related to these special interest groups. After that point, involvement became less interesting to me.

At this stage, I'm between volunteer engagements and thinking about what I might do next as a volunteer.

Harpham: How did you manage this extensive volunteer commitment in the project management community along with everything else in life?

Tarne: The Board had regular conference calls a few times per month and two face-to-face meetings per year. Generally, we had our meetings in Las Vegas because it is a cheap place to hold meetings. The group would usually arrive on a Friday and depart on Sunday. It took away from my free time to participate. This involvement was over and above my day-to-day responsibilities with IBM.

That said, I've always worked in organizations that have appreciated and supported involvement in professional organizations. To some degree, professional volunteering has supported my career development. I can think of one specific job that I got directly through the networking that I did with PMI.

Harpham: How did that opportunity come through your PMI networking?

Tarne: I was in the Leadership Master Class with a group of about fifteen other project managers who were also PMI volunteers. During the year, we met in person three times over weekends to cover leadership training and discussions. I got to know my classmates quite well during this program.

One of my classmates worked for PM Solutions. At the same time, Sprint was going through some business difficulties and laying off staff due to the telecommunications bust in the early 2000s. My classmate got me in the door with PM Solutions, put in a good word for me with the executive team, and I had a job interview with the organization. PM Solutions hired me!

Harpham: It sounds like this opportunity was a happy surprise rather than a strategy.

Tarne: I didn't have a specific goal in mind when I started volunteering with the organization. At the same time, I knew getting involved with a professional organization wasn't going to hurt and that it would grow my professional network.

Harpham: What did you do at PM Solutions?

Tarne: It's a consulting firm focused on project management. When I joined, they had about one hundred employees, some involved in consulting and others were staff augmentation project managers. They also did project management training. My focus was in the project management consulting—helping clients improve their project management processes. I worked with PM Solutions for five years before joining IBM in 2008.

Harpham: During your time with PM Solutions, what are some of the patterns you would see over and over again on projects?

Tarne: Usually, organizations would recognize that they needed a more formal project management approach. One company in particular had some high-profile project failures. My typical engagement with PM Solutions was to help clients create project management methodologies for their needs. We had an "off the shelf" methodology based on the PMBOK Guide and we would sell that consulting service to the client with customization to meet their needs. Customizing the methodology to suit their needs was a key aspect to these engagements.

Harpham: What was driving clients to ask for formal project management consulting?

Tarne: In one case, their need was driven by some project failures, such as blowing the budget, which woke them up to the fact that they needed to change. In another case, the focus was on time to market—make sure that you get everything done quickly so that you can get new products into the market.

Harpham: After you provide this consulting service to the client, did you ever hear from the client six months or a year later to see how the change played out?

Tarne: With one large project, I helped them with the methodology. In addition, we helped them with a governance model to manage the project management environment. We set up a global project management office for them. Prior to this point, they had regional project management oversight, but no consistency from region to region. I worked with them after all of this was rolled out. One of the other services offered by PM Solutions was a project management maturity assessment.

With these assessments, we would analyze and grade how well the organization did projects. This involved reviewing their project artifacts such as schedules or work breakdown structures and seeing how effective they were. We would also look at project charters and other aspects of the project process. In the case of this large project, we did an initial assessment as the project was starting to give us a baseline. A year later, we did another assessment on different regions of the organization. It was an ongoing multi-year project to provide assessments and give them feedback on their process.

Harpham: Who was the client?

Tarne: The client was a global business software company. Specifically, we worked with the unit that ran implementation projects for end customers.

Harpham: You are active in presenting at project management events and conferences. How did you get into that?

Tarne: While I was involved in the IT & Telecom group, I decided to present on our topics as a way to promote the interest group and attract others to join the group. The first presentation I did was called "Ten Barriers to Communications." Both PM Solutions and IBM look favorably on speaking at conferences.

The conference experience that stands out to me the most was getting invited to present at an event in the Middle East. I presented on different approaches to agile, project leadership and Six Sigma. I was one of four US experts invited to present. We went to Cairo, Egypt, for four days to deliver a conference. We ended up doing the conference over several years [2008–2010]. It was a lot of fun to do. It was fun to be featured speaker at the event.

Harpham: Did you engage with the country's leadership on project management?

Tarne: On our first trip, we had a meeting with His Excellency Dr. Ahmed M. Darwish, Minister of State for Administrative Development. The government was interested in fostering Egyptian project management expertise through education. It was the first time I've been in a meeting where I had to address someone as "Your Excellency." That was quite the experience.

Harpham: You presented on communication failure at one of your presentations. What are some of the communication failures that you see most often in the project management field?

Tarne: I have seen cases where people leave a meeting with a different understanding of what was discussed—and there are no meeting minutes. In other cases, I see unclear status reports—or the failure to provide one at all. Overly complex status reports are a problem in some cases. I take pride in being able to write an effective status report. An effective status report should note accomplishments, highlight risks and issues, and call out dependencies that we are relying on the customer to deliver. If you need something from your customer to move ahead, you need to tell them. Make it clear what you need and when you need it.

Harpham: What else have you seen go wrong with project management reports?

Tarne: The "watermelon report" is a classic example. Everything looks green [i.e., the project is going well] on the surface yet it is red [i.e., the project is in serious trouble] on the inside. In that case, the report writer is overly optimistic, dishonest, or incompetent in communicating the project's status. I think that approach is driven by the idea that you can fix the problem soon, so there's no need to communicate about it.

Harpham: How do you detect these "watermelon project reports"?

Tarne: I can't always detect that there's a problem from reading just the report. If I'm close to the project and you see what's going on, that helps. For instance, I may hear a side conversation about certain activities being late and yet that information doesn't make it to the report. That gives you a signal that something isn't quite right. Another sign is if the team seems to be under a lot of pressure but there's nothing in the report to indicate why.

Agile emphasizes short iterations in part to prevent project problems from festering and becoming overwhelming. If you have not completed a piece of work in two weeks, you know you're behind. That's better than going a month or two before you bring it up on a status report.

Harpham: Is that specific technique—the two-week sprint—something that opens the door to introducing the agile methodology?

Tarne: Demonstrating how agile works is a strong way to show the value of agile. I recently came off a short project—the development window was just six weeks. We did two-week iterations and provided a demo to the customer at the end of each of those two-week units. If you manage it properly, you can get work done quickly.

The daily stand-up meeting is another technique that helps to improve results for the project. The key points to cover in a stand-up meeting focuses on three questions: What did you accomplish since the last meeting? What do you have planned for today? Is anything blocking you from moving ahead? It should not be a meeting to discuss issues. Just identify the issues and who needs to be involved in resolving them. It is a mini-planning meeting for the day.

It's a way for the team to hold each other responsible for the work they're going to get done. You never go more than a day without knowing that somebody has a challenge or a block. That means you can get involved and help the team more often as the project manager.

Harpham: From your experience, the daily meeting tempo has a significant impact?

Tarne: Yes, it makes a difference.

Harpham: How did you first get exposed to the agile approach?

Tarne: As a PMI volunteer, I was part of an outreach program to connect with other organizations such as the Scrum Alliance. At first, PMI was resistant to the idea of agile. Eventually, we helped to bridge the gap and see the value of agile to running projects. Eventually, PMI allowed us to launch an agile community of practice and they introduced the Agile Certified Practitioner [ACP] certification to promote these methods. I was also part of the team that launched the agile community of practice for PMI. I also helped by writing some of the ACP certification exam questions. When it came time to update the ACP exam, I was part of the team that reviewed the content after the questions were written.

Harpham: Based on your input, did you see changes to the agile certification?

Tarne: They didn't change too much. The focus was on updating the content and the bibliography related to the certification.

Harpham: Let's turn to listening skills and the role it plays. Public speaking skills tend to get a lot of attention. In contrast, listening gets less attention. What does effective listening look like in your experience?

Tarne: Watching body language is helpful. Are people engaging with the speaker? During the daily stand-up meeting, everyone actually stands in a circle. That means everyone is facing each other. That means that everyone is engaged with the process. Ideally, the meeting is quick—about fifteen minutes long. If somebody is not paying attention and misses something, it is clear that they're not engaged.

Harpham: The quick nature of the meeting could also be a selling point. You could say, "If we all focus during this meeting, we'll be done in fifteen minutes."

Tarne: Yes, that's a benefit.

Harpham: What is your approach to leadership and how has it evolved through your career?

Tarne: The Navy tends to be a command and control environment—it needs to be in order to achieve its mission. Through the PMI leadership program, I've learned a lot about leadership and that includes understanding how I lead.

I advocate the servant leadership approach where the leader serves the team, so that the team can be successful. If we're doing a software project with a lot of smart people ready to work but something is stopping them, it is my role as the leader to clear the impediment. I advocate the self-directing team concept.

The situational leadership model is also helpful to keep in mind. Teams go through a number of stages starting with the forming stage. When the team is forming, the leader needs to be more direct to get started. Later on, the leader can take a step back and the leader's role changes to emphasize delegating, coaching, or support.

If I'm working with a team that is unfamiliar with agile, I tend to be more directive to show them how work is done. If it is a more senior team that has been around the block a few times, I will step back a bit and see how they do things. In the case of the senior team, I may occasionally comment, "Did you think about trying this approach?"

Harpham: Have there been any books that have made a significant impact on your thinking?

Tarne: Stephen Covey's *The 7 Habits of Highly Effective People* [Simon & Schuster, 2013] has stood the test of time. I have gone back and re-read it several times over the years. He has a good model for how to go from defining your vision and then translate that vision to your daily activities.

Harpham: What opportunities and technologies have captured your interest? What do you see when you look ahead over the next several years?

Tarne: I recently helped a team that gave a presentation on cognitive computing, so that's an interesting trend that I'm following. In addition, understanding the why behind your project will become as important as being able to technically deliver the project. I've started using some of the principles of Design Thinking to help in this area. For me, Design Thinking is making sure you have the right problem before you start working on the solution. I also see a general trend to deliver projects faster. There's an expectation that companies will deliver improvements and innovation quickly.

Harpham: For the reader who is looking to break into project management from another field, such as software development or engineering, what do you suggest they do to get started in projects?

Tarne: My volunteer history has been a major contributor to how I have developed my career. Volunteering with the PMI organization is a great move. You can also volunteer with other organizations where you have an opportunity to work as a project manager, even if it is outside of your normal field of professional work.

My wife is a talented project manager, even though she doesn't see herself that way. She's got good skills for organizing and keeping track of the details of large-scale activities. For example, she ran the high school band trip a few years ago, which involved a lot of coordination to move over one hundred students to the right place for a five-day trip.

You can also apply the volunteering approach within the organization you work for. You might volunteer to do something that goes beyond your usual responsibilities. Look for a way to demonstrate that you have project management skills.

Chapter Summary

- Recommended books include *The 7 Habits of Highly Effective People* by Stephen Covey.

- Career transitions: Seek outside resources (e.g., MBA programs and specialized recruiters) to support your career moves.

- Courage: As the project manager, you have a key role to stand up for the project's success and your approach (e.g., agile). Tarne's experience shows that traditional solutions, such as assigning more people to a project, does not always help.

- Professional development and volunteering: Tarne grew his career as a volunteer leader at the Project Management Institute and as a speaker. This activity also led to new relationships and career opportunities.

- Communication failure on projects: Examine your project documents, such as weekly status reports, and ask yourself if these documents provide clear and transparent information to the reader.

Ray Grainger

CEO, Mavenlink

Ray Grainger *is the co-founder and CEO of Mavenlink, where he is leading the mission to reinvent the way businesses do work. He has dedicated his career to helping clients succeed, and brings over 25 years of experience in software and high-technology consulting to Mavenlink. Grainger began his career at Accenture, where he spent 17 years honing his expertise in professional services management as global managing partner. During his time at Accenture, he also invested in several technology companies through Accenture Technology Ventures, including enterprise knowledge management vendor InQuira. He later became Executive Vice President of Professional Services and Strategic Alliances at InQuira (acquired by Oracle in 2011), where he met his Mavenlink co-founders, Roger Neel and Sean Crafts.*

In his spare time, Grainger is a true adventurer. He is an avid diver and a world traveler. He served on two expeditions to Antarctica with the National Science Foundation (for which he earned the congressional Antarctica Service Medal). He holds a BS in engineering, with distinction, from Harvey Mudd College, where he is also a trustee.

Bruce Harpham: What career lessons did you learn from starting your career at Accenture?

Ray Grainger: Starting my career with Accenture had several benefits. It's a good mentoring organization. You learn a lot from your immediate supervisors who are close to you in age and therefore have recent experience with your type of work. You learn supervisory skills, managing people, communication, and related foundational skills to be a good manager in the context of client services. Asking good questions, managing tasks, and getting clarification are some of the other skills you learn over the first four to six years at the firm. It takes about that much time to become a project manager in the organization.

© Bruce Harpham 2018
B. Harpham, *Project Managers at Work*, DOI 10.1007/978-1-4842-2668-1_18

Harpham: What kinds of projects were you involved in with Accenture?

Grainger: My early projects were technology related—applying technology in large companies. In my case, it was in the aerospace and defense industry. In the late 1980s, the industry was going through the first wave of MRP [material requirements planning] implementations, the predecessor to ERP [enterprise resource planning]. This technology supported a broad range of planning and execution in manufacturing in the aerospace and defense industries.

Harpham: Would this be Lockheed Martin, Boeing, or Airbus? Those kinds of companies?

Grainger: Yes, exactly. Northrop Grumman Corporation was my big first client when I joined Accenture out of college. I was working on large-scale, complex manufacturing, planning, and execution systems.

Harpham: Was that your first exposure to the aerospace industry?

Grainger: Yes, it was the first time I had worked in that industry. I had worked on large-scale projects prior to joining to Accenture. I had worked with the National Science Foundation in Antarctica earlier. Each season, there was a portfolio of projects. It's a whole different experience down there. In that environment, you have significant resource constraints and you are working with people from around the world. I learned how to operate in large-scale projects and I found that work interesting. I had to collaborate with new people I've just met and work together to get a project delivered.

Harpham: What was it like to get work done in this extreme environment? What did you work on?

Grainger: I worked on many projects while I was there—some took several years and others were short term. The longer-term projects were a challenge because you had to take hiatus for part of the year. It was dark and you couldn't get anything done.

One notable project was to build an emergency camp at the South Pole. Each year, there is a winter group that keeps the South Pole station operational and does some winter-related science work and experiments. If the main station goes up in flames, they need a backup place to live for the rest of the winter.

The team and I built an emergency camp that needed to support about seventy people for the winter period—about four months—without any support from the rest of the world. We needed to figure out what types of facilities were needed. Logistically, it was very interesting. We prefabricated much of the project deliverables at another location, dissembled it, put everything on giant sleds and then on a C31 airplane. We had to get it done on time—there's no flexibility on schedule in that world.

It was also interesting to work with a variety of disciplines like carpenters, plumbers, and so forth. None of them had ever worked together and they had to come together quickly. There was no room for failure. Everybody knows that we had to succeed—there is no other choice. The deadline is fixed and there is no way to get more resources. It forces you to be resourceful and get along well with others.

The people you have on the team are also fixed—you can't bring in someone new! You're not only working together, you're also living together. You're in the same environment with the team twenty-four hours a day. I encountered real differences between people but I had to find a way to work through that.

I went through this experience between graduating from high school and starting my college studies. I learned how to do projects through this experience. My life has been made up of projects ever since then.

Harpham: It's clear that you have succeeded in different environments. First, it was Antarctica. Then you moved into management consulting. Today, you're running a project management software company. How do you navigate the transition from consulting to the software field?

Grainger: As you move through different career stages, you gain different skills and ideas that you put into your career "knap sack." Looking at the first consulting projects I did at Accenture, I took several skills away from that. I learned about project metrics—tracking time, the importance of accurate tracking, and estimation methods. Those insights were independent of the specific industry I was working on.

As you move up in your career, domain expertise becomes very important. In the aerospace and defense industries, that may mean learning the manufacturing process and how it will be impacted by technology projects. After six or seven years in that aerospace and defense, I moved to another industry. That transition was partially driven by a substantial decline in US defense spending in the early 1990s.

We applied the insights we learned from aerospace and applied it to the high-tech industry generally. For example, I can apply the same framework to manufacturing network routers for Cisco. It also applies to building and managing the lifecycle of software products. I migrated from big industrial manufacturing to fast-paced high-tech manufacturing. That was a transition for me from a domain perspective.

That said, I always had expertise in technology deployment. I knew a lot about software from that work. As I moved into the high-tech field, I acquired clients in the software industry. That included clients like BAE Systems. You can apply similar processes—product management and design—to a different field. You can always find analogs between your experience in the past and the current domain you're working in.

Over nearly twenty years, I was exposed to software companies on various consulting assignments. Those experiences informed my approach when I decided to run my own software company.

Harpham: As you described your industry transition, I'm reminded of the concept of the "peace dividend." The idea that defense spending could be reduced after the Cold War and those funds could be put into tax cuts or other spending. In your case, it was a dividend of knowledge that you could apply to other industries.

Grainger: Yes, I was able to transfer those ideas and processes elsewhere. The aerospace and defense industries have excellent processes to ensure quality and reliability. The industry also has a high need for project control and accounting—funding was always well understood in that world. All of those skills were transferable to my current work—building software for the services industry.

Harpham: Let's turn to the origins of Mavenlink. How do you come to start the company? What was the first year of Mavenlink like?

Grainger: It was a white-knuckle experience for that first year!

Prior to starting Mavenlink, I invested in an enterprise knowledge management company called InQuira, through Accenture Technology Ventures. I joined that company as the Executive Vice President of Professional Services and Strategic Alliances, with the idea that I would later start my own software company.

When we decided to start Mavenlink, it was the fall of 2008. I persuaded my co-founders, Roger Neel and Sean Crafts, to join me and we were excited. I sold some of my Accenture stock in order to fund the business with seed capital. Roger left InQuira shortly after I left the company. He got married, left on his honeymoon, and then came back to work on the company. Two weeks later, October 2008 arrived and everything started to crater.

Fortunately, the timing went well in one respect. We had set up our seed capital earlier in the year before the stock market took a dive. We had sold while asset prices were high and had a lot of cash on hand. We dodged the bullet from that perspective—had we sold assets later in the year, there would have far less to work with in getting the company underway. In the broader environment, venture capital was drying up fast.

In January 2009, we started to develop the product. At the same time, the financial crisis and recession were underway. We took our seed capital and spread it across multiple bank accounts so that no single account was over the FDIC limit for deposit insurance. There were worries we could lose money if a bank happened to go under. It was a wacky experience! On the other hand, certain expenses became much more affordable. We could take flights within California for about $29 each way on Virgin America and get a hotel room for $59 a night. We were able to stretch our capital a long way.

You have to remember that we didn't know how long the recession was going to last. Some thought it might become a depression. We were committed to building the company and going for it. We made sure to handle money carefully throughout, however.

By July 2009, I remember talking to my co-founders and saying, "Well, the world didn't end. It looks like the recovery is starting. Let's keep building our business." The first year was tough!

Harpham: When did the first paying customers come in?

Grainger: We had the first paying customers in January 2010. During 2009, we were building the product. We had to define the breadth and boundaries of the product. How many business processes were important to cover? We went through a lot of product iterations based on feedback from the market during the first year.

Harpham: What was the product development process?

Grainger: We knew we wanted to target creative and professional services—notably marketing agencies, IT services firms, management consultants, and professional service providers—basically companies that perform services for a fee to clients. We felt that the existing software for this market was not good enough. We first pushed the product to everyone in those industries we knew through our network.

Initially, we pushed out the product on a free basis. People at Accenture would use it to run their projects. In total, we had one thousand people try the product out. This was all people from my network and other people involved in the company at the time.

Consultants were frank in providing their feedback, which was helpful. They didn't say vague positive comments. They would tell us, "This sucks!" Or, "If you don't make this, my clients will never use the product with me." This feedback made a difference in improving the product during the trial period.

In some cases, we would bring people into the design stage and tell them, "Here's what this feature would look like. Is this what you had in mind?" Then we would get back comments like, "Yes, that's what we asked for but it's not what we really need." That meant more changes to fine-tune the product and trying to make it better with each iteration.

Harpham: When you got on the phone with these early users, what were they telling you?

Grainger: We would hear comments in this general theme: "We love the concept but the product seems raw." I remember being hurt by those kinds of comments. Digging deeper on those comments, they meant that "the product has to do so much more to be valuable to us." I was surprised to hear that people wanted more depth in order to use the product. I had thought this is SaaS [software as a service] product and that fewer features would be a good fit. However, there was demand for more features. The expectations for project management software are high—higher than I would have thought.

Harpham: There are a lot of project management software offerings on the market. Who is the ideal user for Mavenlink?

Grainger: I came from the professional services industry and that informed my approach. What I found is that there are good tools for the professional project manager, such as Microsoft Project. However, I noticed that many projects were run by people who were not full time project managers. Yet, those people had to manage multiple stakeholders, including client participants and subcontractors. The project software addressed the needs of the project manager, but everyone else was using email and other tools.

I envisioned a multi-stakeholder application to manage the business of professional services companies. There were some existing tools that addressed scheduling, time capture, or accounting. There was nothing that brought it all together in the way we envisioned.

Harpham: What is the interplay between improving results with software such as Mavenlink and the people side of projects? Some people assume that their project problems will go away if only they had the right software.

Grainger: If the business has clarity on one or two overarching goals with adopting a tool like Mavenlink, that makes a tremendous impact. For example, if a company has the goal to make all of their projects more profitable with a motivated CFO, that helps. Without that clarity, people sometimes struggle with the change, because adopting Mavenlink processes can be quite different from what they're using today.

That's true for any project. You need to be able to answer, "Why does this project matter to the business?" With that motivation, you can engage people to work on the project. It doesn't work well to provide the software and say, "OK, get started!" The underlying behavior needs to adjust as well. All of the stakeholders need to be engaged.

Harpham: Let's explore change management further. There have been many horror stories in technology projects where the project team builds something great and hands it off to the business only to find that nobody uses it. What have been some of your lessons learned in doing change management well?

Grainger: At the start of the project, you need to understand the magnitude of the change. Some changes are large and some are not. What are we changing to? How big of a change is it? Risk is another factor to consider. You may have a small change that impacts a critical business process—that will need to be managed closely. In contrast, you may have a big change underway where there will be limited negative impact if it goes poorly.

You have to spend to the time to understand the stakeholders on the project to get change done well. After that, understand the project's change details and what does it impact. Does it impact everyone in the company globally or does it have a local impact?

Duration also needs to be considered. If you are doing a multi-year technology project, there is a high likelihood that you will get fatigue for the project at some time. It could be fatigue on the project team itself or the business. During a project of this length, the business itself may change substantially due to an acquisition or divestiture.

Harpham: What have been some of your project management lessons learned over the years?

Grainger: In working with clients, I understand the pressures involved. Some of the projects involve large amounts of money. Some of them are "bet the business" projects. In order to achieve success in those settings, you have to understand the client's expectations.

What are their expectations of the project?

What are their expectations on how you interact with them?

How frank do they want you be?

What is their communication style?

If there is an issue, how do you want they want that addressed? Do they want to be personally told? Or handle it through a steering committee?

Addressing these questions help you to get off on the right foot. On these large projects, trust needs to be developed quickly and maintained during the project. It's often effective to seek to build a personal connection that goes beyond the project.

It's important to lay this foundation before you hit the first speed bump on the project, because problems will occur no matter what. You just don't know when it will happen. When you have a strong relationship, you will be able to get through the problems better. If you successfully work through the problems, trust is enhanced further.

Building trust and managing expectations are essential project management activities. It takes a while to get really good with trust and expectations.

Harpham: Expectations are interesting to manage. My definition of fast and your definition of fast may be very different. Can you share a story where your client had significantly different expectations and how do you manage that?

Grainger: Client perceptions of speed were often different than my view. They thought something could be done much faster than my experience said was possible. They might think the project would take three months while I consider it more like six months. That's double the time and probably double the cost as well.

The confidence builder for me in addressing these conversations came from early in my career. I was wrestling with how to deal with this challenge. I didn't want to just capitulate to the demand, because that would cause other problems. A client partner told me once, "You have done twenty technology implementation projects by the time you're a client partner. In contrast, your client will have done maybe two in their entire career. You will have so much more experience than the client. You will have examples to draw on. The client knows their business better than you, but you understand this type of project far better than the client."

Nearly every time, the client would come in with a time estimate that sharply disagreed with my view of what was possible. That meant a conversation with the client to challenge their assumptions. Of course, you don't want to challenge them in a condescending way. Simply refer to past examples of similar projects and point out what was involved in them. Steer the conversation toward risk. Explore the magnitude of the changes being considered and the assumptions in play.

I would often make comments like, "Moving a project like this fast doesn't give people the opportunity to make the change effectively." Ultimately, that could translate into the project taking longer to complete.

Harpham: How did you have conversations about project trade-offs?

Grainger: I had one big client where we were doing a technology implementation for their customer support organization. The customer support unit had thousands of employees so this project would have a significant impact in terms of people. The company was selling expensive technology projects around the world that were complex to configure and maintain.

The client needed the support center to be operational in three months. My experience said it would take six months, but they said they needed it in three months because they were committed to supporting a new product. So I looked into the trade-off implications. I reviewed the scope and looked at what could be done. I proposed to move the training and change management activities to after the technology implementation. That's usually not a good idea to do. In this project, the schedule was set and there was no flexibility.

I explained that we could offer a post-implementation change management service for $600,000. The client signed up within thirty minutes of the discussion. They knew it was necessary for long-term success. Ironically, if they had done the project differently, that service probably would have cost one-third as much. However, they were committed to meeting their schedule. The date was the date.

Harpham: The question is not "Will we do change management?"—but rather when and for how much?

Grainger: If you skip change management, you're likely to fail. As the project manager, you have to assess and understand the organization's risk tolerance for disruption. In this case, they were willing to tolerate stress and disruption to meet their date. In practical terms, that meant managers at the client had to tell their people: "We're going to go live with this on this date. You're not going to get training on it until a later time. I'm going to ask you to be adaptable and understanding to the situation."

Harpham: What goes into your personal productivity practice?

Grainger: Start with the fundamentals. If the project manager arrives late and disorganized, it creates a bad impression. So personal productivity impacts how you are perceived as well as how effective you are.

Taking a systematic approach is one method I have practiced to boost productivity. Back at Accenture, some of our technology implementation projects, such as implementing a SAP product had certain common points. Everyone had clarity on the goal and how projects like this are run. When you start the project with clarity on the goal and the process, it creates a good impression. Look for plans, templates, and processes that can be reused.

Harpham: How do you recommend project managers succeed in a matrix environment?

Grainger: Some matrix organizations handle this well. At Accenture, the project manager would provide comments on your performance directly to the line manager. That would give you the chance to shine based on your project contributions. In that environment, your project manager determines the difference of your career through the feedback they provide.

Harpham: What other insights have you learned about project best practices that we haven't covered?

Grainger: I think it's important to give people flexibility and find ways to minimize the stress of business travel. Both of those factors have influenced the creation and design of Mavenlink's products.

Providing clarity on what you want people to do is incredibly important. Your priorities may change and you need to let the team know that. It's understandable to change your mind. When you do, make sure that decision is clear to the team.

You have to deeply understand the stakeholders. I'm surprised at the number of project managers that lack that understanding. If this is missed, the project may be shut down or you may be removed as the project manager. Creating a stakeholder map where you take note of who holds power and how communication needs to flow is part of the picture. It goes beyond creating a document. For important stakeholders, a personal touch goes a long way. In a way, you almost have to act like an account manager even if you are exclusively dealing with internal stakeholders. You may need to meet with people on the project individually to understand their needs and win their support.

I recall cases where the CIO is at odds with the business leader. There are cases where the CIO and the business leader have a different agenda and a different career objective. The CIO may see me as a vehicle to achieve a certain career objective. In contrast, the business leader is focused on the business outcome of the project. At the ground level, these observations translate into actions like helping the CIO prepare for a critical presentation and taking the business leader out for some fun at the ball game. Treating both of them in the same way would have been ineffective.

Chapter Summary

- Lessons learned from consulting: Grainger developed subject matter experience in technology implementations in a variety of industries. These experiences laid a foundation for future success.

- Team work in extreme conditions: Grainger's experience includes working on projects at the South Pole. If you had to find a way to work effectively with people in a closed environment, how would you do it?

- Starting Mavenlink: Developing a project management and collaboration software tool like Mavenlink was full of surprises and required adjustments to better meet the needs of users.

- Change management: This "last mile" effort makes a major difference in a project's long-term success. Without it, your stakeholders and users are likely to experience greater stress.

- Understanding the needs of key stakeholders: Find out what your most important stakeholders are interested in (e.g., exposure for career growth, personal growth, or some other goal) and look for ways to meet those needs with the project.

Seth J. Gillespie

Senior Project Manager, Apple

Dr. Seth J. Gillespie *is currently a senior project manager at Apple. Gillespie has experience in information technology and management within a variety of industries, including hardware and software engineering, pharmaceuticals and biotech, motion picture films, natural and renewable energy generation, and management consulting.*

Gillespie earned a PhD in organization and management, specializing in information technology management; an MBA, with an emphasis in technology management; and a BS in molecular biology, with a minor in economics. In addition, he holds PMP (Project Management Professional), PMI-ACP (Agile Certified Practitioner), CSM (Certified ScrumMaster), ITIL (Information Technology Infrastructure Library), and CISSP (Certified Information Systems Security Professional) credentials.

In his free time, Gillespie enjoys traveling and assisting in social justice causes benefiting under-served groups worldwide.

Bruce Harpham: How did you first get involved in project management?

Seth Gillespie: I started my career as an IT systems engineer after finishing college. My first job out of college was a small biotech company called Agouron Pharmaceuticals, which developed and manufactured unique protein molecules that play a role in treating serious diseases like cancer, as well as novel and life-saving antiretroviral drugs impacting millions worldwide. I wanted to get my foot in the door and learn about the biotech industry. I had some consulting experience in IT work previously, so this role was a good fit. I worked at that company for about four years as a systems engineer primarily involved in data center design, networks, and computer build-out and maintenance. In addition,

© Bruce Harpham 2018
B. Harpham, *Project Managers at Work*, DOI 10.1007/978-1-4842-2668-1_19

I gained great experience building networked labs at several field sites for science and office staff, which sometimes required donning a hazmat suit!

It was during this first job out of college that I realized I did not need to be stuck in a profession that my degree in science would lead to. I was really empowered in the realization that I enjoyed working in IT—and the rest is history. Working at Agouron was interesting and fascinating for me, especially since the company was small [i.e., under 500 employees] when I started. As it turns out, Agouron was acquired by Pfizer, a global pharmaceutical company in the Fortune 500. I had the opportunity to work on the integration required to merge the two companies' back-end systems together, with a focus on data center services.

Around this time, I received a recruiting call from a biotech company in the San Francisco Bay Area. I credit the cold call to my volunteer and industry talks, which gave visibility to my work and accomplishments outside of my company. Even though I grew up and went to college in the San Diego area, I hadn't spent much time in San Francisco. It turns out that the company was actually right across the Bay from San Francisco and in the same city as Pixar headquarters. The hiring manager at the company told me, "We like your technical background at Agouron and what you did with the Pfizer merger. We'd like you to interview for a project manager position in our IT group. We think it would be a great fit for you."

When I heard this, I thought to myself, "Well, I've never had the project manager title. Does it make sense for me to take a flight to interview for this job—even if they are paying for it?"

Harpham: At this point, you were wrestling with the career change to move into a project manager role. How did you think about it and make a decision?

Gillespie: I was nervous about it because I didn't think that I was qualified. On the other hand, I had experience with IT hardware and software deployments, data center management, and procurement in my previous roles. I had worked with project managers through my career, and I understood their value to the organization. In a way, I always looked up to them. In the first few years of my career, I was in an individual contributor role.

In moving to project management, I was able to have a greater impact than what I could achieve as an individual. Moving to project management was a major breakthrough for my career.

Harpham: Given your concerns, how did the job interview unfold?

Gillespie: The hiring manager told me that my technical background and accomplishments were great. They wanted me to build on my experience and take it to the next level at Chiron, a mid-sized biotech firm in the San Francisco Bay Area. They asked me to fly up to their location, spend the day with them, and put my hat in the ring. I really needed that push from the company, because I didn't feel that I was qualified at first. I interviewed with the team and learned about their projects. They were pleased with me and I accepted the role. That's when I officially became a project manager.

Harpham: The transition to this role involved building on your prior accomplishments in technology?

Gillespie: It wasn't as if I came to that role directly from college with a degree in molecular biology and started working as an IT project manager. My undergraduate degree was in science and that led me to the opportunity at the first biotech company. While there, I excelled in IT work for several years. Eventually, I was recognized for my IT work and then hired into the project manager role. It was a great role and included international travel! I worked with Chiron for about four years, before my next pivot.

Interestingly, I did not have a PMP certification or an MBA degree when I started the project manager role. Therefore, I chose to pursue both a PMP and an MBA degree on my own. I felt that I needed more knowledge to continue growing my skills, especially now that I had greater responsibility for projects of increasing complexity and cost. I enrolled in UC Berkeley's project management certificate program. Completing that program started me down the path of lifelong learning. I kept learning and studying in various advanced programs in the years ahead, including Stanford University. I also sought out other professional programs, including Toastmasters for professional speaking, which I recommend to this day.

It was a seminal move for my career. For about six months, I was a bit uncomfortable. I didn't know if I would make it or if I would be a good fit for the role. Fortunately, my manager, who had himself earned a PhD, saw my potential, in addition to the great work I had done through past accomplishments, and believed in me enough to enable me to succeed as a project manager, which I did.

While at Chiron, I had the opportunity to travel extensively within the United States, Germany, and Italy on various business trips to lead data center expansion projects. During this time, my expertise in biotech matters, such as the FDA's [Federal Drug Administration] IT record keeping and software development requirements, helped me to add value to the business.

Looking back, I realized early in my career as a systems administrator that there was a limit on what I could contribute to the organization as an individual contributor. There are only so many hours in the day after all. As a project manager, I could work those same hours and make a much greater impact by leading the project team. But it's not for the faint of heart. It's hard work and sometimes long hours, but it is well worth it. I felt a greater sense of accomplishment along with recognition from that work.

Harpham: What is your approach to project management?

Gillespie: I believe that project management is both an art and a science. The science side includes the best practices described in the PMBOK Guide and related training resources. For example, how to set up a project schedule, how to set up a project charter and a Gantt chart, and how to use project management software. All of that is only half the story of project management.

The art side of project management is interpersonal skills. For example, empathy comes to play a major role. I had to develop these interpersonal skills to a much higher level to be effective. It was very different from my science background and my analytical side. To be successful, you have to master empathy and interpersonal skills, as well the science-side skills, such as scheduling and cost accounting.

Often, you will find yourself asking a person to do something that is challenging or unrealistic for them to do. For example, to deploy a large project impacting millions—with many unknowns or with a high level of complexity or uncertainty—in a very short amount of time.

As a project manager, I'm there for my team. I'm not there to throw anyone under the bus. If I am doing my job right, I'm there to shield them, to defend them, and to empower them, so that they can get the impossible done. In addition, my role is to remove blocks that are standing in their way to become successful. At the end of the day, even if it is a stressful or drawn-out project, I want my future team members to see my name as the PM and be excited to work with me—not because it will be easy all the time, or that I will know all the secrets, but because together we will do great things.

Some project managers may emphasize one aspect more than others. A people-oriented project manager may be deeply connected with the team, but lose sight of the analytical or science side, such as the schedule and documentation. I feel that you need to have the analytical and the interpersonal aspects [or the "art and science"] to be successful in this field.

Harpham: What does it mean to remove blocks that are impacting the team? Can you share an example of what that looks like?

Gillespie: My analytical side will break down blocks into two categories. The first category—it's either an ability problem or it is a motivation problem. If there is an ability problem, that means there is a tool, a process, a procedure that the individual cannot manage on their own. Ability problems can be solved by providing the technology, training or additional help required to do the task. If we're working on a software development project, an ability problem could be solved by pairing the person with somebody else who has the skills, so that they can learn what is required, or by giving them mentorship or other technical help.

A motivation problem means that the team member has the ability and expertise to do the work, however, they don't understand where they fit within the schedule. The person may object that the schedule is unrealistic. Or, you may get no specific feedback at all. That's more common in my experience. You just don't hear back from the person, so you have to guess about whether the activity is being worked on.

When there's a motivation problem, it may not be any fault of the individual. In fact, they may be very senior in their role. To address the motivation problem as the project manager, I help explain the significance of their contributions and how what they do impacts others downstream in the project.

The project team member may not realize that if they complete the task by Friday at five p.m., this will not allow the offshore team to complete critical work downstream. They may not realize how their contributions [or lack thereof] impact other people working on the project. By showing how their work—big or small—fits into the big picture, they better understand how their contribution to the project and to other people matter. That's how their deliverable came to have its deadline. It's not just a made-up deadline. Typically, the motivation problem is solved by giving the person greater context and encouraging them to see how their contribution fits into the overall schedule.

Harpham: In a large company, you may need some input or an approval from another department to move forward on the project. In a bank, you may need to engage and obtain approval from information security and internal audits to move ahead on a project. Thus, the block on the project could be some other department failing to pay attention. How do you address that challenge?

Gillespie: I would diagnose that situation as a motivation problem. In my view, the project manager should own the communication—in terms of both the formal communication plan and the stakeholders. The project manager is responsible for making those tough calls: "Look, we need sign off on the risk management plan by next Wednesday. If we don't get it by then, we are in danger of missing our deadlines in Q2." Typically, the project manager has the unique insight and understanding of the downstream activities to be able to make that call and push through that kind of barrier.

Mindset is important here. It's not a question of blame or making another group look bad. It's just a question of stating the facts and the consequences of inaction. The communication needs to bring visibility to the task.

Let's say you foresee an issue. You can proactively prepare for it with an email. Write a note that says: "A sign-off is coming. You will get the materials on [this date]. Here's the high-level goal we're working on with the project." In the case where you get no feedback from the stakeholder and you're worried about the deadline, then a phone call is a good move. A short call to the leader or an ally with influence can help. Ask if they are on schedule to complete the activity by the deadline and ask if they need any clarification or additional information to move ahead. This kind of iteration not only helps as a gentle reminder, but also makes the communication more interactive than one-way, which is always good in my experience.

If the other person is at the same office location, I like to visit them in person. For some stakeholders, if you are out of sight, you are out of mind. Make yourself known. I don't consider following up diligently to be "bugging" the person. I don't apologize for it either. I'm there to ensure the project's success for the organization. I've never been told I'm too persistent, because I do it with tact and empathy.

I've found time and time again that varying the communication approach is valuable. Some people prefer a phone call. Others like email. Some like text messages or IM [instant messaging]. It's important to learn those preferences and act accordingly. If you do that, people will be thankful for the reminders. I get compliments and positive feedback that people appreciate my diligence as a project manager. The team knows that I'm helping them to be successful.

Harpham: You made a good point about the follow-up being a proactive strategy to ensure success, rather than seeing it as complaining.

Gillespie: Absolutely. There's an art to the follow-up. The analytical side of you may want to check off the task as done and move on. However, the art side can include learning the skill to read between the lines. What is the person saying? What is the person not saying? Sometimes chatting about the weather and other topics helps you to connect with the person. I see the value in chitchat to connect, but I do keep it to a minimum—not only out of respect for my time, but their time as well.

I've seen some project managers who are incredibly friendly. It seems like they want to become your best friend. They'll talk about their family or the weekend for twenty or thirty minutes. That's great on the social side, however, that approach is too much of a good thing. On the other side, you don't want walk up to someone and immediately say, "Hey, what is the status of your task?"

Harpham: What have you learned about running projects through formal study versus hard-won experience in the trenches?

Gillespie: I see great value in the structure and documentation that PMI and other organizations advocate in running projects. In my view, it's mandatory to learn about these frameworks, especially in the IT sector. Understanding the project management framework is important. The next step is to think through how this framework applies to the organization and the people on your team. Some people have a "take it or leave it" approach to these frameworks and structures.

In my experience, I have come to realize that each organization is different and I need to keep that in mind in how I run projects. For example, companies vary on the degree of documentation they require on projects. Let's consider two cases.

One organization values a high degree of documentation: there's templates, status reports, A significant amount of project data is collected, detailed schedules, and so forth. As the project manager, I will take care of all that documentation. For the project team members, I will shield them from that burden as much as possible so that they have more capacity and energy to do their work.

If the organization requires paper documents to be signed or approvals to be managed, I will take care of those requirements. If I didn't have the PMI understanding, I would not be successful in a highly documentation-oriented environment, such as the pharmaceutical/biotech industry. Those industries require a high degree of documentation, because your work has implications on patient safety and there are compliance considerations.

When I led projects in the pharmaceutical field, we had five- to six-inch-thick binders for each project. We had detailed project charters, data on software releases, user acceptance testing, and much more. The formal project management training is simply required to be successful in that context.

On the flip side, I have been in start-ups and companies with a lower level of project management maturity. There's nothing wrong with that culture. In this context, I can still excel as a project manager. Instead, I will maintain the schedule, the work breakdown structure, roles, and responsibilities for my own purposes and not showcase them. That documentation helps me to be successful. I know who to contact and when to keep the project moving along. By keeping that process documentation on my desk, I don't insist that people use project procedures, such as submitting changes via signed change orders. In that culture, change management is fast and customer driven. It's more agile and I'm OK with that. However, if I didn't have the training and education in project management, I would be running around in circles trying to stay organized and I would get frustrated fast.

Finally, I don't try to encourage everyone to adopt a highly detailed approach to project management. Those processes help me to be effective and keep me sane. I respect that some companies have a culture that does not recognize those processes and formal structures. Some organizations may not understand the purpose or value of a RACI [a chart listing an individual's relationship to the project in one or more of four categories: Responsible, Accountable, Consulted, And Informed] chart, for example. In that case, there's no need to fight or try to make them adopt it. Just maintain it for your purposes if you find it helpful.

Harpham: Is fine-tuning your approach to the organization's culture and risk appetite important in deciding how and when to apply formal project management processes?

Gillespie: Yes. I do look for opportunities where it makes sense to surface a project management best practice. However, I'm not going to push it too far. I think it's great to introduce one or two processes to improve results, instead of pushing to adopt a whole project management methodology. If the organization is failing or struggling, you may have a mandate to implement significant change or an improvement program. In that case, you have a "moral authority" to implement a more extensive change to adopt formal project management processes.

Harpham: What is a project management strategy that you've learned the hard way?

Gillespie: Empathy is something that I've had to learn over time. Earlier in my career, empathy was less of a requirement because I was simply focused on my tasks as an individual contributor. When I moved to my first few years as a project manager, my greatest lesson was realizing how much I had to learn.

As a new project manager, I would put together a project schedule or a Gantt chart. I would put deadlines for tasks and deliverables on the schedule based on my understanding of what was involved. I didn't consult with other people. I imagined that other people were too busy to provide their input. The fundamental problem with that approach is that you're creating the project plan and schedule in isolation. Even if you have personally done the work, you may think that you don't have to get estimates or validate your estimates with other people. I had done data center projects previously, so I thought I could estimate them based on my past experience. In reality, it is critical to get estimates and feedback from the project team. Even if the project team comes back with estimates that directly match your estimates, it is still important to do it.

More often, you find gaps and blind spots in your thinking. You may underestimate some areas and overestimate other areas. Believe it or not, people will be forthright if you ask them how long an activity will take to complete, versus simply assigning a deadline.

Harpham: There are two benefits from this engagement. First, you get the immediate benefit of a higher-quality estimate. Second, you gain greater engagement from the person who provided their input.

Gillespie: Let me expand on that. If I know of a better way to do a project or a task, and I have a team member who may differ from that opinion, I will generally defer to the team member. If they fail at that task, they will learn from that experience. It's better for them to learn from that experience rather than me simply telling them how I would do it. That's important because we have to allow our team members to make mistakes and own them. This is assuming that the task has some leeway on it. Obviously, you don't want to put anybody in danger or cause a critical failure.

Believe it or not, these different ways of doing things can often lead to innovation. If I had insisted that that person do it my way, the project may have gone more slowly. The schedule may suffer as well. Overall, I find the benefits of letting people go their own way is well worth it. I don't want to tell people how to do their job, for the most part.

Harpham: How do you deal with third parties on project, such as outside vendors?

Gillespie: I believe the authority to do project work is granted by the project sponsor to the project manager. A vendor may have a contract with the organization. However, that contract may not spell out expectations for the project specifically. In any case, I may look to the contract for agreed upon SLAs [service-level agreements] so that I can understand what the vendor is expected to do. For example, I will push to have access to senior technical staff from the vendor's side in case we need assistance or need to escalate an issue.

I will then analyze the agreements and vendor documentation along with my authority as the project manager. Then I can put the vendor into my framework and understand what the vendor's expectations. Fortunately, I haven't had many problems with third parties over my career so far. Reading and understanding the contract or other written agreements is critical. That information informs what you can and cannot expect from the vendor.

In terms of day-to-day work, I treat vendors like they are part of the team. Only in the worst case will I have to investigate the relationship in greater depth to understand penalties and similar clauses related to the SLA. In the event of a serious problem, it is important to keep calm, seek advice from a trusted colleague, and work through the situation.

Harpham: Let's turn to your PhD. What was your focus of your PhD research? How does that connect with project work?

Gillespie: Let me put that in context of the other educational activities so that you can understand where I'm coming from. I started by obtaining a certificate in project management from Berkeley. Next, I earned the PMP certification from PMI [Project Management Institute]. Later on, I took on an MBA degree specialization in technology management and several other certifications along the way, such as ITIL and the PMI Agile Certified Practitioner.

I was very interested in conducting in-depth research through my PhD. Earning the degree ultimately took around eight years. It was a long and drawn-out process. It was a significant investment of time and energy. I don't encourage people starting out in project management to obtain a PhD degree, unless they are gluttons for punishment. For me, it was a personal goal. I wanted to do research and expand the body of knowledge in my field. I do see application in the workplace from my research. My communication has become more strategic and I have unique and valuable insight into evidence-based management that few others have. My PhD was in organization and management, with an emphasis in information technology management.

For most people interested in project management, a MBA or a master's degree would likely be the best terminal degree. I would also highly encourage project managers to earn the PMP certification, or if just starting out, the CAPM [Certified Associate in Project Management]. Even a few years ago, there were not many master's degrees available in project management. Now there are many choices and good schools to choose from.

Harpham: Tell me more about your research focus in your PhD.

Gillespie: It was a correlational study of risk management and its impact on information technology project success. I surveyed approximately one hundred project managers regarding a specific project they choose to comment on. In the survey, I asked them which risk management techniques they used on their project and how successful their project was. Success was measured in terms of achieving their specified scope, schedule, and budget.

Next, I did a statistical analysis to learn about the correlation between using various risk management techniques and whether or not the project was successful. Based on this research, I've done presentations and several publications, including a book, *Risk Management: An Enterprise Dilemma* [DBC Publishing, 2016]. All of my results are in Chapter 4 of the book, as well as a follow-up discussion. I think the book is an excellent read and a good investment for its price.

Harpham: Based on your research, what works in risk management on projects?

Gillespie: In my experience and research, project risk management practices are often done informally or not at all. Risk management mitigation, budgeting for risk, and analyzing positive and negative risk in advance of a project's execution phase are rare. The study showed that project managers who used risk management techniques were correlated to higher levels of project success. I advocate using project risk management in the planning phase—even more so than in the execution phase of the project, where it is often too late to migrate your most important risks.

Harpham: If this approach to risk management contributes to success, why do you think it is done so rarely?

Gillespie: It's not well understood as a practice. Organizations don't tend to promote or encourage it. Other project managers do not tend to showcase it either. A failure in mentorship may be part of the story. In the PMBOK Guide, let's remember that risk management is only one of several knowledge areas. If you're a brand-new project manager, are you going to dig into that area when other areas appear to be more exciting?

Aside from certain industries, like banking and construction, I see an organizational aversion to doing risk management. That aversion is likely because risk management has not been proven to be beneficial and relevant to a particular company. Risk management also identifies weaknesses. Who wants to reveal or identify their problems or that they're underprepared for a potential problem?

Harpham: What are the methods and techniques that go into your personal productivity system?

Gillespie: Meeting notes are a key activity for me. For every meeting that I hold, I send out an email of the notes for the meeting within about an hour after the meeting. That holds true whether I have one or five meetings a day. In today's environment, if I wait a day or two to send out the meeting notes, there could be other meetings going on that change the discussion or action items. This is an insight I've developed over time.

When I say "meeting notes," I mean meeting minutes, like action items—tasks with a responsible person and a due date. I also include a high-level summary of the issues discussed in the meeting. "Meeting minutes" sounds so formal and dry. That's why over the years my *colleagues* and I have called them "meeting notes," but they are essentially the same thing. However, I would say that, as a best practice, you don't have to be chronological in the "he said, she said." Rather, be topic driven and action-item focused.

In terms of communication, I think it is best to send out your meeting notes in your first post-meeting communication, rather than saying, "Thank you for attending the meeting. The minutes will be sent out shortly."

When you make a promise like that, it often sets you up for failure and sometimes there are delays that will prevent you from doing that. It's better to set a personal deadline and get it done, that way, the first thing they get from you is an actionable communication.

Turning to email, I'm a strong believer in getting email to "inbox zero." I don't use email as a task manager which means that I try not to keep an email in my inbox as a way to remind me to do something, since this does not scale for the work that I do. I know some people—more than a few— that use that approach for email. They often have elaborate folders and rules to manage the information—so it can be done. I generally prefer to manage tasks in a spreadsheet with multiple tabs, organized just the way I like it. That way, I don't have to fight with folders and I can add additional context, status, or other notes to a task, such as a due date. Any input I receive from email, or other means, needs to be distilled and analyzed for action. It can't just sit in my email inbox. But that's my own method.

Finally, I keep an ongoing PowerPoint file for all of my projects. I have a set of slides that I keep for myself that makes sense to me. This material helps me to quickly prepare for presentations, written, verbal, and ad hoc communication on each project. I know that there are great software tools to help with these processes. However, when it comes to generating material and maintaining my own sanity, I prefer to use spreadsheets and presentation files.

Harpham: There's value in using tools that you know and understand well. It's not always necessary or helpful to use new software.

Looking ahead over the next few years, which technologies and trends are you following with interest?

Gillespie: Waterfall project management is on the decline. It's not going away, because it does fit with certain cases. I see a greater interest in moving toward scrum and agile methods though some argue that agile is being taken to an extreme. For example, SAFe [Scaled Agile Framework], has its own unique challenges. Today, the PMBOK is mainly focused on waterfall project management. PMI does have an agile certification, but it is still relatively new. But I expect that it will become more popular over time.

Chapter Summary

- Recommended books include Gillespie's *Risk Management: An Enterprise Dilemma.*

- Generating career opportunities: Gillespie attributes some of his career opportunities to raising his profile through speaking engagements and volunteer work.

- Transition to project management: Gillespie moved into the project field after delivering great results in IT and data centers. Despite that success, adjusting to the demands of full-time project management took some time.

- The art and science of project management: In Gillespie's view, a successful project manager needs to combine the "science" of project work (e.g., schedules and budgets) with the "art" of project work (e.g., leadership, empathy, and communication skills).

- Risk management: Aside from a handful of industries, Gillespie has found that risk management practices are often poorly developed. This presents an opportunity for project managers with strong risk skills to add value.

- Continuing education: Gillespie has developed his knowledge and capabilities through extensive education, including earning an MBA, a PhD, and numerous professional certifications.

Frank Crescenzo

Manager, Brookhaven Site Office, Brookhaven National Laboratory

Frank Crescenzo is the manager of the Brookhaven Site Office at Brookhaven National Laboratory (BNL) in Upton, New York. He is a federal employee and member of the Senior Executive Service (SES) with the US Department of Energy (DOE). Crescenzo was appointed site office manager in February 2013. He is also responsible for the DOE's management and operating (M&O) prime contract to assure all activities at BNL are completed to DOE expectations.

Crescenzo has 37 years of experience performing and managing technical activities and personnel, including 27 years managing the prime contract for operation of BNL, 6 years regulating commercial nuclear power reactors, and 4 years managing overhaul and testing programs for US Navy nuclear reactors. He was the DOE's federal project director for the NSLS-II project, from shortly after approval of mission need in 2005 through approval of project completion in 2015. Concurrent with these duties, Crescenzo was also the site office manager at the Princeton Plasma Physics Laboratory from October 2014 through December 2015. From 1990 until February 2013, he was the Brookhaven deputy site office manager; for nearly four of those years, he also served as acting site office manager. Throughout his tenure with DOE, Crescenzo was responsible for the delivery of many capital projects, including new scientific facilities, infrastructure projects, and environmental cleanup projects at BNL.

In the 1980s, Crescenzo served with the US Nuclear Regulatory Commission. From 1980 until 1984, he served with the Department of Navy, Norfolk Naval Shipyard, as a nuclear test engineer. He was responsible for planning and execution of nuclear plant overhaul and testing programs for naval nuclear submarines.

© Bruce Harpham 2018
B. Harpham, *Project Managers at Work*, DOI 10.1007/978-1-4842-2668-1_20

Crescenzo has a BS degree in engineering from the University of Massachusetts, Amherst, MA, and a JD degree from Touro College, Jacob D. Fuchsberg Law Center, Central Islip, New York. He is also certified as a Level IV DOE federal project director, a senior-level role held by a small number of senior professionals.

Note: The statements, opinions, and recollections expressed by Mr. Crescenzo for this book are solely his and not those of the Department of Energy, its Office of Science, or the Brookhaven Site Office. Furthermore, Mr. Crescenzo's participation with this publication is not an official governmental endorsement of this book.

Bruce Harpham: What is the focus of your current role?

Frank Crescenzo: I am the site manager for Brookhaven National Lab, a US Department of Energy–owned lab located on Long Island, in New York State. The Lab is 5,300 acres in size with about 2,700 scientists, engineers, technicians, and support personnel performing scientific research and related activities. In addition, thousands of scientists from around the world visit BNL each year to use one of the many scientific "user" facilities located at BNL. Excepting the visiting scientists, almost all personnel at BNL are contractors to DOE employed by Brookhaven Science Associates [BSA]. I, along with my site office of about thirty-five personnel, manage the DOE's prime management and operating contract with BSA. The contractor's responsibility is to do all the work required to keep the Lab running effectively. The value of the M&O contract for BNL is about $600 million per year.

The Lab's scientific user facilities include the only collider in North America, one of only two in the world [the other being the Large Hadron Collider in Europe], a multi-function center for nanoscience, a computational science facility, and a few small, specialized particle accelerator facilities. The Lab also has a newly completed synchrotron radiation facility known as National Synchrotron Light Source II [NSLS-II]. I served as the federal project director in creating the NSLS-II.

The Brookhaven National Lab is part of a national network of government-owned contractor operated [GOCO] labs. The Department of Energy has responsibility for seventeen national labs across the country. Some of these labs, like BNL, are multi-program labs performing research across a wide variety of topical areas with multiple scientific facilities. Others have a singular scientific focus, such as on high-energy physics, plasma physics [fusion energy], or nuclear physics. Still other labs are both multi-program but have a large mission to support nuclear security research. In many cases, the labs collaborate with each other or with industry and academia to accomplish goals or to complete capital projects.

Harpham: What type of scientific work is done at the Brookhaven facility?

Crescenzo: Brookhaven's principle mission is to design, build, and operate large complex and unique scientific facilities for the broader science communities of users, which include scientists from BNL. The Brookhaven facilities are focused mostly on basic science, but in some instances, like at NSLS-II, can have applied focus. By basic, I mean "fundamental" or distinct from applied science. An applied science question might be: How do we make a better battery? A basic science question might be: What did the universe look like a fraction of a moment after the Big Bang? At Brookhaven, we can actually re-create the state of the universe at that early moment using our collider, the Relativistic Heavy Ion Collider [RHIC]. There's also a large and important portfolio of applied science work done here as well, but in terms of dollars spent, the majority supports basic science.

The Department of Energy's Office of Science has several scientific programs in different areas. These programs support research activities at the national labs, at or with universities and in some cases at overseas facilities. Some are focused on basic energy science—materials, condensed matter physics, chemistry and related points. Basic energy sciences are a major area of work at Brookhaven, and support the operation of NSLS-II and the nanoscience facility. Nuclear and high-energy physics programs support the RHIC facility. Another DOE program supports research into advanced scientific computing technologies and strategies. Other programs support fusion energy and research on biological and environmental questions as these relate to energy. Typically, a science program's budget will support research activities, operation of research facilities and construction of new facilities.

The National Synchrotron Light Source II [NSLS-II] is akin to a gigantic microscope: it creates and stores a current of electrons, which emit beams of light mostly in the X-ray range of the spectrum. These X-ray beams then illuminate samples of matter, which supports investigating and analyzing various phenomena. This facility can be used for energy research, biology research, chemistry, and many other types of scientific investigation. Just about every basic science—and many applied science areas—can use the NSLS-II facility for research.

In many cases, the areas of focus for a national lab are driven by the scientific facilities that are available at that location. You might ask why the federal government is investing resources into scientific research programs and facilities. The short answer is that the government is the only organization with the resources to fund and operate large, complex scientific facilities with purely scientific value. Private industry will generally not build these facilities, as there is inadequate financial return on investment. Universities typically don't have the resources to build and operate facilities like these. It's important to note that there is usually a large yearly operating expense that, over a facility's life cycle, which can exceed thirty years, often far exceeds the initial construction costs. Building a facility like NSLS-II requires is a long term commitment of resources.

Harpham: I'm curious to understand how you came to have these responsibilities. How did you get started in your career before you were running National Labs?

Crescenzo: I graduated from college with an industrial engineering degree in 1980. My first job was in the nuclear industry as a civilian in the US Navy's Norfolk Naval Shipyard in Portsmouth, Virginia. It was a very interesting job! At that time, I was often working seven days a week for months on end. At Norfolk, my focus was on testing nuclear submarines. The submarines would come into the shipyard and they would be serviced or upgraded. My role was to ensure that the nuclear steam supply equipment was properly operated and maintained and that all the systems were correctly tested to assure correct operability afterwards.

After three to four years at Norfolk, I went to work for the US Nuclear Regulatory Commission [NRC]. The NRC is a government agency that is best known for regulating commercial nuclear power plants. In order to manipulate or direct the controls on a nuclear power plant in the United States, an individual has to obtain and maintain a license from the Commission. During my time there, I administered tests to applicants for these licenses to operate nuclear facilities. Following that, I was a senior resident inspector assigned to represent the NRC at commercial nuclear facilities on Long Island and in Westchester County, New York. During this time, I also went to night school to earn a law degree.

Harpham: Why did you decide to pursue a law degree?

Crescenzo: In the late 1980s, I was thinking that I might like to be a lawyer. It was a great experience to study the law and I enjoyed the curriculum. I found the material intellectually manageable. The greater challenge was the physical aspect. Working all day and then going to school at night for nine to twelve credits a semester is strenuous. I graduated from law school but never ended up practicing law.

I came to Brookhaven in 1990 while I was earning the law degree. Soon after moving here, I became the deputy site manager in early 1991. It was similar to the job I have now except then I was the number-two person. The 1990s were a very different time compared to today for the labs. There was a major effort that was begun at that time to improve safety, business, and environmental management, so it was a bit of a transitional era. That effort has continued until today. However, safety and environmental management are now top priorities engrained into the culture of BNL. At any given time, there are a number of such projects underway at a national lab.

Harpham: Would these projects include building large scientific instruments?

Crescenzo: Exactly, that's one example. Since I've been here, I've been involved in a number of projects. Around the time I joined the DOE at BNL, the effort to build the Relativistic Heavy Ion Collider had begun. In today's dollars, that project was about $1.5 billion to carry out [at the time, it was approximately $750 million]. I wasn't the project director for that project but I was responsible for it. I had a federal project director [FPD] who worked for me on that project.

The DOE requires that every capital project over $5 million have a certified FPD assigned to it. An FPD is always a federal employee and is overall responsible to the project sponsor for project delivery. The FPD leads an integrated project team consisting of other federal employees and contractors to manage the project planning and execution phases. DOE maintains a robust and disciplined training and certification program for FPDs. An FPD is certified and assigned to projects by DOE to levels I through IV commensurate with his or her training and experience related to project management.

Harpham: Can you elaborate on the environmental projects?

Crescenzo: We had a large environmental cleanup project starting in the 1990s and extending until about 2012. Recall the history of this site - government operations on the property that became Brookhaven Lab in 1947 dates back to the Army's Camp Upton and the First World War.

Up until the 1970s, laws and standards for environmental protection were limited. A lack of knowledge concerning the effects of environmental actions or inactions resulted in past practices in industry and at government facilities that would not be tolerated today. Facilities for treatment of hazardous materials did not exist and waste streams considered hazardous and highly regulated today, were commonly disposed of in onsite landfills or discharged to surface or groundwater bodies around the site. For example, the Army cleaned its trucks with volatile organic cleaning fluids and allowed the runoff to collect in the groundwater which created plumes. Mercury, a common element in research, was typically dumped into drains, ultimately finding its way through the sewage treatment plant to a sensitive river that runs through BNL property. There were also cases of radioactive materials from BNL's reactors getting into the soils and groundwater.

Starting in the 1990s, there were a number of projects to stop further releases and to clean up legacy impacts in the soils, groundwater, and rivers at BNL. The cleanup effort took a number of years with a budget over $500 million. It was one of Brookhaven's larger projects and it had nothing to do with science. It was a highly structured project that used earned value management, project reviews, and other processes.

In addition to the major projects to create new scientific instruments, there are a number of other projects underway at Brookhaven at any given time. For example, a building may be under construction, another building being demolished, or an existing science facility may be installing a new instrument. Brookhaven also has ongoing projects to support other labs, including a very large neutrino experiment in Illinois and South Dakota, a large digital telescope being constructed in Chile, and a $300 million upgrade to a detector at the Large Hadron Collider in Europe.

Harpham: What was the origin of the NSLS II project?

Crescenzo: Creating a large scientific facility like NSLS II takes a great deal of time and resources. Typically, people start thinking about the project around fifteen to twenty years before it is finished and operational. People start to ask questions like, "What kind of scientific research capabilities will we need in five or ten or twenty years?" I personally recall first hearing about a next-generation light source for BNL sometime in the late 1990s.

Harpham: In brief, what was the objective and rationale for the NSLS II project?

Crescenzo: In the late 1990s, there was a realization that the synchrotron radiation facility at BNL was getting old. It was understood that a new instrument would be needed to support the large number of synchrotron science users at BNL and to a certain extent in the Northeast. At the same time, other questions come up concerning budget matters and timing. When could it be done? These early steps of developing the idea at a high level didn't involve me given the role I have. These are planning activities that are reserved for the program officials I spoke of earlier.

Generally, the Department of Energy's science program budget and priorities are divided into three areas. These include a budget to support research at national labs and academia, a budget to support operating existing research facilities, and a budget to support building brand-new facilities. Determining when and how to fund a large project like the NSLS II from the "build new facilities" budget is challenging in part because the decision makers have to be mindful of all the other programs and projects in their portfolio. Typically, funds become available for new projects as other projects are completed. New operating funds become available as older facilities phase out or shutdown.

As you can imagine, the early thinking about such projects tends to be informal and ranging in scope and costs. Many people come to the table with ideas for scientific research. With NSLS II, informal support for the project really began around 2003 with formal DOE support via the Critical Decision process starting in 2005 and substantial financial support from DOE starting in 2007.

Harpham: What is the Critical Decisions process?

Crescenzo: On any large project [and some other projects], there are certain "critical decisions" to be made. On each project, there's usually five pre-defined critical decisions.

The first critical decision [Critical Decision 0] involves the mission need - the sponsor has to make a decision or a declaration for the mission. For a DOE science program, this is typically described in terms of a scientific capability. The particular mission need that spawned the NSLS-II was the need to "image materials at the single atom scale." Critical Decision 0 for NSLS-II was completed in August 2005. You can consider that moment as the formal beginning of the project. I became the federal project director shortly after Critical Decision 0.

The next step—Critical Decision 1—is to answer the question: how do we best satisfy the mission need? Specifically, we start to create conceptual designs showing different ways to fulfill the need. Several options were considered at this stage, including building a brand-new facility, upgrading an existing domestic facility, utilizing an overseas facility and, as always, a "do nothing" option. Critical Decision 1 also authorizes financial support for preliminary design efforts.

The next Critical Decision, 2, to approve a baseline, locks in the cost, scope, and schedule for the project. This is followed by a Critical Decision 3, which authorizes physical construction to begin. Lastly, there is a Critical Decision 4, which signals project completion and authorizes the facility to begin operations.

Harpham: It's interesting to see that choosing an international facility to carry out the scientific mission is one of the options.

Crescenzo: Absolutely. Every year, there are more and more great scientific facilities established around the world. If there is a great facility in Japan or Europe we could partner with, that might be a great option to achieve the mission. Every scientific field has its own community. The nuclear physicists from around the world know each other, for example. They all keep informed on what facilities are available and what questions would be worthwhile to explore next. Generally, any scientific community will have many more science questions and new facilities in mind than there are resources to pursue them. So, they have to prioritize and they try to avoid duplicating facilities.

In many cases, it quickly becomes obvious that you need to build a new facility to achieve the scientific mission. Unlike some highly specialized facilities designed to answer narrow questions, light sources are workhorse science facilities servicing a very broad user community. The United States operates five and just about every major nation has at least one with more under construction, all oversubscribed by users. You almost can't have too many Light Sources [if you could afford them]. However, it's important to go through the exercise of generating a variety of options to meet the mission need and giving each option careful consideration. If that work on defining and analyzing options for the project is skipped, you might fall into the situation where you build the project just because somebody asked for it. You may end up with the proverbial "white elephant" that nobody really needs or wants. That wasteful scenario can be prevented by using this type of options analysis.

Harpham: What was the next step in the project's development?

Crescenzo: In 2007, we went through Critical Decision 1. That's when we decided that building the NSLS-II would be the best way to fulfill the mission need to image materials at the single atom scale. At that time, the high-level specifications were also created and design funds were released to the project.

The federal project director role means that I am the senior federal person on site with the project. In this case, I was managing the project through the contractor.

Harpham: In your capacity as the federal project director, what kinds of decisions come across your desk?

Crescenzo: For example, I would authorize the use of contingency funds on the project. If the project encounters a cost that was higher than planned [or if it will take longer than planned], those decisions would come to me for a final decision. I would also make decisions regarding scope changes on the project. For example, just before we started physical construction of the building to house the NSLS-II, we realized the experimental floor would be very cramped so we decided to broaden it about 10 meters. Sounds simple but it's a round building so it was 10 meters wide by 800 meters round. It cost about 12 million extra so I had to approve this scope change and release contingency funds to pay for it.

In many cases, the contractor would have the authority to make some of these decisions. In this arrangement, significant authority was delegated to the contractor to make smaller changes. However, very large changes might have to go to my customer for a decision. If the change was very, very large then that change might be brought to the Secretary of Energy. In this project, there was no need to contact the Secretary, but it could have happened. Some situations—known as a "baseline breach"—may call for the Secretary to get involved as well.

Harpham: Do "baseline breaches" on the project happen often?

Crescenzo: My working definition of a project breach is where the cost or schedule is projected to significantly exceed the approved baseline considering contingencies or the baseline scope cannot be delivered. The NSLS-II never approached a baseline breach situation. It happens fairly frequently in other projects. For example, some projects have enormous technical challenges that cannot be solved as initially planned, often funding profile changes cause progress to slow and total costs to skyrocket, and sometimes, unforeseen challenges emerge. These situations can have enormous impacts on project cost and schedules. In my experience, it's more often than not that a project breach is caused by forces external to the project. To the extent that a project team is responsible for a breach, it is usually because it failed to plan for risks properly. NSLS-II was a very successful project. We didn't encounter these types of problems.

Harpham: It sounds like Light Source II was a near perfect project. It was delivered on time and on budget. That's an impressive accomplishment given the complexity of the project. How was that achieved?

Crescenzo: We had an excellent customer or sponsor to work with on the project. For NSLS II our sponsor was the DOE's Office of Science program for Basic Energy Sciences [SC-BES]. If you study projects enough, you will find that the customer's involvement [or lack thereof] is extremely important to the project's success—or failure. A good project customer is someone who is interested, engaged, and committed to success on the project. They will give you the resources required to achieve the objective. They will understand that risks are part of the project and will provide resources to cover risks. Finally, a good customer will also hold you accountable to deliver the project.

If the customer doesn't hold you accountable to deliver the project, problems tend to linger and don't get solved. Here again, we had an exceptionally good customer: Basic Energy Sciences at the Department of Energy.

We also had a great project team. The project leadership was exceptionally good at leading but also in the "business" of project management. Below the leadership the technical staff, the scientists and engineers, who designed and built the machine were among the best in the world. There were countless technical challenges on this project and the technical team overcame them all.

Lastly we had a great project baseline and plan to deliver the project. We understood the risks involved in the project and could plan accordingly. Every day brought a new problem, but we mostly anticipated these problems through risk management and worked through those problems, such as problems with vendors. At the end of the day, we were able to solve the problems by using additional staff, money, or other approaches. Our solutions always were well within our contingencies.

Harpham: The role of the customer is a great perspective to highlight. Some explanations of project success or failure put all pressure on the project manager's side of the desk. Can you give examples of actions the customer did that made you think, "We're going to win because we have a good customer helping us!"

Crescenzo: We had a good funding package to build this project as a starting point. I've been involved in other projects where the customer was not interested in success per se. In those cases, it seemed like the customer was more interested in looking successful. In the latter case of "looking successful," the customer would dictate the budget and project deadline. If the team pointed out that the project will take longer or cost more, this kind of customer would respond with "That's the wrong answer!" In that case, the project will be destined to fail.

Harpham: What was your approach to planning the project with the customer?

Crescenzo: It's important to go through the pre-planning stage to achieve success. Our customer was engaged with us during the planning work. I would talk with my program manager almost daily though this time. My program manager, a member of my integrated project team, was located in headquarters and worked in the sponsor organization [SC-BES]. Typically, the program manager would monitor my performance and my contractor's performance on the project and communicate this to his superiors. He also assisted the project by attending to HQ tasks, such as budget issues or handling project-directed inquiries from external entities. That's another example of the customer being committed to true success rather than simply looking successful.

Harpham: Can you explain more about the difference between a project customer who's interested in success and one who is interested in appearing successful?

Crescenzo: The good customer has to be committed to provide the resources for the project to be successful. The customer has to be engaged and knowledgeable enough to effectively hold the project team accountable for results. The customer has to be prepared for and understand the nature of project work: uncertainty, risk, and changes to cost and schedule. The customer has to be willing to accept project changes as they occur. At the same time, it's my job to stay on top of the contractor and ensure that they are delivering according to plans, considering risks and contingencies. In this case, everyone was comfortable with the project baseline in terms of budget and schedule. Creating that baseline and obtaining agreement on it was Critical Decision 2 with our process.

In contrast, a not so good customer might force a contractor to agree to a baseline that the contractor does not believe is credible. The customer will declare that the project will be successful because it will be delivered at such and so time for some cost that they can afford—i.e., it looks successful now. Often these customers will rotate folks through the project, so they fail to remain adequately engaged. As these project execute, they run over budget and schedule, create crisis, then the customer throws the contractor under the bus for failing to deliver.

Harpham: What was the next important point on the project?

Crescenzo: In 2009, we arrived at Critical Decision 3 on the project. It happened to occur right at the same time as the 2008 to 2009 economic crisis. The conventional construction market collapsed in terms of demand. That construction market collapse had a two-fold impact on the project.

First, we went out for bids for the buildings and related items [conventional construction]. Generally, with projects like the NSLS-II, scientists design the machine they want and an external civil construction design firm or architect engineer is contracted to design a new custom building to house the machine. Often the building, or "conventional construction," is on or near the critical path and must get started first or very early on the project schedule. In many past projects, the bids for conventional construction would come in much higher than expected causing baseline problems at the very start of construction. This was a large risk for the NSLS-II. However, the economic situation contributed to the outcome that bids came in at great prices—right on target with what we had planned. This allowed us to retire a large risk on the project early.

Second, in response to the so-called great recession, the federal government, through its "stimulus" program released a large amount of funding for "shovel ready" projects to stimulate the economy in 2009. Originally, NSLS-II was to receive about $103 million in 2009 to get started with construction. The stimulus program accelerated an additional $150 million in fiscal year 2009 to our project, so we ended up with a total of about $253 million in 2009. It is important to note that this $150 million was accelerated funding, not additional funding. The total project cost in the approved baseline did not increase above the original $912 million. Rather, the $150 million added to 2009 was subtracted from later year budgets in the project's multi-year funding profile.

With those resources available at an earlier point, we were able to solve some of the technical risks in the project and accelerate the project's completion. Overall, this added funding made it possible for us to reduce risk on the project and facilitate the opportunities to add scope to the project.

Harpham: After Critical Decision 3 in 2009, what was the next significant point in the project?

Crescenzo: We had Critical Decision 4 next. At this point, the buildings, instruments and everything requested was delivered. We demonstrated that the facility and instruments were fully functional to complete the project in December 2014.

Harpham: It looks like you had excellent opportunities in terms of government spending and an oversupply in construction capacity to move the project ahead quickly.

Harpham: What do you mean that you used some of the budget to "buy down risk"? Can you describe that in further detail?

Crescenzo: An enormously important question in a federally funded project is how much money do you have each year to spend?

Practically, if a project's schedule is "funding limited" that means its progress will be determined by how much funding is available to commit over the life of the project. The project will need to defer work and procurements to later points on the project schedule when funding is available.

On the other hand, a project schedule can be "technically limited" meaning progress will be determined by how fast work can be done in the most optimal schedule. Any given task has a limit on how fast it can be done and cannot be accelerated even with unlimited money. It may take a vendor a year to make a thousand magnets or an engineer a certain period of time to design a structure. In almost all cases, a funding limited project will take longer and cost more in the end than a technically limited project.

This concept is particularly important for federally funded projects, as US government budgets are approved annually. A federal project sponsor may need to limit a project's funding in a given year to less than optimal in order to fulfill commitments elsewhere in its program. While a program can plan on a future funding profile, it's not certain until the annual budget is enacted into law. The annual budget process can change the funding from the baseline plan in a particular year.

The possibility that the funding profile would be "stretched" on NSLS-II was the single largest risk that we carried for most of the project's life. Thankfully, it was never realized. Most large projects that I've been involved with are funding, or close to funding limited. NSLS-II was an exception, the acceleration of the $150 million essentially shifted the schedule from near funding limited to technically limited. With this accelerated funding, we actually had more money on hand than we could spend for the first few years of construction. This is a very rare circumstance in government projects.

Any part of the technical scope may carry risk. For example, the vendor may be late in delivering to the project. With the added budget we were given, it was possible to bring some of the technical scope earlier in the schedule than we had originally planned. Completing those technical components earlier meant there was a reduced need to hold a portion of money for risk management.

Let's say you had originally planned to do certain project work five years from now. Then, you are able to make changes and start on that project work tomorrow. It changes everything. You have the capacity to get started on something else earlier. We were able to add additional scope that wasn't in the initial baseline.

Harpham: Did adding scope to the project prompt questions or objections?

Crescenzo: No, this was not a gold plating scenario. With NSLS-II, we were able to accelerate the project's progress as additional resources became available. The facility was originally designed to ultimately have sixty-five beamlines and five lab office buildings [LOBs].

A beamline is a scientific instrument where the visiting scientists illuminate their samples, the working end of the facility so to speak. An LOB has office and lab space to support thousands of scientist users who would visit the facility to use the beamlines. As a reference, a state of the art beamline might cost $20 to $25 million and a fully built out LOB $15 million. The initial baseline plan was to build six beamlines, two fully fitted-out LOBs, and one "shell" LOB [walls, roof, HVAC]. This approach—to deliver partial capability on day one with the intent to add capability later—is very common on DOE science facility projects. As risks were retired, and we saw a funding opportunity, we were able to finish the LOB shell and add two more shells. We added significant parts to the technical scope to facilitate future beamline construction. Again, everything we added was envisioned within the end state facility design approved with Critical Decision 1. Therefore, these additions cannot be termed gold plating.

In contrast, gold plating on the project would look quite different. That would be something like: "We're going to add something that will significantly increase or change the capability envisioned in the original design or possibly to build an unrelated or ancillary facility somewhere else nearby." Again, for NSLS-II we were simply building out the original design more quickly.

Harpham: So the scientists were pleasantly surprised when they heard about the expanded facilities?

Crescenzo: The sponsor was happy about the progress. And in general, the sponsor represents the scientific community of users.

The actual scientists were focused on different capabilities. The stakeholders interested in the beamlines include physicists, chemists, environmental specialists and many other professions. At Brookhaven, it's a diverse community of different researchers and scientists as opposed to a facility specialized in a specific area, such as nuclear research. The scientists knew they were going to receive a certain capacity and simply wanted it to be available for use. I am sure that in the end everyone with a stake in NSLS-II will be more pleased with the extra scope we delivered from what we planned to deliver initially.

Harpham: I'm curious to understand the project chronology. When was construction completed on the project?

Crescenzo: Construction was ultimately completed in 2014.

Harpham: What are some of your lessons learned from your role in the Light Source II project?

Crescenzo: A key lesson for me is that many of the non-technical problems ultimately stem from communications. There were a lot of communication problems between those doing the project work, my office, and the customer. One of my biggest contributions to the project was to raise the quality and accuracy of project communications. Certainly, bad news is bad news. However, I hate surprises on a project. If there was bad news, it should not come as a total surprise. Also, the customer doesn't want surprises either. If I suspected a problem might develop, I would provide early warning about those situations.

I also learned lessons about the importance of planning the project well at an early stage. That includes defining the risks and establishing a risk management plan.

Harpham: Can you illustrate the communication problems you encountered? What does that sound like?

Crescenzo: Surprise! If the customer is surprised about an issue or problem, it is likely that there was ineffective communication earlier. Sometimes communication problems were connected to roles and responsibilities issues. For example, you might have the customer telling the contractor how to do business. It's not the customer's responsibility to tell the contractor how to run their business. Instead, the customer's role is to say, "There is a problem here. You need to demonstrate how you will solve the problem." Ultimately, some people would get confused about the boundaries of their role in the project and I was often called upon to straighten this out.

Harpham: How can the "Surprise!" situation be prevented? Is it a case of project managers delaying saying anything until they have a one hundred–percent complete picture of a situation?

Crescenzo: There is a tendency for everyone to delay informing others of problems until they have complete understanding of the problem or maybe the solution to the problem. This approach or philosophy must be avoided at all times as it can erode trust.

Let's say a part of the project suddenly has a cost of $5 million higher than what was planned. You will need to inform your customer—hey, it's $5 million more than planned. Once they get over the surprise, the customer may start to dig into the situation. If the customer then finds out that you've been struggling with a vendor for six months and the likelihood of increased cost has been discussed for five and a half months you lose the customer's confidence. Finding out such a back-story makes your customer wonder, "What else is going on with this project that I don't know about?" Losing the confidence of your customer is very bad for many reasons.

You want your customer to know about potential problems even those that are on the horizon. When you communicate enough, the customer has greater confidence about your approach to problems. They are likely to think, "OK, here comes a problem on the project. Nothing unusual about a problem happening here. I also know that my project manager has been successful at addressing problems in the past and will keep me informed about the situation."

Harpham: It comes down to anticipating problems or spotting early warning signs.

Crescenzo: On any given day, there will be problems big and small as you work through a project. However, effective project planning means that you will anticipate most of the significant problems. For instance, you know for certain that some, but not all, of the vendors will be late in their delivery or more expensive than planned. You must plan for this risk, partly with mitigation strategies, but also with time and money. A well-designed project will carry or plan for a lot more risk than ultimately gets realized. For example, you may plan for a million dollars' worth of delays from vendors and some will be late and some will be on time, so maybe it costs you only $500,000 to address. Now you have $500,000 to apply to other risks, or maybe added scope.

Harpham: What are the upcoming trends and opportunities in the next three to five years that you see coming up in science and technology?

Crescenzo: I'm not an expert in predicting the direction of science. I will say that there are effective processes in place for the DOE programs to communicate with the various scientific communities to develop the strategic directions for science and the DOE's role in those plans. Keep in mind that the DOE is the largest funding source of basic scientific research in the United States. That means many different scientific projects are explored at any given moment. Also, whatever DOE does, or wants to do, will need to be authorized by the President and the Congress, and I am certainly no expert on predicting the outcome of those processes.

I would like to address a related question as to why should the government should support science. Take the Apple iPhone as an example. Some folks might say, "Look! What a wonderful high-tech product developed by private industry! Who needs the government to fund R&D?" Well, most of the foundational technologies [e.g., GPS, Internet, cellular, touch screens, lithium ion batteries, LCDs] that went into that product were based on ideas and technologies developed at their earliest stages by the public sector's science and technology research. Government funding for basic science, especially at the early stages—where the risks are high and the benefits are unclear, plays an essential role in furthering our nation's technology base and in turn competitiveness.

Harpham: What does your personal productivity system look like?

Crescenzo: In order to be productive in my decisions, I need to be well informed. Therefore, a key practice for me is seeking out information from my team and other sources. I also made it a priority to ensure that the right people worried about the right issues at the right times. Of course, there are many other useful tools to use in projects, such as earned value management. However, it's important to understand the limitations of a given tool. Earned value management reports can be misleading.

Harpham: In what way, would earned value management reports mislead a project manager?

Crescenzo: Take NSLS-II for example. Early on, we were spending huge amounts of money on conventional construction. If you looked at our spending versus our planned spending, it was ahead of schedule. However, you might have a key vendor who is delivering their important but less expensive contribution late. Earned value measures may not take into account the importance of small budget items that play a critical role in the project's success. Without those parts, you cannot finish the project. We had that issue with certain parts that were difficult to produce. They required absolutely clean production conditions and this was a serious challenge for the vendor. An earned value or financial report on the project would not clearly identify this delay of a lower-cost item as a critical issue.

Earned value management information is useful, but you need to supplement it with other resources. An experienced project manager once told me that earned value management analysis is "like trying to drive a car by looking in the rear-view mirror." You certainly need to check the rear-view mirror periodically to drive safely, but looking forward is more important.

Chapter Summary

- The role of the project sponsor in project success: Crescenzo attributes much of his success on NSLS II to having an excellent customer/sponsor. Such a sponsor cares about the project's success and engage in discussions on risk.

- Changing the world with projects: NSLS II, an award-winning project, enables new types of scientific research. That research cannot happen, however, unless project managers deliver an outstanding facility.

- Finding opportunities in crisis: NSLS II's success in terms of staying on budget was facilitated by obtaining great prices from vendors and accelerated funding during the 2008–2010 recession. What opportunity can you find in your next crisis?

- The productive leader: In order to make good decisions on your projects, make it a habit to seek out quality information in reports and in other resources. Biased or incomplete information will quietly sabotage your decisions.

- Critical decision points: The NSLS II was governed with several processes, including a number of "critical decision points." How can you adapt these process and questions (e.g., How do we best satisfy the mission's needs?) to make sure that your organization builds the right projects?

David Kollm

Enterprise Agile Coach, Accenture

David Kollm *is an enterprise agile coach at Accenture, where he has worked on multiple client projects in the telecom, insurance, defense, healthcare, retail, software, Internet/ASP (Application Services Provider), computer manufacturing, and high-tech industries. Before Accenture, Kollm founded a design and marketing company, whose clients included Massachusetts General Hospital and many of Boston's top law firms. Prior to this, he worked in senior product management, project/engineering management, and engineering roles in the computer, packaged software, and Software As A Service (SaaS) industries. Kollm has extensive expertise in product planning and delivery and management with agile processes and methods in large multinational (onshore/offshore, multicultural) environments. He also has expertise in bimodal development, interfacing agile projects with existing waterfall dependencies.*

Bruce Harpham: How did you start your career?

David Kollm: I started my career at NCR as a hardware engineer. While in that role, I worked on PC2PC [a 1 megabit local area network], RetailPC [NCR's first PC-based cash register], NCR's Token Ring LAN board, and NCR's first personal computers targeted at consumers. I worked my way up through the various engineering levels and eventually obtained a consulting engineer position at NCR. The company decided to move our group from Dayton, Ohio, to Minneapolis. This proposed move—to a new location and role—was not a good fit for my family as we were expecting our first child, so I looked around for other opportunities.

© Bruce Harpham 2018
B. Harpham, *Project Managers at Work*, DOI 10.1007/978-1-4842-2668-1_21

Ultimately, we moved to South Carolina where I made a lateral move to a project integration manager role. I had eleven years of experience as an engineer and engineering manager prior to moving over to project integration management. That was my first formal introduction to project management. While I was in that role, I started an executive MBA degree from Clemson University. My goal in achieving my MBA was to learn the "business side" of the product development business so that I would be able to understand and see the non-technical side of work. My next career move was to product management.

Harpham: Why did you move into product management?

Kollm: I wanted to make a bigger impact and contribution to the company. As a project manager in that context, I had a limited opportunity to make a bigger impact on a product's vision and roadmap. I was simply expected to implement the pre-existing plan. I remember working on one project night and day for three months with the project team. The project was to implement a local area network. At that year's Christmas party for the division, the vice president of the group gave a glowing speech about a specific product and the extra effort put in by its leader to bring it in on time. At first, my project team thought the VP was referring to me. As it turned out, the VP was referring to the product manager who he called up for additional recognition. This person had only visited the engineering team once and didn't appear to work any overtime. Yet, the VP handed him a briefcase full of money at the event. In reality, he had never even set foot in our development area or spoken to our team. We did all the work and he got all the credit.

Harpham: An actual briefcase filled with cash?

Kollm: Yes, it was briefcase with cash! I'm not sure how much, but it looked like a lot. Then another product manager was called up to the stage by the VP and received a briefcase of money. At this point, my wife looked at me and said, "What do you think about this product manager role and why were they being recognized when you and your team did all of the work?" Certainly, the product role was attractive in part due to what I saw at that event.

I also realized that I could do a much better job as a product manager— knowing firsthand the impact and responsibility I would have in leveraging a company's engineering resources. I felt that if product management and engineering could work together more closely—instead of just throwing specs over the wall—the company would produce better products in shorter timeframes with less death march overtime.

Harpham: What was your first year of work in the product field after coming up through project and engineering roles?

Kollm: In some respects, my technical background was a disadvantage. As a product manager, you should be looking at what your customer wants and work toward that. That perspective contrasts to an engineering outlook that takes technical capabilities as the starting point. It was challenging to take the view that I had to set the vision and then challenge the engineering team to meet that vision.

Harpham: How did the product management roles unfold?

Kollm: Ultimately, I ended up working in several product management roles at NCR, AT&T, and elsewhere. Eventually, my division was acquired by Compaq. Unfortunately, we were far from Compaq headquarters, so I felt isolated from the company's management. The company invited us to move to their headquarters in Texas. I didn't want to move there. As a result, I moved to a role at Parametric Technology Corporation as a marketing manager. Shortly afterward, the dot-com bust hit the technology industry.

Harpham: How did you navigate through the dot-com crash?

Kollm: I worked in various roles in this time, but none of them seemed to work out. Eventually, I co-founded a web design and marketing company with a focus on serving healthcare and law offices in the Boston area. Within three months, I had booked two years' worth of business and was on the qualified vendor list for Massachusetts General Hospital! We delivered over fifty external/internal websites along with traditional branding designs—logos, stationary, etc.—to Massachusetts General Hospital and multiple large law and accounting firms in the Boston area.

Harpham: What did you do after running the business?

Kollm: After running my own business for four to five years, I decided to switch back to the employee role. I was surprised to see how much employer expectations had changed compared to when I was last an employee. I recall interviewing for one job where I thought I was a great fit. Unfortunately, I didn't receive an offer. When I asked why, I was told that they were seeking a person with deep project management expertise and my résumé showed a combination of project and product experience. As they put it, they didn't want a jack-of-all-trades. I realized that the market had shifted.

Harpham: How did you respond to this shift in the job market?

Kollm: I learned about the Project Management Institute and decided to earn the PMP certification. I learned that there was a need to develop your own professional brand. It was no longer enough to say that you had successfully worked at a Fortune 50 company like NCR. Prior to moving into engineering management and product management at NCR, I had achieved the career level of consulting engineer. However, that was not enough. Companies do not want to take risks when they hire. One way to reduce hiring risk is to look for indicators, such as if the person has a PMP certification.

After passing the exam and updating my résumé, I found myself in a project management position within two weeks!

Harpham: Earning the PMP certification made a major positive impact on your career?

Kollm: Obtaining my PMP had an immediate impact on my career prospects. Before I obtained the PMP certification, I secured multiple job offers simply by stating that I had taken a PMI PMBOK–based project management course. Prior to this, I kept getting passed over for project management positions that I was overqualified for.

Harpham: What lessons have you learned along the way on how to navigate through large organizations?

Kollm: I recall learning about the importance of transparency and politics when I was working at a large insurance company in the Boston area as a project manager. The organization had a highly political environment, including the IT organization. At one key meeting, a business stakeholder showed that he missed all his deadlines for the project; however, he was still expecting IT to meet the overall delivery. I called him out saying, "This lack of information is putting the project at risk. We can't move ahead with this level of information and support."

After the meeting, I was called into my boss's office. I was told off for making the business partner look bad in the meeting. I responded by saying, "I just reported the project's status." There was a subtext: the business partner had a higher rank than me and I was criticized for pointing out his shortcomings. At that point, I realized that I wanted to move to a different environment.

Harpham: It sounds like the organization was dysfunctional.

Kollm: It was dysfunctional. If you can't tell the truth at a status meeting, how can the organization's management change course or make good decisions? While the company was doing reasonably well, I noticed that they were not number one, number two, or even number three in their industry. Their dysfunctional corporate culture contributed to reduced performance.

Harpham: I can certainly see the connection. If I'm an executive in this organization, this kind of corporate culture may reduce the quality of information I receive. Without crucial information, how can I make good decisions for the company?

Kollm: You're one hundred percent right. People wouldn't speak up when they saw problems. There's the adage that by the time you become an executive, all the status reports you receive will be positive. Everybody below you will massage information before it reaches you.

This reminds me of a recent agile coaching project I led at a large telecommunications company. I led an effort to have all the scope systemically tracked within our agile project management tool and then review that directly, instead of producing and reviewing status reports. However, some managers at the company didn't like this approach because this system exposed that they were behind schedule on the project. Transparency cuts both ways. It's better to be transparent than not, but don't expect everyone to say thank you!

If you think someone is going to be negatively impacted by an upcoming report, you may want to proactively offer to help them before the report is released.

I once heard Alastair Cockburn put it this way at an agile seminar: agile is like a mirror. It will reveal what's working and what's not working very quickly. If you move to agile with bad processes, those bad processes will be revealed in detail.

Harpham: What do you see happening when organizations adopt agile?

Kollm: I've seen companies start to adopt agile and then measure this activity with metrics. When they don't like what the metrics tell them, they change the metrics to ones that do. To be fair, they still make some improvements, but playing with the metrics slows down progress considerably.

In other companies, there's a whole different attitude. Management will say, "These metrics show we have a major problem. We need to take action to address the situation." As you might expect, this attitude leads to faster transitions to agile and increased productivity. Fundamentally, those organizations are successful in changing their culture.

Harpham: In your training and consulting activities, what are some of the mistakes you see made by novice agile practitioners?

Kollm: Metrics and measures are one of my areas of expertise. I certainly see mistakes in that area. In agile, everyone is familiar with story points—a way to describe progress on scope. However, the story points are relative and based on each team's progress. Unfortunately, these measures are not well understood.

I have seen procurement people write RFPs with statements that define story points as a productivity measure. For example, the measure could be "each team will deliver fifty story points per month or per sprint." That procurement wording changes them into an absolute measure rendering the use of them useless.

Maintaining story points as a relative measurement of effort is key, because in agile, you measure progress in working software per team. The key word here is per. Each team understands and completes the needed work at its own pace. Keeping this measure relative and at an individual team level provides a useful measure of delivery predictability based on past results.

A waterfall project approach assumes all teams are uniform in capability and therefore assumes a certain hourly estimate for a type of work that is then applied uniformly to all teams doing that type of work. The benefit of keeping story points relative is that we get a much more realistic "rate of delivery" of work per sprint per team. This rate—the team's velocity—can then be used to more reliably predict when the team will complete its overall set of work. This is key because most business partners would rather have predictable reliable delivery of work to base their business plans/product launches on.

However, this does not provide a single simple productivity measure for procurement. Many times, their position is "we'll translate a story point into a certain number of work hours." If you do that, the metric is no longer a relative measure of effort. As a result, it's no longer a team measure and it may become a death march.

Harpham: Speaking of misunderstanding agile, I sometimes see the term "agile" vaguely used to mean "we'll just go faster," while leaving our culture and processes largely unchanged.

Kollm: Agile is a totally distinct way of working. It is a cultural shift. Fundamentally, I see agile adoption as an organizational change management project. It is not just a software development methodology. If agile is treated like a development framework and its adoption is not extended to the business side of a company, it can become a mini-waterfall situation. Even worse, you may get "zombie teams." These are teams with no ownership of their work and without any ability to push back on unready work. They're told what to do and they get yelled at for not getting it done, even when it is not their fault.

Adopting agile is not like ordering off a menu in a restaurant—you can't choose item one, item four, and item seven. Agile is an interdependent system of processes, measures, and cultural shifts that needs to be adopted fully if you want to obtain the benefits.

Harpham: What happens when a waterfall organization attempts to adopt agile in a partial way?

Kollm: That happens all the time. You might have this one group that is adopting agile processes. However, they may report to a PMO that requires traditional project management reporting metrics. As a result, the agile teams must do their work in agile and redo everything to satisfy the waterfall requirements. Consequentially, the teams get burned out from having to serve two different systems. In most cases, the agile experiment collapses and the group resumes using the waterfall approach.

At this point in time, waterfall project management is the incumbent methodology still used in many organizations. To really get the benefits, you can't run a single agile project and say, "We're an agile organization." Organizations must continually work on it. If there's no ongoing effort to adopt agile—both methods and culture, groups that initially do adopt agile will end up like a rock in swift river—worn down over time eventually reverting to waterfall because it is the path of least resistance.

When I arrive at companies today, I find that most of them have experimented with agile in some form. However, many are still treating agile as strictly an engineering/IT activity and haven't tackled the hard problem of involving the business. Because of this they're not getting the benefits they expected to receive.

Harpham: What goes into the agile assessment process you use? Does it explore culture and change management?

Kollm: Let's start with the premise that adopting agile involves an organizational change management process. It's also notable that agile, scrum, and related ideas were not created by consulting firms. They had grassroots origins from various developers.

Agile and scrum were first identified and elaborated on by people doing the actual software development. They saw what worked and what didn't. Further research and experiments at various companies fine tuned the process. Agile gained popularity and notoriety because it works—not because it's the next great idea.

The first question to explore is: Is this company following the generally accepted definition of agile, or are they simply using bits and pieces of it? Next, we look at the roles. Do they have the right roles in place, such as scrum master, product owner, scrum team, and so forth? Do these roles have the right responsibilities and are the people empowered to get their work done? Next, I start to look at the rest of the organization. How do other groups operate? How are requirements developed and passed back and forth?

With all the assessment information in hand, you can then place the organization into a maturity model. This will also include a breakdown looking at subareas like leadership, methods and tools, planning and delivery, people and community, supporting processes and areas, and continuous improvement opportunities. The organization may have sprint activities partially in place, for example. Or the organization may not have a backlog.

One interesting point of note is that while the set of exhibited dysfunctions may be unique to an organization, the underlying principles to correct are universal.

Harpham: What kind of response do you receive when people receive these assessments?

Kollm: Let's assume that the organization is interested in developing their agile capabilities. In many cases, changes are required at higher levels of the organization. It may also involve changes in interactions between departments.

I recall working with a telecommunications company that had been doing some work in agile. They asked me to come in and do an assessment. While interviewing staff and reviewing documentation, I noticed that their burndown charts had a hockey-stick effect. That means that progress is made throughout the project, but nothing was accepted by the customer until the last few days of the sprint. I found out that the quality assurance group would not start testing until all the development work was complete.

Harpham: Why was the quality assurance group doing that? It sounds like they were holding back the process.

Kollm: It turns out that the QA group had an unwritten rule that no QA work could be done until all development work was done. It was a waterfall project management concept! Even though the organization had moved to agile and had merged the QA group with the development team, their systems and processes were still using the old way.

Harpham: That's a great example of the challenges in adopting a new way of working like agile. They are often long-established procedures and unwritten rules that govern how work gets done. Unless those practices are deliberately identified and changed, the old way will stay in place.

Kollm: Right. I also find that agile adoption usually starts as a grassroots effort. There's rarely an edict from "on high" commanding the adoption of agile. Usually, a few people here and there hear about agile. They get excited about the benefits and start to adopt it. Meanwhile, the rest of the organization is operating in the old way. There was no organizational-level effort to change systems, processes, and methods.

People thought of agile and scrum as operating at the level of an individual team. There was no effort to think through how it impacts the rest of the organization's value chain.

Harpham: Let's turn to teaching agile. I understand that you've taught agile within Accenture and elsewhere. What is your approach to teaching agile?

Kollm: As an agile coach, you often get involved in delivering training. In many cases, the teams simply have not had enough or any training when it comes to adopting agile. After an initial assessment, I create a curriculum of classes that addresses specific skills and understanding gaps. At a minimum, you need an experienced agile professional to guide the transformation process.

If you're going to spend a million dollars or more to transform your organization, the cost of a coach is quite a small addition to that budget. Assigning a full-time coach to your organization for six months is often enough. Unfortunately, there's often a lack of thought that goes into finding people with agile expertise. Agile training and development appears to be a field where some people think they can read a book or two and proclaim themselves to be experts.

Harpham: Speaking of books, what are some of the books that you've found highly valuable?

Kollm: There are several books that I would recommend. Let's start with agile books.

Coaching Agile Teams by Lyssa Adkins [Addison-Wesley Professional, 2010].

Agile Estimating and Planning by Mike Cohn [Prentice Hall, 2005].

The Principles of Product Development Flow: Second Generation Lean Product Development by Donald G. Reinertsen [Celeritas Publishing, 2012].

Scrum: The Art of Doing Twice the Work in Half the Time by Jeff Sutherland and JJ Sutherland [Crown Business, 2014].

User Stories Applied by Mike Cohn [Addison-Wesley Professional, 2004].

Essential Scrum: A Practical Guide to the Most Popular Agile Process by Kenneth S. Rubin [Addison-Wesley Professional, 2005].

Beyond agile and project books, here are a few other books I have found helpful, including:

The Power of Habit: Why We Do What We Do in Life and Business by Charles Duhigg [Random House, 2012].

Joy, Inc.: How We Built a Workplace People Love by Richard Sheridan [Portfolio, 2013].

Emotional Intelligence: Why It Can Matter More Than IQ by Daniel Goleman [Bantam, 2006].

Crossing the Chasm: Marketing and Selling Disruptive Products to Mainstream Customers by Geoffrey A. Moore [HarperBusiness, 2014].

Flight of the Buffalo: Soaring to Excellence, Learning to Let Employees Lead by James A. Belasco and Ralph C. Stayer [Warner Books, 1993].

The *Flight of the Buffalo* informs my thinking on leadership.

Harpham: Are there any other methodologies or frameworks that attract your interest?

Kollm: I have also been working on the Scaled Agile Framework recently. I find that many companies are interested in that concept because it is highly prescriptive. It gets them into agile, scrum, kanban, and related methods.

Harpham: The prescriptive nature of the Scaled Agile Framework is appealing?

Kollm: For large companies, that prescriptive aspect is appealing. They can make a complete change in a few years, versus other methodologies that are more difficult to adopt.

Harpham: What is your daily productivity strategy to stay on top of your work and responsibilities?

Kollm: Some of my most productive days are days when I feel like I've done the least activity. In my role as a coach, there's a tension for me to navigate. On the one hand, I'm secretly a "command and control guy." On the other hand, I'm well reformed and see the value in using the coaching approach. The big challenge is to get people engaged with the agile process.

In the military, there's the concept of "commander's intent." The commander makes sure that everybody understands that objective so that people can respond and move as events develop. However, it's critical to avoid telling people exactly how to do it. People should adapt as events unfold. If everybody is clear on the objective, the organization heals and moves ahead. From a productivity standpoint, it continues to amaze me how people will come back with great work if you give them the objective and then set them free to get it done however they wish.

My productivity approach is informed by focusing in the right areas. In terms of work activity, I focus my attention on strategy and process. In terms of people, I focus my attention on managers and team leaders. Once they are equipped, they can direct their teams. At the end of the day, we then use metrics and measures to determine if we are performing well. I developed this high-leverage approach because it is often the only way to achieve the objective. Otherwise, I simply do not have enough bandwidth to work with everyone. This also allows people the ability to step up and take ownership of their work increasing their engagement.

Harpham: Your approach to significant change—like adopting agile—is interesting. You may look at the fifty-person department and say, "I don't have time to manage all fifty people." Therefore, my question becomes "Who are the four or five people that should be the focus of my efforts?" Is that type of thinking part of your approach?

Kollm: Yes, that's fair. It all comes back to the span of control management concept. Any single person can only meaningfully lead five to eight people.

People often forget about training when it comes to agile adoption. A single burst of training at the beginning of the project is not enough. You need to continue the training activities during the project. In my experience, I find it effective to have at least two training sessions per week during an agile project. This continuous training is important—both to reinforce the concepts and to help new people on the project get up to speed.

The continuous training process gives everyone a common frame of reference. If somebody was unclear, almost anyone on the team could bring them up to speed. Training in this way goes a long way toward building team cohesion as well.

Harpham: Looking ahead over the next three to five years, what are some of the economic and technological opportunities that are most interesting to you?

Kollm: I don't think anyone has fully exploited the development value chain from inception to delivery. This includes user experience design as well. I'm also interested in further adopting the continuous integration/continuous delivery [CI/CD] framework, a concept from DevOps. As agile has matured over the past five years, with many companies implementing agile project teams, they are seeing that their next bottleneck is in DevOps. The only way to get the power of agile delivery to market is to streamline and fix their sub and production release environments and processes.

This is where DevOps and CI/CD comes in—focusing on these areas so that work can "shift left" up the food chain of development and release. For example, some phone apps are updated continuously to improve results. Unfortunately, large organizations are struggling to adopt this fast, continuous improvement approach.

Chapter Summary

- Recommended books include (not a full list!) *Coaching Agile Teams* by Alice Akins, *Agile Estimating and Planning* by Mike Cohn, *The Power of Habit: Why We Do What We Do in Life and Business* by Charles Duhigg, *Emotional Intelligence: Why It Can Matter More Than IQ* by Daniel Goleman, and *Crossing the Chasm: Marketing and Selling Disruptive Products to Mainstream Customers* by Geoffrey A. Moore.

- Moving to product management: Building on his experience with project management, Kollm moved into product management, where he could make a greater impact.

- Understanding employer expectations. Employer demands change over time. Kollm found that earning the PMP certification made a positive difference in communicating his value to employers.

- Signs of dysfunctional management: If you cannot openly raise project problems, risks, and issues to your management team, you may be in a dysfunctional organization. Achieving project success will be difficult in that environment.

- Challenges with metrics: Adopting agile (or any other new practice) requires thinking through your established metrics and measures. Your metrics may need to be changed to support your business transformation.

Hilary Wilson

Project Manager, EUMETSAT

Hilary Wilson *joined EUMETSAT's Sentinel-3 project in 2008, initially to manage the organization's contribution to the development of the Payload Data Ground Segment (PDGS). In January 2015, she took up the role of project manager.*

Wilson holds a degree in engineering geology and geotechnics from the University of Portsmouth (United Kingdom) and a master's degree in remote sensing from University College/Imperial College London. She launched her space journey back in 1989, working at the UK Processing and Archiving Facility (UK-PAF) in Farnborough, responsible for processing data from the European Space Agency's ERS-1 and ERS-2 satellites. This led to her holding the post of technical manager at the UK-PAF.

*In 1996, Wilson moved to Darmstadt, Germany, to join EUMETSAT (**Eu**ropean Organisation for the Exploitation of **Met**eorological **Sat**ellites), working first on the development of the Meteorological Products Extraction Facility for the Meteosat Second Generation program, and later as the EUMETSAT Polar System (EPS) data processing team leader. In 2016, Wilson continued her association with the Sentinel-3 project when she was appointed EUMETSAT's Sentinel-3 mission manager.*

Bruce Harpham: How did you get started in your career?

Hilary Wilson: Originally, I was interested in becoming a medical doctor. I got to age eighteen and my grades were not high enough for that path. In looking around for something else to do, I realized that my interest in geology might provide a good choice. Therefore, I embarked on a degree in

© Bruce Harpham 2018
B. Harpham, *Project Managers at Work*, DOI 10.1007/978-1-4842-2668-1_22

engineering geology, which included elements of satellite remote sensing. I particularly enjoyed these aspects because I could still do geology but from the warmth and dryness of an office instead of standing in the middle of a cold, wet, and often muddy field.

Building on this interest, I went on to earn a master's degree in remote sensing, discovering just how much I enjoyed the subject. When I finished my master's degree, there was a major space program underway in Europe—the European Space Agency satellite program [ERS-1], which I was fortunate to join. My first role in that project was as a scientist/programmer working on algorithm development, eventually rising to the position of technical manager at the UK-PAF.

In 1996, I left the UK to move to Darmstadt, Germany, where I initially went back into a more technical role relating to processing meteorological satellite data. As part of this role, I managed the procurement of facilities for EUMETSAT programs. In 2008, I moved to working on the European Commission's Copernicus program.

Harpham: What was your initial role with Copernicus?

Wilson: I served as project manager for the Payload Data Ground Segment. This is the part of the ground infrastructure that processes the Sentinel-3 satellite data and delivers data products to our users. In January 2015, I took over the project manager role for the whole of the EUMETSAT part of the Sentinel-3 mission.

Harpham: What is your current assignment?

Wilson: I still retain the project manager role, but in addition, I am also the "mission manager" for Sentinel-3. I'm responsible for two facets of Sentinel-3: operations for the Sentinel-3A satellite, which is already in orbit, and development activities on the Sentinel-3B satellite, planned for launch in early 2018. In the future, we will have further satellites launched as part of this program.

Harpham: How did you get started in project management?

Wilson: I brought several important qualities to bear. First, I was the most technically knowledgeable person on the work in question. Second, I also had strong organizational capabilities. My managers realized that. "Hilary, you know the most about this area of work technically and you're able to organize people to get this work done. Therefore, would you like to act as a project manager?"

As a single parent with four children, I have to be good at managing life! Over the past twelve years, with a demanding full-time job and four small children, I've had to be highly organized. For example, managing the very different needs of toddlers versus teenagers is similar to managing the conflicting and varying needs of a project. Thus, I joke that I brought these family organizational skills to my professional life.

If you can manage a family like mine, then project management is a breeze! At work, people will largely do what you say because you're "the boss." They don't tend to argue back too much either, whereas you sometimes face that challenge at home. By inclination, I'm a people person and I like to bring people together in an organized fashion.

In my first project management job, I think there were doubts from my boss about whether I could actually do it. However, in 1993 I completed the altimeter product correction and upgrade project successfully, on time, and on budget. At that point, my managers were convinced that I was capable and gave me additional management responsibilities.

Harpham: You also had the willingness to take on the project management role, even though there was some uncertainty or risk associated with it.

Wilson: I was in my mid to late twenties when I took on this altimeter upgrade project, so I had the enthusiasm and "experience" of youth to help take on this project. I was convinced that I could do it! I believed I could do it, and I did it. I didn't really see the risks at that point!

Harpham: You mentioned that you are a people person and that this capability helps you to succeed. What are some of the practices, habits, and behaviors that helps you perform as a "people person"?

Wilson: There's an advantage to being a woman. I believe that identity gives me a stronger approach to collaboration than others appear to have. I'm working in a male-dominated environment and I have been for my entire professional career. I'm usually the only woman in the room [though that situation is gradually improving]. My approach is to build collaborative relationships, because you are always going to achieve more together than on your own.

My colleagues appreciate that I'm going to build them up. I'm not one of those people who tears down other people in an effort to make myself look better.

If I have good team members, they make me look good. In the past, I have worked with managers who were difficult or who had a bad reputation. Their lack of "competence" really frustrated me. However, I have come to realize that reputation goes both ways. If I have competent people working for me, that performance reflects well on me. If my team has a competent boss, they also look good. Thus, it's in my best interest to ensure that my boss succeeds, because that will enhance both their reputation and mine. That's a lesson I recommend to young people for career development. They're often too focused on their individual accomplishments. In fact, you can look better by helping others achieve success.

I do not know everything on this complicated project that I'm working on. I'm well known for saying, "I'm not an expert on that but I have brought the expert on that topic to the meeting." I don't see many of my male colleagues acting in that way. They don't seem to want to say, "I don't know about X," because they believe it makes them lose face. In contrast, I believe it enhances my reputation to be honest. People know that I am credible if I express an opinion.

In my view, an effective manager empowers the people below to do their job. That includes supporting them when they make a mistake and helping them to make it right.

Harpham: Anything else to add on your approach to connect with people?

Wilson: People know that my work matters to me. It's not just a job to me. That reality is both a positive and a negative. I work very long hours because I want the project to work. People know that I work hard on the project because I want it to succeed. If you're enthusiastic about what you do, it is easier to bring other people with you. In fact, some people may not like the specific project or work very much, but they work hard anyway because they don't want to disappoint you.

It's also important to take the time to understand the different motivations of people on the team. Some people are motivated for example by a need for glory. You have to find ways for them to satisfy that need. Other people are more interested in financial rewards. Still others have a focus on the project simply working out successfully.

Harpham: Let's turn to Copernicus and Sentinel-3. Can you define the objective of the program?

Wilson: Copernicus is a European system for monitoring the Earth, funded by the European Union. It consists of a set of different systems that collect data, including satellites and in-situ observations—for example, shipborne sensors, balloons, buoys, etc. The goal is to produce data products to support different thematic areas: land, marine, atmosphere, climate change, emergency management, and security.

Turning to my project work, my role is to ensure the production of reliable and timely data products for our users—for example, national meteorological services, marine monitoring services, and climate services. For some applications, timely release of the data is the priority. In other cases, data accuracy is the priority. For emergency management, you need information as fast as possible. For example, understanding how a forest fire is spreading – week old data is unsuitable in that context. In other areas like climate change, very high accuracy data is prized. Therefore, taking more time to produce a high-quality data product is acceptable.

In Copernicus, we provide data through a series of satellite missions called the Sentinels. These are dedicated to different types of remote sensing. Sentinel-3A and B are primarily dedicated to monitoring the oceans. We are measuring sea surface temperature, ocean color, sea level height, wind, and waves, and so forth. The Sentinel-3 mission is a combined development between the European Space Agency [ESA] and EUMETSAT on behalf of the European Commission. ESA is responsible for providing data to the land users and EUMETSAT covers the marine users. The project requires both establishing the ground infrastructure and the satellites themselves. ESA provides the satellites and both organizations work together on the ground infrastructure.

Harpham: What is your current focus within this program?

Wilson: There are two areas we're working on. We have one satellite that is already in orbit that is ramping up to its full, routine operation launched just over a year ago [Sentinel-3A in February 2016]. The second satellite [3B] is due to be launched at the beginning of 2018. We are preparing the systems and getting ready to operate both satellites in parallel.

We are going to use a tandem operation model for the first few months that we have both satellites in orbit. This means that we will fly the Sentinel-3A and the Sentinel-3B very close together, with only a thirty-second separation. Nominally, we will then fly them with a separation of 140 degrees, which amounts to a minimum separation of thirty-eight minutes.

Harpham: You had mentioned that you had recently taken on the role of mission manager. What does that involve?

Wilson: The mission manager role is a new one to the EUMETSAT organization. In brief, the goal is to make sure we are providing the best quality of service to our users. That involves many different facets: communicating with our users, proactively explaining quality issues, and making sure that the satellite operations are going smoothly. It's a big team—of around 120 people—that delivers on all of these responsibilities. I also review recommendations and suggestions from our users on how we can improve our products and quality. In operations, we do not like surprises. We like changes planned well in advance so everyone can be properly informed.

Harpham: One of the challenges you face is delivering data products on time. What are some of the schedule pressures that you find particularly difficult?

Wilson: Schedules are an interesting problem for space projects. On the one hand, space projects have a long duration. You can easily spend ten years in the development phase on a project and twenty years operating a satellite. In the beginning, not much happens. Then suddenly you may have a situation where you have to react quickly if something goes wrong—or face a large impact on your costs or schedule.

There's a misconception in some areas that the space industry is always on the cutting edge of technology. That isn't true, because it takes years to get a project ready for space. Technology launched into space is often ten years behind the cutting edge for that reason. On Sentinel-3, when we came close to the official launch date, we were constantly changing the project schedule. For example, delays in testing the ground processing software, delays due to the proper launch permissions not being signed, and bad weather at the airport in Russia delaying the transport of the satellite from France to the launch site.

Harpham: Do you face challenges with stakeholders?

Wilson: For the first time, we are working jointly with our colleagues in the European Space Agency on the development of the ground segment. Originally, EUMETSAT was part of the ESA, so there is a shared history. However, Sentinel-3 was the first time the organizations collaborated together on the ground segment aspect of the project, having always worked together on the space segment. You have two organizations with different philosophies and different methodologies. Despite these differences, we had to marry these different approaches and develop a joint way forward. That was quite the challenge!

At first, there was a perception from both sides of "Why wouldn't the other side do it our way?" You have to realize that just because you think your way is best, that doesn't make the other way wrong. You have to learn to compromise where you can and to hold firm when it is important. Getting one's head around the idea that they are different—rather than better or worse—took some work.

Harpham: Given that you work with an international organization, do you face cultural challenges?

Wilson: It is both challenging and enriching. You have to be aware of the cultural sensitivities with certain behaviors. For example, I once corrected a manager in a meeting because he said something factually incorrect. That action would have been perfectly acceptable in the UK, where I'm from. Afterwards, the person was furious with me. He said, "If you had done that in France, one of us would have had to leave the organization!" I found that surprising. It demonstrated that there are very different attitudes on whether it is culturally acceptable to correct a manager or authority figure in public.

It was a lesson with broader implications for me. Just because I know how to operate in the UK doesn't mean that I can use the exact same practices elsewhere. Likewise, one often hears jokes about British humor. Sometimes that sense of wit or sarcasm doesn't translate well. When you work internationally, you realize that many of the practices you consider to be natural or normal are simply cultural practices from where you are from.

After living in Germany for a number of years, I've adjusted to some of the practices here. For instance, it is common to kiss a close friend or business associate on the cheek when you meet them. That's absolutely standard. Yet, when I travel to the UK and use that same practice, British colleagues are surprised. There are many differences like this, large and small.

Harpham: Let's turn to your leadership philosophy. How has your approach to management and leadership changed over time?

Wilson: Emphasizing collaboration is the major change in my management approach. When you're starting off in management, you feel that you have to prove yourself and outperform everyone else. I'm sure in some industries that approach is still considered the way to go. There's an old joke that the word "team" actually means "together everybody achieves more." I regularly say that to my team to emphasize the importance of working together closely. Building on that concept, it's best to surround yourself with people who are interested in collaboration and providing support to each other.

Over the years, I have learned the importance of being myself as a leader. I've always worked in male-dominated environments all the way back to my university studies. Therefore, there was always a subtle pressure to fit in with the men. In contrast, my approach is naturally informed by the fact that I'm a woman and a mother. For example, I have quite strong maternal instincts, which means that I am protective of the people who work for me. I now see this as a positive quality because I'm trusted and people are happy to work for me. They know that I will support them, but also I will hold them accountable when they have not done well.

Not long after I started my current position, one person on my team commented that I had continued "to be me," rather than trying to copy the style of the previous manager.

I used to wear a "suit of armor" at work so that I wasn't hurt by others. However, people started to treat me differently when I had that approach. They thought that everything was bouncing off my armor. It took me a long time to realize that if other people were unaware they were hurting me, how could they change their behavior and interactions with me? I had to take the armor off and make people see me as a vulnerable human being who can sometimes be upset when things go wrong.

That was a hard lesson because it meant a lot of personal change for me. When you're managing relationships with others, you have to realize that others may not want or be able to change. That means the onus is on you to change first. Taking on the persona of somebody else is ineffective and stressful. Now I understand that just being myself is much easier and the armor has been officially retired.

Harpham: The armor metaphor makes me think of feedback. If somebody does something that you don't like, but there's no reaction—positive or negative, the person has no feedback from you on what to do next.

Harpham: What does personal productivity system look like?

Wilson: I don't have a set-in-stone routine that I use every day. I do rely on written lists to stay organized with all of my work. I regularly review my lists and ask myself, "What's important and what's urgent here?" I also make appointments with myself on my calendar in order to plan and organize my work. If I don't do that, I will be fully booked in meetings with other people all day. I agree with the saying "If you fail to plan, you plan to fail."

From a project-planning perspective, I'm fortunate to be supported by a great team. We have weekly meetings to review the projects. That covers both short-term tasks on the project [i.e., to be done in the next week] and long-term matters. That advance planning is important because we want to make sure that we plan user communications well in advance of implementing a change. There is also a need to keep some free time available on my schedule, because there are sometimes emergencies to be handled with satellite operations and related issues.

My two main productivity tools boil down to my calendar and keeping lists. If I had overly rigid systems, it would not cope with emergency situations that periodically occur in my world. After all, satellites operate on a 24/7 basis. As you move further up into management roles, you have to expect greater demands on your time, including some expectations you may have to work periodically on evenings or weekends. After all, if it is a Saturday and the satellite is in danger of collision, that problem needs to be addressed right away.

Harpham: Which books have you found the most professionally valuable?

Wilson: Two books come to mind. *Feminist Fight Club* by Jessica Bennett [Harper Wave, 2016] is excellent. This book deals with how women undermine themselves professionally. For example, let's say you perform well and earn a bonus at work. In that scenario, there's an unfortunate practice where women are likely to tell people that you were lucky rather than saying you earned it. For me, it's important to be a good role model as a senior manager and show how to succeed and still be yourself. The book has a tongue-in-cheek approach to careers and how to manage your career effectively.

The other book that comes to mind is *An Astronaut's Guide to Life on Earth* by Chris Hadfield [Little, Brown and Company, 2013], a Canadian astronaut. There are a lot of good lessons there for management and leadership. The book had a great lesson about having not the goal of being the best at everything but rather seeking to be a "zero," meaning you perfectly fulfill all your responsibilities within the team or a "plus-one," where you do a bit more, rather than a "minus-one," where others have to support you. It's a metaphor for looking for ways to see your contribution in terms of its impact on the team goals, rather than competing with others to outshine them.

Harpham: For the reader who is interested in moving into project management, what advice would you give them to make that move?

Wilson: Start small. Manage a piece of work in a field that you know well technically. If you already understand the technical details of an area, you are then freed up to develop your project management skills on that piece of work. After you successfully complete a project in your area of expertise, you can then look for opportunities to manage projects in other areas. This was the strategy that I used to develop my career.

I learned a great rule of thumb from my father about leading work and teams in new areas where you are not the expert. Make your first goal to learn enough so that you can ask three intelligent questions about the work, and then build from there. That level of knowledge gives you a base to build on.

Finally, you have to like working with people to succeed in project management. You can't get the job done without directing and engaging the team. Some people miss the fundamental reality that your project team does the work for you as the project manager.

Chapter Summary

- Recommended books include *Feminist Flight Club* by Jessica Bennett and *An Astronaut's Guide to Life on Earth* by Chris Hadfield.

- Breaking into project management: Start on small projects where you understand all of the technical details. As you build success on those projects, you will be well placed to pursue additional opportunities.

- Master self-awareness as a leader. Wilson became more successful as a manager when she used her own approach rather than copying the approach of other managers.

- Two-way reputation dynamics: If you perform well, it makes your superiors look good. If your project team members perform well, that will reflect well on you. It is in your best interest to make your boss succeed.

- Understand different motivations. If you are managing a team of people, you will be more effective if you take the time to understand each individual's motivations.

Sarina Arcari

Vice President of Enterprise Program Management, Amtrak

Sarina Arcari, *PMP, is Vice President of the Enterprise Program Management Office at Amtrak. Prior to Amtrak, she led a 27-person team of project and program management professionals at Amerigroup (now part of Anthem Inc.) to provide access to health care for Medicaid and Medicare populations. In 2014, her team at WellPoint was awarded the PMO of the Year award by the Project Management Institute (PMI). Arcari holds a Bachelor of Science degree in marketing from the University of Connecticut. Arcari is also a graduate of PMI's Leadership Institute Master Class.*

Bruce Harpham: How did you get started in project management?

Sarina Arcari: When I teach project management, I always tell people you can learn project management skills and knowledge from classes and resources. However, I believe there's a subset of the population that can't help but work on projects. It's the way they're wired. We think in work breakdown structures. We make lists and check them twice! I think I'm one of those people.

Thinking back to my parents and childhood, I had some early experiences that made a difference. My dad is a mechanical engineer by training and worked in the US Army Corps of Engineers. He was managing projects his entire career. At home, he was constantly working on do-it-yourself activities and I became his assistant. My mom gets equal credit. As a military wife, she was

© Bruce Harpham 2018
B. Harpham, *Project Managers at Work*, DOI 10.1007/978-1-4842-2668-1_23

extraordinarily organized. In fact, I recall my first "project plan." Before I learned how to read, my mother prepared a chores chart with pictures that explained what I had to do each week. I was wired for this kind of organized project thinking from early on.

I was always that person who had a project of some kind going on during college and afterwards. I always enjoyed solving problems and taking on responsibilities beyond my day job. As I acquired a reputation for being the go-to person to get work done, my career progression took off.

Within the healthcare field, I worked at a variety of health insurance companies. Joining Great-West Healthcare was a key turning point for my career. At Great-West, I was brought in to help them with a "buy or build decision" related to a national behavioral health product. Management didn't want anyone from inside the organization—such as those with turf to protect—to get involved in this work. As a result of the assessment, we decided to buy a system and I led the implementation project. By successfully implementing that project, I was then asked to stay on and work on other projects.

Harpham: How did you come to work at Amtrak?

Arcari: For the first twenty-five years of my career, I was in the healthcare industry. In 2015, I won a PMI award and listed that on my LinkedIn profile. Amtrak ultimately discovered me through LinkedIn and that's how the hiring discussion began. I told them, "I don't know anything about trains." Their response: "We've got over 20,000 people who know how to run trains, but we don't have anybody who knows how to run a good project." And the rest is history.

Harpham: Did formal project management training play a role in your career growth?

Arcari: I recall having a conversation with my boss at Great-West Healthcare on that topic. He encouraged me to get certified in project management. These were the early days of PMP certification. There were something like 100,000 certified people at that point. I was resistant to going for the PMP. My response was: "Either I'm good at this or I'm not. Putting three letters after my name will not impact how well I do my job." Eventually, I went on to earn the certification.

Harpham: What happened after you earned the PMP?

Arcari: Shortly after I earned the PMP, I moved to a new organization. My assignment was to create a project management office [PMO], though they called it by a different name. This company worked on government contracts related to Medicare and Medicaid. The company was winning contracts faster than it could implement them. The project management group was charged with implementing these contracts into production.

I mentioned to Amerigroup that it sounds like they wanted a PMO. Surprisingly, they forbade using the term "PMO" because they had had a very bad experience attempting to set up a PMO in the past. Several years before I got there, they had invested millions of dollars in an enterprise PPM system. They had no process to support the system, so it didn't generate much of an improvement in terms of getting projects done.

As I set up the "implementation management office," I realized that I would need a team of people to do the work. Further, I realized that I needed a common language and frame of reference to do the work.

Harpham: It's interesting to see that the "PMO" term was associated with this terrible failure at the organization. Yet the organization you led there would be called a "PMO" anywhere else. Is this a question of terminology?

Arcari: I find that many organizations set up PMOs because they're suffering. Projects are not getting completed. Therefore, the organization is looking to bring some organization to the chaos.

The "IMO" in that organization ended up winning the 2014 PMO of the Year award from PMI. I pushed internally to nominate our organization for the award, even though the leadership didn't like the "PMO" term. Ultimately, I sold the idea of applying for the award by pointing out that, if we won, we could use that award in our sales and marketing material, including proposals to the government. Management then saw the value in pursuing the award.

The company's prior effort to create a PMO encountered problems for several reasons. There was no process or methodology developed. There was no dedicated project management staff. Likewise, there were no supporting policies or procedures in place. Essentially, the organization was sold a bill of goods by a slick vendor who promised that using their PPM software would solve their problems. For a PPM implementation process to produce results, you need to start with the premise that you're automating a process that already works. If not, then you're going to produce mistakes and failures faster.

The company began to grow—up to forty-eight percent annual growth! We were able to handle that increased work without significantly increasing our staff. That was possible because we had a repeatable methodology to implement contracts as they were won. My work with this company and winning the PMO of the Year award is one of my greatest career accomplishments so far. We grew the company from $3 billion in sales to $12 billion in sales in a few years. We were acquired by the second largest healthcare insurance company in the country—Anthem—in 2012.

Harpham: That's a huge increase in volume. How did you manage that increase while maintaining project delivery quality?

Arcari: There are several reasons. First, we specialized in a certain category of business: Medicaid. We also put major effort into developing a solid, repeatable project management process that could be used over and over again.

Harpham: Let's go into the before-and-after changes involved in setting up the PMO and its impact on the organization. If I were an executive at the organization, what was my experience like with projects before you came in?

Arcari: The company's founder had just stepped down from the CEO role and moved to become chairman of the board. The former chief operating officer became the CEO. It was the perfect time for a transition. It takes one set of skills to found a company. It takes another set of skills to keep growing the company to new heights and bring it to the scale of a Fortune 500 company.

Shortly before I arrived, the company suffered a major blow from a lawsuit. While the lawsuit was settled, it was an expensive settlement. It was also a wakeup call to revisit how they approached the business. It turns out that the company missed a critical step in their work and this led them to experience significant problems. They lost a contract for an entire state. Much or all of that problem can be traced back to a project management or implementation flaw. That pain motivated the new CEO to look for ways to improve the organization's implementation capabilities.

Harpham: Were there project managers on staff when you arrived?

Arcari: When I arrived, there were no credentialed project managers on staff. There were no people who had the project manager title either. Since the company had a start-up culture, there were people doing projects "off the side of their desk." For example, you might have someone in the claims department who would work on implementation when the company won a new contract.

Harpham: What were your priorities when it came to starting the PMO?

Arcari: I tend to act as a people-first manager. First, I spent ninety days investigating the "as is" situation at the company. I wanted to know how the organization was currently doing projects. Was anything working? I have the view that there's almost always something good at an organization that you can recognize and build on. I found a few places where people put forward heroic efforts to get the work done, for example. One department had a full-time person dedicated to implementation work, and they were performing better than other departments.

I proposed that further improvements required dedicated project management staff with deep expertise. I was able to secure twelve positions for project implementations. I handed out those roles to various functional areas to support implementation. My negotiation point with the functional managers was: "I need your best thinker and execution person to serve on the implementation work. You can use this new position to backfill the position with a new hire." I made it clear that I could not take somebody inexperienced to work on implementations.

Harpham: How did those negotiations with the functional managers unfold, since you were asking for their best people?

Arcari: If I learned nothing else in my career, it's this: no PMO can be successful without executive support. Ideally, that support should go all the way to the top, including the board of directors. I had that support, which helped tremendously. Some managers were simply happy to get an "extra body" in their department and they were willing to do whatever it took to make that happen. Overall, the managers understood this arrangement would ultimately serve them and the company. I made it clear their person would continue to report to the functional manager. However, that top performer had to be fully dedicated to my implementations.

Harpham: Once you had these people, how did you direct them to work on projects?

Arcari: I sent them out to lead projects in various parts of the company. Over time, the project implementation team grew. Early on, there were major struggles. We actually started off with one Microsoft Project license for the whole company. That meant one person had to manage all the schedules and related information. People would print the reports, fax them out, and receive updates back by fax. This whole process—fax-based updates—was used in 2008 and 2009.

Harpham: Why were they using these manual processes?

Arcari: The company was in the start-up phase at that time so resources were limited. In the Medicaid business, you plan for a one- to three-percent profit margin. That means that there are limited resources available to invest in software licenses. Fortunately, as we proved our process, we gradually obtained more resources and could become even more productive.

Harpham: How did you further develop the organization's project management maturity?

Arcari: We started to offer two-day internal classes on project management for everybody who worked on our projects. More and more of our staff earned the PMP certification as well. I also wrote the policy and procedure manual to guide our work, which defined the five phases of project management with our company's spin on it. It was a step-by-step process: first, do this, then use this template, and so on. It was a highly prescriptive approach. I even specified items, such as the meeting agenda format for project meetings.

We were very prescriptive because there was so far to grow in our project management maturity. By adopting this disciplined approach, we were able to keep up with the growth in 2013 and beyond. Eventually, it became a well-oiled machine.

Harpham: It's striking to note the value of executing on the fundamentals of project management consistently. It gives you the capability to propose further improvements and obtain resources, like training and software licenses.

Arcari: Right. It's interesting because nobody wants to focus on the fundamentals. They want to focus on the "sexy" items like a five-million-dollar project management software system. In my present role, I'm going through a similar experience of building up the organization's project management capability.

Harpham: How has your thinking on project management certification evolved? How does it relate to your "people first" leadership philosophy?

Arcari: My thinking on project management certification changed after I finished the first ninety days at the company. During that time, I investigated the organization's current situation and capabilities. I realized that people were using the same words and terms with different meanings. There was no common ground when it came to project management.

One person might say, "I need a project manager." It turns out that they actually wanted one thing that was quite different. I recall one person saying something like, "You're not a project manager. A project manager would sit with me in my department and do the work right here." Their understanding of project management was based on hiring an outside consulting firm and having that outside person sit with them to do the work.

I quickly came to the realization that a common lexicon and methodology was needed before I could do anything here. I decided to go with the certification and standards offered by the Project Management Institute. I'm grateful to PMI beyond measure for the great resources that they have. At the same time, I consider the PMBOK Guide rather difficult to read yet there is great material in there. I focused on the five phases of project management starting with initiation and planning. That was enough for us to get started. I also found great project management job descriptions from PMI, which helped me to build the organization.

Harpham: How did you approach defining project management roles at the organization?

Arcari: I went to the organization's human resources department and asked to see all of the project management job descriptions. There were eighteen job descriptions on the books! They all said the same thing with minor differences, like "finance project manager" or "IT project manager."

In order to attract great project managers, they want to know what's next for them in terms of career path. When I walked in the door, I didn't have a good answer to that point. I fixed that situation by adapting PMI's project manager job descriptions to the organization. I also used the PMI salary survey to work with human resources to come up with the right compensation level for each role. Fortunately, human resources was cooperative and liked the fact that I came to the table with all of PMI's resources.

Harpham: Have you ever seen that situation with multiple job descriptions and an unclear career progression for project managers anywhere else?

Arcari: When I arrived at Amtrak, there were hundreds of project management job descriptions. I'm working with HR right now to revise and simplify the job descriptions for project management.

My "people first" focus led me to ask how I could boost the credibility of project managers in this organization. Part of the answer was seeking professional training, like the PMP. Part of the answer was to create a project management career progression.

I want to show the outside world that we're an employer of choice for project management professionals. We recognize it as a profession at Amtrak and we want top-notch talent. That employer of choice concept extends to supporting volunteering with PMI and providing training. We also sponsor the local PMI chapter.

Harpham: What are some of the mistakes that you see novice project managers make?

Arcari: When you lack professional working experience, you try to find a guidebook that will tell you what you're supposed to do. I see younger project managers open the PMBOK Guide and expect to find a "how to" process to answer the question "what should I do tomorrow?" The PMBOK Guide is not designed to provide that kind of answer. It's a guide to a body of knowledge assembled by many project managers.

There's also a related mistake: attempting to apply the entire PMBOK to each and every project. They haven't learned the art of assessing how much process to use on a particular project to achieve success. Based on my experience in the healthcare field, I came up with a metaphor to describe this approach: we need to practice "minimally invasive" project management just enough process to get the project completed—no more and no less.

The missing piece at Amtrak's project management right now is a lack of resources to help new project managers. We have standards, policies, and a career path, but there is not yet a detailed manual that lays out all of the processes and procedures. For example, what should a project manager do on day one of a new project? That is not yet in place here.

Harpham: How do you decide how much process to use?

Arcari: I developed what I called a "T-shirt sizing" model—a way to classify your project as small, medium, large or mega. For each of those levels, there's an accompanying amount of process recommended to successfully complete the project. When people are early in the career, they don't have enough experience to do "T-shirt sizing" approach. As a result, they feel the need to do everything on the project.

The other point to keep in mind for this "T-shirt sizing" model is the level of talent required to manage the project. You need one kind of person to lead a mega project and a different kind of person to work on a smaller project.

Harpham: If you have a six-week project, it doesn't make sense to use a three- or four-week planning process.

Arcari: That's right. A twelve-page communication plan would not make sense for that kind of project.

Harpham: You mentioned "mega projects" as one of the categories. Do you have any mega projects in your portfolio?

Arcari: When I arrived at Amtrak, I had to adjust my definition of small, medium, large and mega projects compared to my previous organization. In my previous organization, a long and involved project might have lasted eighteen to twenty-four months. In contrast, there are Amtrak projects that will take years and years to complete. Some may take up to thirty years to complete.

It's been a growth opportunity for me to think about how do I approach mega projects where the completion date is years into the future. How do I get excited about those?

Harpham: Do you have any of those thirty-year projects underway right now?

Arcari: There's the Gateway Program. The objective is to increase train capacity in the northeastern United States—starting from New Jersey and continuing further north. Right now, train capacity in this region is limited by two one-hundred-year-old tunnels that go underneath the Hudson River [which separates New Jersey and New York]. Those two tunnels currently handle twenty-four trains per hour in each direction—one going north and the other going south. These tunnels are safe, but they require immense maintenance efforts to keep in good condition because of their age.

Unfortunately, these train tunnels cannot be taken out of service for upgrades. Taking these tunnels out of service would economically devastate the Northeast. Therefore, we have to build at least one new tunnel before we can take one of the older ones out of service. Eventually, we are going to have four tunnels in the region, which means we will have doubled the capacity.

However, we will then reach another roadblock. Once you cross into Manhattan, there's a constraint at Penn Station. There's a limited number of train tracks that go into the station. So you can't simply push more trains into that station. As a result, we have to purchase an entire city block in Manhattan in order to expand Penn Station. That will allow us to add eight more underground train tracks into the city. All of the approaches, train yards and more will need to be expanded for greater capacity. Finally, keep in mind that this project is not limited to passenger rail. Freight rail is also in scope. This is a huge project. I will probably be retired well before it is completed.

Harpham: How does this project compare to other large projects you know about?

Arcari: This is probably one of the largest projects of this kind currently underway in the United States. Compared to Dubai or China, there's not as many mega infrastructure projects underway in the US right now. The US needs to do more of these projects actually. At the very least, we need more repair projects to keep our infrastructure in good condition.

I'd say this Gateway project is one of the biggest and sexiest projects currently underway in the United States.

Harpham: How do you get people excited about a project where they may not see it through to completion?

Arcari: I've learned that engineers and people at Amtrak love these long-term mega projects. For me, simply being around these people has helped me realize it is a great project to work on even if you're not here when it is finished. It's inspiring to be affiliated with a project that will probably still be here one hundred years from now. The existing tunnels are just over one hundred years old. Given the much better technology we have today, the new tunnels might last two hundred years!

I've never worked on projects that will have that kind of legacy. I had not previously worked in construction projects so this is a new world for me. These Amtrak projects serve the public good and function as economic enablers.

The young engineers I talk to are excited about this project because it is a special opportunity. Right now, if you're an engineer and want to work on a mega project, many of the opportunities are in Dubai, China, and other countries. To be able to stay at home in the US and still work on a mega project—there's not many opportunities like that.

There are also a number of people who are train fanatics. They just love everything about trains—building them, running them and beyond. Some people can quote baseball statistics from memory. I know people who can do the same for trains. That enthusiasm makes them easy to work with because they're so motivated.

Harpham: I'm curious to understand more about Amtrak and how it came to play its role as the main US passenger rail service. Can you briefly explain how Amtrak came about?

Arcari: Amtrak came into existence in 1971. Prior to that time, there were many different railways serving different parts of the country. Today, there are still a number of very large railway companies in the United States, like Union Pacific and BNSF. All of these independent railroads carry some combination of passengers and freight.

Everything changed in the 1970s when the railway companies decided to exit the passenger rail business. The US government realized this was a problem. It's a big country and there's value in having passenger rail service. Amtrak was created by Congress with participation from the existing railway companies. Today, Amtrak is the only national-scale passenger rail operation serving the US. We only own the rails in part of the Northeastern region—between Boston and Washington, DC.

Structurally, Amtrak is a private corporation that cooperates with the government. For example, some of our large projects to build or improve facilities and infrastructure are funded through grants. However, most of our operations, revenues, and expenses are handled independently.

Harpham: Over your career, you've moved through several roles. You've had the role of the individual project manager who is delivering the project. Today, you're in the role of managing and developing project managers. How did you navigate the transition to a management role?

Arcari: When I coach and mentor people going through this transition, I tell people that it's the most difficult professional transition you will ever make. Going from an individual contributor role to being a leader of people is challenging. As an individual project manager, you may think that you have direct control over the project. It's an illusion. You do not have control.

Learning how to be comfortable with discomfort is the number one point to transition to a leadership role. You will reach the limit of your personal work capacity at a certain point. If you're asked to do more work than your personal capacity, you need to be able to work through people. Therefore, you need to get ready for those requests by training your people to be just as good or better than you were as an individual contributor. Then you have to set them free to get working.

When you have ten different project managers each going in their own direction, you're never going to know what exactly they're doing. That's different from being deeply involved in the details of a single project as a project manager. When you're running a project management office, you tend to pay attention to projects that are in trouble—those with red status. Your job becomes teaching people to become as smart as capable as possible so that your project portfolio stays in good shape.

For me, I took a full year to make the transition into a management role. The transition was harder than I thought it would be. It's harder than it looks! When you watch your boss from a distance, you might think, "How hard can that job be?" I think it's more difficult mentally and emotionally than an individual role. From time to time, I wish I could go back to being a project manager, because it would be easier to manage compared to what I do now.

Harpham: What are some of the aspects of your role that you find especially challenging?

Arcari: At Amtrak, we have over a dozen labor unions and many different contracts. This week, I spent half a day meeting with the general chairmen from the unions to discuss their concerns. I also happened to be the only woman in the room for that meeting. It was a tough meeting. There was a lot of bravado to get through.

Harpham: Speaking of tough meetings, let's turn to the topic of conflict. How do you approach and solve conflicts productively?

Arcari: My approach has changed over time. Earlier in my career, I usually avoided conflict. However, I've come to understand that conflict is part of human nature. In many instances, it's healthy and should be encouraged. That's doesn't mean starting fights though.

The better approach is to foster an environment where people feel comfortable bringing up problems and questions. I believe that there's always a path to yes. We might not all be happy with the solution but we should be able to get everybody some of what they're looking for.

I've also noticed that there are some people who are "negative scanners." On one level, they drive me nuts because their perspective is so different from my view of "there's always a way to make this work." That said, I've come to appreciate and cultivate the "negative scanners" in the organization when I find them. They're the people who find problems that nobody else is talking about. I find that the quiet ones often have a lot to say but you have to draw it out of them.

From time to time, I act as the devil's advocate in some discussions. That approach is especially important in risk management where it is valuable to think about what can go wrong on the project. It all goes back to that idea of "you have to comfortable with uncomfortable situations."

Harpham: It's interesting to see the preferences and interests of people drawn to project work. Some people are drawn to the field because they love to achieve and ship big projects. Others like the order and process-oriented nature of the work. What do you think draws people into project work?

Arcari: Problem solvers are drawn to the field. Project managers tend to be very achievement oriented. They want to get this project done. Then they want to know what's next for them both in terms of their career and upcoming projects.

Harpham: What does your personal productivity system look like?

Arcari: Everything starts with my calendar. I use Microsoft Outlook. I live and die by the calendar! As a general practice, I aim to keep at least two hours per day free from meetings during business hours. It was important for me to articulate that rule as I have worked with assistants since 2010.

In terms of the details, I don't manage my calendar. My assistant runs that from me based on principles that I set up. My assistant and I meet every morning to review the calendar and address any conflicts.

In terms of scheduling, I avoid working outside of normal business hours as much as possible. I expect the same from my team as well. There's no expectation to work on evenings or weekends. You need to get away from work completely in order to recharge. When I occasionally break that rule— like sending a late-night email, I make it clear to my staff that I don't expect a response until the next business day. I also use color-coding on my calendar so I understand upcoming commitments easily.

I also consider my appointments with my staff, such as the weekly team meeting, to be engraved in stone. I want my staff to be able to rely on knowing when the staff meeting is so that they can plan accordingly. I don't sacrifice that commitment to the staff meeting just because a request comes in from somebody else, even if it's an executive. Likewise, I work to maintain several other standing meetings, including one-on-one meetings with my direct reports. The next priority level involves interaction with my boss: his staff meeting and my one on one with him.

I've also learned to delegate and to say "no" more often to stay focused with my time. Likewise, I teach my staff to say no to requests. For example, if my boss asks to meet with me during the my weekly team meeting, I will say "no" and suggest to meet another time.

Harpham: What color categories are you using to organize your calendar visually?

Arcari: I have a color for the federal railroad administration—they're the organization that funds the organization. I have another color for my boss. I have a color to represent time in transit—when I'm traveling between offices or other places—that helps me to decline meetings while I'm in transit. I also block an hour for lunch to keep that time for me. I also put personal appointments in another color so those are easy to track. Before I leave the office at night, I quickly review the next day's calendar so I have an idea of what's coming up.

Harpham: What would you say your biggest productivity challenge is right now?

Arcari: Right now, it's regularly setting aside time for strategic thinking. In previous roles, I usually had the opportunity to set aside about an hour a day to think, plan and work on strategy. In this role, I haven't had that opportunity, because I've been focused on learning the organization and the industry. When I regularly take that strategy time, it makes me a better leader.

Harpham: What goes into your strategic-thinking time?

Arcari: I like to start with large Post-it Notes as a thinking tool. With that in hand, I start to work through open questions. What do I need to capture? What ideas, tasks, and questions do I have to get out of my head? It could be work items, personal items—anything that comes to mind. Much of my work takes a great deal of thinking time to create, because there are new processes and methods to create, like project charters. I often come up with school tasks as well since I'm working on a master's degree right now. In part, it's a way to highlight the most important tasks and concerns that are taking up my attention.

Harpham: Are there any other activities that go into these strategic-thinking sessions?

Arcari: There are all kinds of topics and questions. For example, I periodically review my organization chart and ask myself, "Is this the right structure for what we're being asked to do? Do we need additional talent in the organization?"

Harpham: This is an interesting practice for project managers to think about. It's a reminder that there's value in setting aside time to explore strategy and big questions.

Arcari: In a way, this is anti-project manager behavior. Many project managers are "programmed" by habit to think that they have to be achieving tasks all the time. One of my earliest bosses taught me, "Sometimes, you need to sit and think." If I omit this thinking time and simply "do, do, do," life and work start to feel more chaotic.

Harpham: Are there any methods that you find helpful to get this strategic-thinking activity?

Arcari: On occasion, I find it helpful to head off to a coffee shop. By physically getting out of the office for half an hour, I can focus on the activity without interruptions.

Chapter Summary

- A mistake that novice project managers make: Arcari notes that some novice project managers make the mistake of seeking a guidebook that will address all of their questions and applying the *PMBOK Guide* in its entirety to each project.

- Early project management inspiration: her parents. Arcari's mother kept the family highly organized. Her father shared lessons from his experiences in the US Army Corp of Engineers.

- Use Project Management Institute (PMI) resources. Arcari has benefited from using numerous PMI resources, including the PMP certification and job descriptions.

- An evolving approach to conflict: Early in her career, Arcari avoided conflict. Today, she sees the value in conflict and seeks out "negative scanners" who may detect risks in the organization.

- Navigating industry transitions: Transitioning to the rail industry was easier because Arcari led an effort that resulted in a PMI award.

Mehmood Alam

Senior Project Engineer, Costain

Dr. Mehmood Alam *is a chartered mechanical engineer and an experienced EPC (Engineering, Procurement, and Construction) design and project management professional. He is an APM qualified Project Management Practitioner with more than 16 years' experience in the Oil and Gas, Nuclear Power, and Aerospace sectors— from concept and FEED (front-end engineering design), through to EPC and operations, on projects worth millions of pounds.*

Alam is the winner of the 2014 IPMA Young Project Manager of the Year Award and the 2011 International Project Management Association (IPMA) Young Researcher Award. He is internationally recognized for his commitment to research, his project management expertise, and for successfully delivering end-to-end solutions. This includes project definition and strategy; bidding, selection, and appointment of contractors; engineering design and procurement; project planning; monitoring and controls; delivery; close out; financial management; and the provision of strategic and tactical advice to clients involved in project management activities.

Alam is also a visiting faculty member at the School of Mechanical Aerospace and Civil Engineering (MACE) of the University of Manchester in the United Kingdom.

Bruce Harpham: How did you first get started in project management?

Mehmood Alam: After my graduation in early 2000, I started my career as an aerospace design engineer. In my first job, I designed electronic warfare systems installed on a variety of aircraft for the Ministry of Defence.

It was a multi-billion-[British] pound project to develop the design, manufacture, production, and installation of an electronic warfare system on military aircraft. My focus was on design side of the work. I modeled the mechanical units of the system using Pro/ENGINEER and carried out stress analysis using ANSYS. As an engineering graduate, I built up my experience and carried out technical design work. It was a great opportunity to learn about the industry, understand engineering problems, and provide design solutions. My role gradually expanded as my project manager involved me in more project management activities.

I produced product specifications, proposals, delivery schedules, cost estimates, risk registers, and integration plans, and rolled out systems from design into production and integration. This included the design and manufacture of systems' prototypes, supplier selection, quality inspections, and factory acceptance testing. I conducted post-modification safety and operational tests, and flight trials. In addition, I evaluated effectiveness through post flight debriefs and systems troubleshooting. I coordinated training sessions for users and produced system integration and operator's manuals. I learned the fundamentals of project management on the job with the support of my senior managers.

During these years, I developed interest in project management and decided to undertake formal education in this discipline and understand more about its principles, practices and tools people management, team dynamics, and corporate culture and leadership.

Harpham: What was your focus in the aerospace project?

Alam: The systems we designed and produced were integrated in military aircraft, namely Mirage. I managed the delivery and integration program of these systems.

In this role, I worked on flight lines and got hands-on experience working on aircraft and system installation and making them operational for use. These military aircraft carry very sensitive aerospace and avionics systems and my team and I had to first fully understand the constraints and these systems before any change can be made. I developed the procedure for system integration in the aircraft. Each aircraft after the modification was subject to ground testing and flight trial. It was a very unique experience.

Harpham: This was one of the first projects you worked on. What were some of the lessons you learned from something that didn't go according to plan?

Alam: I was working to a very compressed program for system design manufacture and integration. I faced several operational issues during system integration that impacted our schedule of activities. One of the key lessons for me was lack of contingency planning to remediate flight operational issues and defects/troubleshooting, as I could not hold the aircraft for longer durations to rectify the problems. Therefore, a quick management response was always required.

Project scope is another classic example of a project management challenge. The scope of work was not very well defined and it was a challenge to meet the evolving requirements of the client in the given schedule and budget. The client came up with a list of requirements and asked us to conduct a feasibility design study and suggest a proposal. The lesson I learned from this government-funded project was that we should consider all risks pertinent to the work and accordingly set up and agree on the type of contract with the client. That approach will give a reasonable allowance to accommodate changes to scope and budget.

Harpham: The initial request was something like, "We're looking to improve our aircraft technology. What do you have in mind?"

Alam: That's right. It was a research and development project leading into production and integration of new systems for aircraft. We came up with various design proposals on what could be done. These aircraft have a certain level of capabilities. We started by assessing the aircraft's existing capabilities and then come up with recommendations and a proposal on what to improve.

There was a lot of back-and-forth discussion with the client about the scope. At times it was frustrating as the scope of works went into several iterations bounded by the constraints of budget. Looking back, I think the contract arrangement could have been improved by using a cost reimbursable model for such a project.

Harpham: When was the project fully complete? Did you have the opportunity to see the systems in production on flying aircraft?

Alam: Yes! We created and tested prototypes to check the functionality. The production process was then subcontracted out to three approved suppliers. There was a fourth vendor assigned to assemble the system. Given the deadlines, we had to run tasks in parallel and work with multiple vendors. It was a challenge to ensure that the products are manufactured, produced and tested as per the standards and specifications. I led the integration team and successfully delivered the system integration program. I carried out system integration, conducted modification checks, on-ground testing, and flight trials. The project was completed in three years. I was also in charge of the after-sales product support program and carried out root-cause investigations of any problems raised by the client, and accordingly provided solutions.

I felt motivated knowing my little contribution was added to military aircraft that are now successfully flying.

Harpham: It sounds like an unexpected aspect on this project was more extensive subcontracting than originally planned.

Alam: That's true. The client had deadlines for the project and we needed to meet those dates. Initially, we planned to have one supplier to help us with additional knowledge and capacity. We ended up going with multiple vendors. As you may imagine, managing multiple vendors is much more difficult—especially when dealing with aerospace-grade design and manufacture. You have to manage them closely to ensure that they meet the project's schedule and quality requirements. The software was developed in-house. The manufacture and assembly of mechanical components was undertaken by the vendors. Electrical systems were provided by us, and their integration and final quality check was conducted by the vendors. FAT [factory acceptance testing] were conducted by our quality inspectors.

Harpham: When you began to study project management, what were some insights you discovered or blind spots you overcame?

Alam: My project management studies filled in several knowledge gaps. For instance, I learned much more about contracts, their types, and their use in different project situations. Commercial management was not something I had covered in my engineering studies.

Regarding quality, I learned much more about the way to approach quality management on projects. My understanding of project quality had been based on the idea of adapting and reusing quality plans from previous projects at the company. I also learned how to quantify and better manage project risks and project controls, including estimating, planning, and monitoring tools and techniques.

The course I took on people and organizations stands out to me. I learned about the business psychology and organizational behavior. The hard sciences of project management—schedule management, project controls, and budgets—were easy to grasp. My greatest challenge was people management. I was interested to learn about intrinsic motivation factors that drive people. I was also interested to learn how to become a better leader—when to delegate and when to become more assertive.

Harpham: Regarding developing your interpersonal skills, what are some of the strategies you've learned?

Alam: I developed my interpersonal skills over the years while working on various projects. I learned to bring composure to the team and adopt appropriate leadership style during meetings to ensure that the team remained well-engaged and focused in the process. On occasions when I feel that the brainstorming is not leading in the right direction, I learned to be more assertive and maintain the focus of the discussion.

I believe in teamwork and valuing people regardless of their culture and background. I have been in situations where I have had to manage personal issues such as holidays and grievances. Project conflicts are another important consideration. I manage these philosophical issues by understanding the underlying cause, collaborating as much as possible and acting assertively as required. For example, I challenged the way progress was being reported on the National Grid FEED project. I directed all leads to provide weekly updates to the planner so a better refection of earned value could be obtained.

An important part of working life is understanding the limits of my own knowledge, and while I strive to improve my level of understanding, I pro-actively seek help and advice from colleagues when appropriate. I have disseminated my expertise to other staff and this is evident from their development and progression.

Harpham: As an engineer, you rely on your expertise to solve problems. When you move to a project manager role, you will be working with different experts, such as legal experts. In that case, you may not understand the details of their profession but you still have to work them to achieve the project's goals. How do you adjust to this new role?

Alam: Yes. In my present role, I face this challenge. My background is mechanical engineering. I've moved to new industries over time—from aerospace to nuclear and then oil and gas. My project management capabilities together with my engineering and design background have enabled me to succeed in these different industries. Project management knowledge gives you the ability to diversify your career and work in different roles and industries.

Harpham: How did you change industries? At first glance, aerospace and nuclear are quite different.

Alam: The first five years or so of my career were focused on the aerospace industry. Over that time, I shifted from a traditional engineering role to an engineering and project management role involving interaction with clients, keeping them satisfied, understanding their requirements and getting them delivered through my team while ensuring that my cost, time, quality, and safety targets are achieved.

I realized that I was doing a project management role rather than a very technical role, though my engineering knowledge and experience helped me a lot to deliver as a project manager. These project management skills are transferable—to a large degree—to other industries. The diversification in experience equipped me to switch between industries.

Changing to nuclear and subsequently into oil and gas wasn't very difficult for me given my background of engineering and design, and project management. The roles I took in these industries were project engineering and project management related, which I fully equipped myself with the key competencies to deliver projects successfully.

Harpham: In the nuclear industry, risk management is a major concern. A poorly managed risk in the nuclear industry can lead to devastating results. What has been your approach to systematically and effectively manage risk on nuclear projects?

Alam: Safety is a top concern in the nuclear as well as in the oil and gas industry. Through each and every component and activity, safety is critical. I am well placed to understand the importance of safety because I have come from the aerospace background, where safety is one of the fundamental concerns in all work we do. I worked on nuclear projects related to safety cases, fault studies, radiological analysis, software development, plant boilers, and fuel cycle optimization and most recently on gas compression stations.

I ensure that all design work is conducted to relevant engineering standards and specifications. All engineering design work is checked and reviewed before it is released. Engineering design assessments are carried out and the design is subject to a gated process before it is released for construction. The selection of only approved contractors is carried out and vendors delivering equipment comply with the defined standards and specifications and deliver as per the Inspection and Test Plans. I ensure that a robust project health and safety file is set out for the project. All risks recorded in the technical risk register are either designed out through the project or transferred over the client on the residual risk register for consideration during operations. All these controls enable me to lead the development and delivery of a safe design for our client.

Harpham: Even a small change may be simple on its own. Yet that change may have second-order or third-order consequences on safety.

Alam: I concur. The work I do involves the design and construction of national assets, such as petrochemical plants and compressor stations. Safety by design is considered a top priority for me while delivering these projects. The cause and effect of every change instigated by the project is considered before its implementation.

Harpham: Let's turn to your project management awards from the International Project Management Association. How did you achieve that award and what are the implications for your career?

Alam: I'm a member of various project management associations and bodies, such as APM [The Association of Project Management, a UK Project Management Professional organization], the International Project Management Association [IPMA], the Project Management Institute [PMI], and Institute of Mechanical Engineers [IMechE] UK.

I have won two international awards to-date. The International Project Management Association [IPMA] Young Researcher award was given on the recognition of my doctoral research work in 2011.

My research established the widely debated link between investment in project management education and benefits to individuals, projects, business units, and the corporate level. The investigation process examined the viability of the five-level Philips [2003] ROI model from a business perspective. However, the extent to which there is a financial return arising from professional development programs is difficult to assess and this brings into question the applicability of Level 5 of the ROI model. The overriding success of this research is the pathway that equates investment with the Return on Value [ROV] concept providing a more pragmatic approach for the assessment of continuing professional development (CPD) programs.

The IPMA Young Project Manager of the Year Award was given to me in 2014 based upon my achievements in delivering projects successfully.

I was very pleased to win this prestigious award. It's a great honor for me and my company. The IPMA is the world's largest professional project management body, so this is recognition on an international scale.

I encourage project managers to join the IPMA and enter for the award and IPMA certification programs. It's a great platform on which to build your career.

Harpham: What are your personal productivity strategies to stay organized and productive?

Alam: Every day is different for me. I don't follow a particular pattern each day. My role demands engagement in many meetings, internally with the team and with the client. This sometimes affects my daily work. I manage this by prioritizing and planning my time for essential meetings only where my involvement is essential.

Earlier in my career, I tended to do all of my work personally. Over time, I have become better at delegating and empowering others on the team to get work done. As a result, I have the capacity to focus on issues that are best suited for me to work on, such as managing stakeholders, project teams, and/ or technical project issues.

Harpham: What is your approach to delegation?

Alam: I'll give you an example from my current project in the oil/gas sector.

I manage a team that includes recent graduates and lead engineers with extensive experience. When someone joins my team, I provide additional support to ensure that they know the project organization and work involved. I also make sure that the lead engineer or another senior engineer of the relevant discipline is available to provide support to the new team member. As the new person demonstrates his or her ability on the project, I gradually give him/her more responsibility and autonomy. If the person joining the team is highly experienced, I take a somewhat different approach and delegate, but I still take the time to express my expectations and explain their job requirements and facilitate as needed.

Harpham: Let's turn to career development. What advice would you give to readers who are interested in breaking into the project management field?

Alam: I have presented a few seminars on this topic to the University of Manchester about my career journey from engineer to project management. People come into project management from different backgrounds. It's not required that you come from a specific discipline.

It's important to take the time and effort to understand the industry and domain context of the project. If you take a new graduate from an MBA program and tell them to run an oil and gas engineering and design project, I don't think they will be able to succeed. In my experience, it is a good idea to start by building your domain or industry experience and subsequently move into project management. On the engineering projects I work on, the project manager is expected to already have the knowledge and understanding of the engineering fundamentals, the design process and construction works. You are not expected to know every detail as the person leading the project, but you are expected to know the basics.

In my view, a technical background or profession gives you a good foundation to lead and manage engineering and design and construction projects.

Coming into project management gives you more diversity and variety in your career. Often, you have a greater opportunity to get promoted to higher levels of responsibility relatively more quickly. You get a sense of what is required to manage and lead people from different disciplines.

Harpham: How has your leadership strategy evolved over time?

Alam: I gradually developed my leadership skills over time. I have learned to adjust my approach based on the context. In some cases, I have to be assertive and take charge. In other cases, I lean back so that others can take the lead. There's a difference between a manager and a leader. If you're a leader, your people look up to you and take confidence from your approach. A key factor for leaders is the ability to inspire the team to work on a common goal. However, I recognize that leadership is an ongoing effort—I am always seeking to improve my ability to lead.

Harpham: What trends and opportunities do you think will be most significant to project management in your environment over the next three to five years?

Alam: Given that client organizations have limited budget expenditures due to current oil and gas market conditions, innovation and moving away from traditional ways of engineering design, management and delivery are greatly emphasized.

Harpham: What books have you found most valuable in supporting your professional development?

Alam: For engineers and project managers, I would recommend the following books: A *Guide to Project Management The Wiley Guide to Managing Projects* by Peter Morris and Jeffrey Pinto [Wiley, 2004], *Business Psychology and Organisational Behaviour* by Eugene McKenna [Psychology Press, 2006] and, *The Innovator's DNA: Mastering the Five Skills of Disruptive Innovators* by Hal B. Gregersen, Clayton M. Christensen, 2011].

Chapter Summary

- Lesson learned: A disciplined approach to managing project scope is critical. Small changes add up over time.

- Vendor management: Alam has managed multiple vendors in complex projects. This is a critical skillset, especially for larger projects.

- How to change industries: Alam has succeeded across several industries as he developed his leadership and project management skills. Grow these skills to increase your career options and flexibility.

- Risk management: In high-risk environments such as nuclear power, look for second- and third-order consequences to your activities.

- Breaking into project management: Alam recommends establishing yourself with industry and domain expertise for a period of time before seeking out opportunities to manage projects.

Alicia Aitken

Chief Project Officer, Telstra

Dr. Alicia Aitken *is Telstra's chief project officer (CPO), responsible for ensuring successful project delivery across the capital investment program. She has worked extensively with organizations across the globe to assess and develop their organizational project management capabilities. Prior to her role at Telstra,* **Aitken** *held the position of CEO at Human Systems International, which was acquired by the Project Management Institute in 2013. Her experience ranges through several industries, including telecommunications, banking and finance, defense and aerospace, pharmaceutical, engineering and construction, mining, oil and gas, and government.*

Aitken is actively involved in several industry groups and peak bodies. She holds a PhD in project management and psychology from Bond University, with a particular focus on how project managers cope with stress. She is a regular keynote speaker at conferences around the world and contributes to academic programs at universities in both Australia and Europe.

Bruce Harpham: How did you get started in your career?

Alicia Aitken: Before becoming chief project officer at Telstra, I ran several companies. My first business was selling specialty coffee online. I started selling directly to consumers and then expanded into wholesale distribution for Australia and Asia. Later on, I expanded into offering online training for the coffee industry.

The next business was a web development company. It was back in the days when almost anybody could be a web developer. Through that work, I learned about the PhD research carried out by Dr. Lynn Crawford. We then went

© Bruce Harpham 2018
B. Harpham, *Project Managers at Work*, DOI 10.1007/978-1-4842-2668-1_25

into business together to create a project manager competency assessment company. The company offered an online self-assessment and follow-up process, which grew into a registered training organization in Australia with a global client base. We did assessments and benchmark work for project managers in large organizations.

Dr. Crawford was also running another business that focused on organizational development activities for project management. We eventually merged the assessment business and the organizational development business together. As a result, I took over Human Systems International's Asia-Pacific business.

In 2013, we sold the Human Systems International business to the Project Management Institute. Shortly after the sale, Telstra approached me and invited me to serve as their chief project officer. It was a brand-new role for the organization.

Harpham: How did you get into the coffee business?

Aitken: During my undergraduate studies in business, I was curious to know if the models and theories being taught would apply to the business world. The best way to test those ideas is to actually run a business. My best friend was working at a local specialty coffee roaster company. At this time, specialty coffee was an emerging niche—Australia was moving from instant coffee to barista-made coffee. She mentioned to me that the company's owners were interested in expanding online, but they didn't quite know how to get started.

I approached the owners of the company and offered to do the work for free if they would give me exclusive rights to sell their product online. They said yes! I started this business in the late 1990s, before many of the services and infrastructure that support ecommerce were in place.

Harpham: How did you transition into your next business?

Aitken: I kept the coffee business going while I built the web development business. As we started up the project management business, I also kept those companies going. In total, I was running three businesses concurrently. When I started my PhD, I realized that I needed to make some adjustments to my workload in order to complete the PhD. I ended up selling the coffee business to a friend in the coffee industry. The web development business was taken over by another friend of mine who was in that industry.

Harpham: Let's turn to the project management assessment business. How did you obtain the first few clients for that business?

Aitken: We were commercializing academic research. As a result, we had several companies and government agencies who had participated in the research. The research participants became our first clients once we developed the first commercial offering. I then went out and sold the product.

One of our first large customers was one of Australia's largest banks. They were going through a transition from decentralized to centralized project management. The company was interested in assessing the capabilities of their project managers. With that success, we were able to continue selling the service to other customers.

Harpham: What were your clients seeking to achieve by working with you?

Aitken: Most of the clients were searching for the root cause of project failure. They had a theory that bad or incompetent project managers might be the cause. The first question from the client might be something like, "Could you come in and tell me which of my project managers are good and which are bad?" Without fail, the assessment process would find some project managers who needed development. On the whole, most of the organization's project managers were fundamentally competent. We found organizational problems and systemic issues that prevented project success.

Harpham: Clients assume they know the answer—we have incompetent project managers—and you respond by telling them a different answer—organizational issues are a bigger problem. How did those conversations play out?

Aitken: One of the advantages to having an assessment business is that you take the opinion out of the conversation. Therefore, the conversation is fact based and you can point to the evidence to discuss. When you're in an opinion-based conversation about project success and capabilities, it's he said, she said. It's hard to make forward progress in that environment. If you take the emotion out of it and focus on the data, you can better understand the problem. That puts both of you in the position of solving the problem in a constructive way.

Harpham: What were some of the patterns you observed in terms of the dysfunctional environment?

Aitken: Lack of sponsor engagement was a common theme. A lack of continuous professional development for project managers was another theme. It's important to set the standard that project management is a profession that requires training, specific skills, and continuous development. I also found a lack of clarity in terms of what is expected of the project manager.

Harpham: What was the focus of your PhD studies?

Aitken: My research focused on the question—how do project managers cope with stress? I've long had an interest in psychology and the human aspect of project management. Interestingly, I found that project managers use similar strategies across their approach to work, home, and personal health. That's unusual compared to most other populations. For example, other populations may have problem-focused coping at work and emotion-focused coping at home.

Project managers tend to start with an acceptance attitude, an emotion-focused coping mechanism. Next, they use problem-solving coping and start to create a plan. The acceptance point was an unexpected discovery. In essence, this means the person realizes that "Something horrible is happening to me that I do not control. Despite that fact, I am going to face the problem and make a plan to get out of it."

Much project management work is focused on gaining control over our world. Therefore, I had assumed that people would feel in control and use problem-focused coping. I was surprised to find that project managers accept the reality of the situation and then make a plan to address it. It's quite heroic!

Harpham: Let's turn to your current role. What is your objective as the chief project officer at Telstra?

Aitken: It's a new role that was introduced about two years ago. In its first incarnation, the role is focused on serving as a change leader. That means a person who can inspire the organization to go on a journey of creating project management as a standalone capability. That means a capability separate from other areas, like IT and engineering.

Let's take a moment to define the organization's structure. Telstra has over thirty thousand employees working in more than twenty countries around the world. For project management, we have a decentralized model. Our project managers are spread among the organization's business units.

The first goal was to create a community of project delivery practitioners. I measure success in that area by how many people attend the events, training, and the other offerings we have. We also carry out a pulse survey to explore how project managers feel about the organization, their sponsor, and other points.

The next goal is to create a group of effective executive project sponsors. It's important to have good project managers. However, the other side of the project delivery success coin is to have good project sponsors. This development effort guides executives on how to run steering committees and make good decisions about projects.

The final goal concerns the success of our project delivery. We use several benchmarks and metrics to measure how successful we are at delivering projects. When I started, we carried out a baseline exercise to evaluate our success. Today—about eighteen months after that initial baseline—we are measuring our success.

Harpham: What were some of the findings from that initial baseline analysis when you joined the organization?

Aitken: Like many organizations, we had a number of solid project management practices in place. There was also an emerging portfolio management practice. We choose to make our focus on professionalizing our project managers and capabilities. We want to make sure that those who fell into the project manager role "accidentally" develop the capabilities to become effective professionals. That professionalization activity was carried out through a combination of training, certification, and engaging the organization's executive sponsors. In addition, we are interested in advancing our portfolio, investment, and benefits management processes.

Harpham: What is the organization's approach to benefits management?

Aitken: Our business cases have both tangible and non-tangible benefits. We track all of those benefits. The final gate in our gating process—gate 5—takes place six to twelve months after the project has closed. During that time, we do a review of the benefits that were achieved and what was planned. To assist with this work, we have a permanent team that owns and manages the "gate 5" process on benefits management in cooperation with the business owner of the project. We don't rely on the project manager to do this work. After all, they are usually long gone and leading a different project.

Harpham: It's interesting to hear that there's a dedicated team that looks at benefits achieved and measuring project success.

Aitken: That capability is one of our strengths. At the same time, I'm aware of other areas where there is still a lot of room to grow.

Harpham: Let's explore intangible benefits and how these are measured. Some organizations struggle with how to define these benefits and determine if they have been achieved. What's your approach to intangible benefits?

Aitken: Customer satisfaction is one example of an intangible benefit. We measure that by using the Net Promoter Score method. The other major intangible is brand protection or reputation. Though it is important, it is relatively more difficult to manage.

Harpham: How might a project impact the brand positively or negatively?

Aitken: On the negative side, if a project introduced a new product and it somehow caused a problem for the whole network, that would result in a negative brand impact. In terms of positive brand impact, a recently introduced product comes to mind. The product is called Telstra Smart Home—it's our Internet of Things product. That was a brand-enhancing project. That product also connects the organization's overall strategy to transform from a world-class telecom company into a world-class technology company.

Harpham: What does the Telstra Smart Home product do exactly?

Aitken: It is a way to manage and access various technologies in the home, such as home security cameras, having a door to lock or unlock remotely, turn power switches on and off, and so forth. You can carry out all of these functions from a smart phone application.

Harpham: Turning back to your work, what does a typical workweek look like for you?

Aitken: I have two teams to manage. I have a delivery team of ten people who deliver large projects. In addition, I have a capability team that carries out functions like training, sponsor training, and so forth. Wi-Fi Nation is one of the larger programs we currently working on. The goal is to create the world's largest Wi-Fi network, which includes creating public Wi-Fi hotspots around the country.

Harpham: What is your approach for developing project capabilities with the organization's executives?

Aitken: The most important thing is to do the pre-work before you even attempt the conversation. I spent the first twelve to eighteen months delivering projects for our executives. During that time, I made an effort to get to know them and develop my relationships.

I also spent a lot of time seeking to understand how they like to learn. I was also curious to learn about their career journey. I learned that our executives like to learn by observing and modeling other executives. They prefer this modeling approach to taking traditional courses. They often look around for other executives to see who is good with a given activity, and then model that activity. At the same time, they also learn from observing what not to do. All of these insights fed into our sponsor capability program.

Taking the time to understand our executives and how they learn was a key factor in the success of our executive training program.

Harpham: It sounds like the traditional training model would not have been suitable. Can you elaborate further on the modeling idea?

Aitken: I learned that this group of people would likely not be interested in attending a training session. Likewise, they would probably not respond to mandates, rules, and similar methods. They're very smart people and they're able to learn their project responsibilities quickly. They don't need a lot of intervention.

What executives do need is exposure to new ideas and new ways of working. The challenge for me and my team is to come up with ways to present those ideas effectively. We have addressed the challenge with several interventions.

Harpham: I've noted that you discuss training and development activities with the term "interventions." Can you elaborate on your approach further?

Aitken: Our interventions are somewhat personalized. At the time, we have to create interventions that serve the needs of more than three hundred executives. One successful approach has been to ask an executive, with a strong track record of sponsoring projects, to give a presentation to other executives. We've also had events where our deputy CFO and executives from other companies come together to discuss project issues. We have also brought in former executives who know serve on boards to provide their perspective—I like to think of them as "uber-sponsors."

We have also created resources, such as a sponsor handbook. This is a reference document that covers key questions that experienced project sponsors tend to ask. For example, how much should my PMO cost? Which people should attend this forum meeting? Executives generally do not want to ask these kind of basic questions publicly. Therefore, it is helpful to give them this resource, which they can study. 2017 is the year of the project sponsor at Telstra. All year, our focus is providing support and assistance to our sponsors to help them on their journey.

Harpham: What mistakes do you see as a recurring pattern for the project managers you interact with?

Aitken: The biggest problem is project managers forgetting to lead their projects. When that happens, project managers fall into administrative tasks. With project management, we have a lot of useful processes that we use to guide our work. If that process is pushed to the front and that's all anybody sees, it is easy to dismiss project management as an administrative function. Truly, project management is about leading the execution of strategy.

Harpham: What is the cause for this tendency to overemphasize administrative activities?

Aitken: Two points come to mind. First, project managers understand the value of project processes. As a result, project managers are highly skilled and comfortable using those processes. However, we do not understand how that process emphasis is perceived by other people outside of the project management world.

Second, there's also pressure from non-project managers. These people don't know what to expect from their project managers. If they see a project manager focused on administrative activities, they may think to themselves, "Oh, this is a person who does my admin. I'll give them more work to do like that." Then you quickly end up in a catch-22 scenario—you do a bit of admin work and then you are given more of that to do. Soon, you have no time or capacity to act as the project leader. Instead of being perceived as a leader, you are perceived as an administrator.

Harpham: Let's look at leadership from the perspective of influence and relationships. What was your approach to relationship development when you joined the company?

Aitken: I have a fundamental belief that nobody is going to follow you into the abyss if they don't first know and like you. My first few months were focused on going to meet people. I thought of this as "making friends at Telstra." In meeting new people at the organization, I wanted to let them know about my role and find ways to help them. I found it effective to ask people how I could help them, rather than telling them. During these months, I put in a lot of effort to travel to various offices in order to meet people face to face. This stage was all about building rapport.

The next stage was to find ways to work with as many executives as I could. I started to interact with some executives directly through project work—they were serving as project sponsors for projects led by my delivery team. However, there were many other executives that we couldn't deliver a project for because we were at capacity.

I used a wide range of strategies to find ways to work with other executives. For example, I looked for opportunities to take on extra work myself. Through doing that work, I had the capability to build their trust and deliver for them. One executive was working on setting up a new business unit—they needed a CapEx function created. I offered to do that work for them. It turned out to become a second job for me! There was a lot of effort involved—above and beyond my "day job"—to find those opportunities.

I also found it helpful to get involved in volunteer activities and groups at the company. For example, we have a Brilliant Connected Women's group, a diversity council, and other groups. By participating on the diversity council, I had the opportunity to build a relationship with other executives and work with them to deliver on the organization's diversity agenda.

Beyond those activities, I also went out for coffee meetings and other informal ways to get to know them.

Harpham: I noticed a few key aspects to your approach. You had the awareness to realize that there would be a limit to how many executives you would meet through your main responsibilities. Therefore, you knew you had to proactively reach out, travel to other locations, and look for these other opportunities.

Aitken: Yes. I knew the executives needed me, but they didn't know I existed when I first joined the organization. Therefore, the chance of them coming to ask for help was limited at first. You have to put in the effort to create awareness.

Harpham: Let's look at your career journey. You had started your career in the entrepreneurial or self-employed area and then moved to join a large organization. How did you navigate through that transition?

Aitken: I was up front with my first boss at Telstra. We actually created a risk register concerning my transition to the company. On that register, I listed the fact that I had never worked for a large company. As a result, I might find the pace of change frustrating. Likewise, I might not have the political skills to effect change in a large organization. Another risk was that the company might not like my approach to getting things done. We talked about those risks during our one-on-one meetings.

The large corporate world was an unknown territory for me. As it turns out, I love working in a large organization. It's great to have access to so many different people who bring such a variety of ideas to work. I find that variety of ideas and people highly stimulating. All of the skills I had developed in managing people in my own companies translated well to the corporate world. However, I had to learn my way around the various systems used in the company: HR systems, procurement systems, and so forth.

My consulting and sales skills have been a tremendous asset in my success at the company. Selling ideas inside a company is much easier than selling a product and getting someone to part with their money. It's actually the same skill set, but doing that process inside the company is much easier.

Harpham: It's interesting to see the risk register practice applied to the context of a career transition. You're showing that project processes and methods can be used in other contexts.

Aitken: It's a conversation I've been having lately with various people. At Telstra, project management is a specific discipline for managing projects. However, the principles of project management have great life applications.

Harpham: What is your approach to leadership?

Aitken: Leadership is a privileged position to be in. If you're going to lead people into the unknown, recognize that you're asking them to go into a scary place. As a leader, you have an obligation to do lead with respect and trust. This work requires self-awareness about your own emotions and the ability to keep yourself in check. I like people to work with me rather than for me.

Harpham: What techniques and methods are part of your personal productivity system?

Aitken: It starts with having a clear operating model for the year. In a way, I think of each year's goals as a large project. What are the major work packages? When will those be done? Once that overall plan is set up, it is helpful to have a number of checkpoints. I like to have weekly or fortnightly one to one meetings with each person on my team, so you can understand the team's progress. By setting the broad goals and schedule, you can then leave people to come up with the best way to achieve those ends.

In terms of time management, this is still a journey for me. For this year, I've started to block out time for certain activities on my calendar. My ideal approach is to break my work time into thirds. One third of my time focuses on supporting the delivery team. The second third of my team is focused on the capability team. Finally, the last third of my time is focused on building for the future—either for my team or the company more broadly. For example, what projects and programs are planned for the future? What capabilities will we need in the future to achieve our strategy?

Harpham: How is the time management system applied in practice?

Aitken: Looking at the last month or two, I would estimate that I'm about sixty-five percent successful with adhering to this schedule. This year has been better than other years because I've made a conscious effort to focus.

Harpham: What books have you found professionally valuable?

Aitken: I recently read *Why Should Anyone Be Led by You?: What It Takes to Be an Authentic Leader* by Gareth R. Jones and Robert Goffee [Harvard Business Review Press, 2015]. It was recommended to me by the deputy CFO. The book itself was great. I'm still thinking about the question in the book title.

Harpham: What advice would you give to someone who is looking to break into project management from another role?

Aitken: There are two streams of work to consider in making this transition happen. First, pursue training and certification—take courses and build skills through project management courses. Second, networking is critical. Making a transition into your first project management job is difficult because you've got to convince someone to give you a job that you haven't done before. In order to find an opportunity, you need a network that includes potential employers and a person who is willing to take a risk on you.

The training and certification part is relatively easy. You just need to spend time and money to learn the knowledge. In contrast, people seem to struggle with networking. This activity may include going out for coffee with new people or cold calling for new opportunities.

Harpham: The networking point is so valuable and yet it is underappreciated. In my alumni volunteer work at the University of Toronto, I regularly encourage students to put $50 on a Starbucks card and then take professionals out to coffee for three months. That activity will pay huge dividends, yet almost nobody will do it. At the same time, students are willing to spend tens of thousands of dollars to earn the degree.

Aitken: Exactly!

Chapter Summary

- Recommended book. *Why Should Anyone Be Led by You?: What It Takes to Be an Authentic Leader* by Gareth R. Jones and Robert Goffee.

- Bring facts to the discussion. Aitken's approach to professional development was enhanced by bringing an evidence-based approach to the discussion. How can you bring that perspective to your work?

- Use project methods for your career. Aitken used a risk register and other project methods to facilitate her transition to Telstra.

- Development is for everyone. Executives, project managers, and everyone else needs development in a variety of forms, including modeling successful people, to reach their full potential.

- Measure your project's benefits. Take note from Telstra's process to measure the tangible and intangible benefits of projects six to twelve months after the project is completed. Telstra has a dedicated team to focus on this activity.

Index

I

© Bruce Harpham 2018
B. Harpham, *Project Managers at Work*, DOI 10.1007/978-1-4842-2668-1

Get the eBook for only $5!

Why limit yourself?

With most of our titles available in both PDF and ePUB format, you can access your content wherever and however you wish—on your PC, phone, tablet, or reader.

Since you've purchased this print book, we are happy to offer you the eBook for just $5.

To learn more, go to http://www.apress.com/companion or contact support@apress.com.

Apress®

81390508R00188

Made in the USA
Middletown, DE
24 July 2018